D1592762

Reconsidering Reparations

PHILOSOPHY OF RACE

Series Editors

Linda Martín Alcoff, Hunter College and the Graduate Center CUNY

Chike Jeffers, Dalhousie University

Socially Undocumented: Identity and Immigration Justice
Amy Reed-Sandoval

Reconsidering Reparations
Olúfẹ́mi O. Táíwò

Reconsidering Reparations

OLÚFẸ́MI O. TÁÍWÒ

OXFORD
UNIVERSITY PRESS

OXFORD
UNIVERSITY PRESS

Oxford University Press is a department of the University of Oxford. It furthers
the University's objective of excellence in research, scholarship, and education
by publishing worldwide. Oxford is a registered trade mark of Oxford University
Press in the UK and certain other countries.

Published in the United States of America by Oxford University Press
198 Madison Avenue, New York, NY 10016, United States of America.

Library of Congress Control Number: 2021032539
ISBN 978-0-19-750889-3

DOI: 10.1093/oso/9780197508893.001.0001

1 3 5 7 9 8 6 4 2

Printed by Sheridan Books, Inc., United States of America

Contents

Series Editor Foreword

The topic of race has been an object of serious philosophical concern starting from as early as the seventeenth century. Work on the topic has included political philosophy, social ontology, the philosophy of science, ethics, the philosophy of art, and the philosophy of language, among other areas. Philosophers have wanted to know what is this thing called 'race,' whether it actually refers to anything in the world, how it is related to other ways of marking group identities, and what its political, ethical, and aesthetic effects have been.

The concept of a "critical philosophy of race," the title for this series, helpfully signals that philosophers do not necessarily take race to be a natural kind, but that there is debate over what kind of "kind" race is. Critical race philosophy sets out to explore the implicit "race-effects" on the conceptual architecture of modern societies, as well as legal hermeneutics, concepts of justice, and the formation of institutions. Race also plays a role in forms of subjectivity, intersubjective relations, and in general, on our varied forms of life.

This series aims to explore the emergence and consequences of the concept of race, as well as its associated practices. It aims to showcase both domination and resistance, the complexity of racial meanings across diverse communities, and the variable ways in which race and racism operate in regard to varied identities. The concept of race is mercurial, as are the ideas that legitimate racism. There needs to be a constant reappraisal of new forms, new ideas, and new efforts at amelioration.

The series will showcase the unique contributions philosophers can bring to this area of inquiry. Two of these involve conceptual analysis and normative analysis. Conceptual analysis concerns how "race-talk" emerges, how it refers and to what, how (and whether) it is distinct from ethnic or other group categories, and how it operates in the pragmatics of everyday speech. Normative analysis concerns the politics and morality of "race-talk," or racial classifications. Beyond these two broad areas, every field in the history of philosophy itself has been impacted by new debates on major figures, from the influence of Aristotle's views about slavery to the debates over Sartre's understanding of negritude.

Linda Martin Alcoff
Chike Jeffers
Series Editors

Acknowledgments

I have an uncountable number of people to thank for this work.

Thanks to my family for their support: my siblings Ibukun and Ebun, and my parents Abiola and Yetunde, all the Taiwos and Sokunbis, and all the Cincinnati Nigerians; Abigail Higgins, the Higgins family, and the Kennedys.

A special thanks to Emma Young, for her invaluable editorial work on this book, as well as to the various editors at Newgen Knowledge Works. Many thanks to Peter Ohlin and Hanah Purslow at OUP, and series editors Linda Martín Alcoff and Chike Jeffers. I'd also like to thank all of my colleagues who did direct research work to contribute to this book: Olawunmi Ola-Busari, Treasa Powathil, Joey Jebari, Chun Hin Tsoi, and Anna Saez de Tejada Cuenca. Thanks to the many departments and workshops that allowed me the space to refine the views and chapters of this book: Stanford Junior Scholars Workshop, Yale Political Theory Workshop, Georgetown History Workshop; the philosophy departments of University of Michigan, Washington and Jefferson College, Rowan College, CUNY, and my home institution of Georgetown University. I also thank individuals who helped review the work on their own: Abigail Higgins, Peter Chesney, Brian Hutler, Matt Lindauer, AJ Julius, Flavien Moreau, Holly Buck, David Morrow, Rose Lenehan, Elizabeth Barnes, Peter Levine, Serene Khader, Jared Rodríguez, Samia Hesni, Vanessa Wills, and Liam Kofi Bright.

A special thanks to supportive scholars whose direct and indirect support made it possible for me to be here at all: including AJ Julius, Daniela Dover, Jason Stanley, Melvin Rogers, Gaye Theresa Johnson, Fred Moten, and Josh Armstrong. To friends and comrades whose support and advice were just as essential: Marques Vestal, Thabisile Griffin, Seye Akomolede, Sutiweyu Sandoval, Lance Lowe, Jynnette Lewis, Alexis Cooke, Sa Whitley, Annie Fehrenbacher, A.r. R, Anuja Bose, Miranda Sklaroff, Pilar González, Jack Suria Linares, Carter Moon, Tobi Akomolede, and Fred Baba. To the many individuals besides these who I may have inadvertently left out (with sincere apologies).

To the institutions and organizations I was able to learn in or from: The Undercommons, UAW 2865, UCLA Labor Center, LA Black Workers Center, and Pan-African Community Action.

To our moral ancestors, without whose struggle and sacrifice none of this would be possible: to the anti-colonial fighters, to the abolitionists, to the workers who demanded more, and to the activists who refused to accept less.

To all of our moral and genealogical descendants, to those who are yet young and those who are yet to come: with love, with hope, and with solidarity.

Reconsidering Reparations

Reconsidering Reparation

The Malê revolt of 1835 was centuries in the making.

It took place in Brazil, but its story starts in West Africa. There, the Hausas and the Yoruba were peoples divided by war. Having been captured in war and trafficked across the globe, people from these same ethnic groups encountered each other in Brazil, where they were known as "Nagô" and "Haussá." Here, they became peoples united by the shared condition of racialized chattel slavery.

The first peoples enslaved in Brazil were Indigenous, Tupi-speaking nations—soon after the arrival of the first Portuguese settlers in 1530. But disease quickly decimated the local population, though the few who survived were often successful in waging resistance. Meanwhile, the Jesuit missionaries among the early colonists preferred to convert indigenous peoples rather than enslave them. Both to pacify the Society of Jesus and to fulfill labor demands, colonists conspired with the crown to traffic in Africans, creating a new population known locally as the Malês.[1] The first slave ships came from Africa in 1570. By the time the Malês revolted, the system they fought against had been in place for three centuries.

Salvador, the site of the revolt, was on the other side of the Atlantic from the political turmoil in West Africa.[2] Yet the politics on both sides of the Atlantic were linked by a resource redistribution system spanning four continents: Africa, the site of the wars whose captives produced slaves for this growing economic and political system; Europe, via the imperial powers that secured and built the slave ports along Africa's western coast; South America; and North America. These wars, and the human trafficking resulting from them, helped build the world we live in.

---

[1] "Reparations for Native Genocide and Slavery—Caribbean Community (CARICOM) Secretariat"; National Coalition of Blacks for Reparations in America (N'COBRA), "The Abuja Proclamation (Pan-African Conference on Reparations, 1993, Abuja, Nigeria)"; National Indian Brotherhood, *Indian Control of Indian Education: Policy Paper Presented to the Minister of Indian Affairs and Northern Development*; Frith, "The Global Push for Reparations"; Scott, "Reparations, Restitution, Transitional Justice"; "Porto-Novo | INOSAAR."

[2] Hébrard, *Slavery in Brazil: Brazilian Scholars in the Key Interpretive Debates*.1

1

Introduction

"Don't go from written bars filled with rage
To prime time television and a gilded cage
Don't forget, it's people in the world still enslaved
I barb wired my wrist, and let it fill the page"

—Black Thought

Injustice and oppression are global in scale. Why? Because Trans-Atlantic slavery and colonialism built the world we live in, and slavery and colonialism were unjust and oppressive. If we want reparations, we should be thinking more broadly about how to remake the world system.

There's been a recent resurgence of interest in the idea of reparations, especially in the United States, where I grew up and where I am based as a scholar. Here, Ta-Nehisi Coates's "The Case for Reparations" has been described as singlehandedly rekindling the age-old debate, setting off a firestorm of reactions across the political spectrum, culminating in a "historic" Congressional hearing where the issue was debated by a subcommittee of the House of Representatives.[1] Coates's piece follows generations of the Ross family and their structurally enabled exploitation at countless people's hands. Over the years, members of the family were enslaved in Mississippi, then forced into debt peonage and sharecropping, and finally preyed upon in the Chicago housing market by unscrupulous lenders. At every stage, racist background social structures aided and abetted slave owners', landlords', lenders', and others' predation upon Black people and communities like the Ross family.[2]

---

[1] Stolberg, "At Historic Hearing, House Panel Explores Reparations."
[2] Coates, "The Case for Reparations."

Reconsidering Reparations. Olúfẹ́mi O. Táíwò, Oxford University Press. © Oxford University Press 2022.
DOI: 10.1093/oso/9780197508893.003.0001

Opposite Coates stand figures like Coleman Hughes, who testified at the same hearing. Hughes takes himself to have exactly the right sort of standing to opine on this issue—his ancestors, he explains, were enslaved on President Thomas Jefferson's famous Monticello estate. Nevertheless, he considers himself privileged—he grew up in the suburbs and attended an Ivy League school. Perhaps more importantly, he argues that reparations has no role to play in the changes that African-Americans need: "In 2008 the House of Representatives formally apologized for slavery and Jim Crow. In 2009, the Senate did the same. Black people don't need another apology. We need safer neighborhoods and better schools. We need a less punitive criminal justice system. We need affordable healthcare. And none of these things can be achieved through reparations for slavery."[3]

Here, Coates, or I myself, might have been surprised. At least some of those things are precisely what we want from reparations. Hughes exploits a haze of ambiguity around reparations: what *are* they about? Adolph Reed, Jr. describes the call for reparations for African Americans as a blend of "material, symbolic, and psychological components."[4] Reed explains that the United States's long history of slavery and racial economic apartheid has cost African Americans in direct and indirect "material" ways, which include racially discriminatory lending practices, as well as the violent exclusion of Blacks from voting and other aspects of public political life. Reparations projects that involve financial payment of some kind might go some distance toward remedying this. But also important are means of addressing impersonal material considerations such as political representation, as well as attempts to counter symbolic injustices, such as monuments and memorials that continue to propagate the ideology of global racism. Finally, some proponents of reparations believe that they will raise collective racial consciousness and provide tools to address social pathologies that are related to the painful history of slavery and racial domination.

Reed thinks the ambiguity caused by these separate categories of goals is a liability, since elites can then exploit it by choosing the

---

[3] Coates and Hughes, "Should America Pay Reparations for Slavery?"
[4] Reed, "The Case Against Reparations."

version of reparations that is cheapest for them: the symbolic. We have already seen this tendency at work: in Washington, D.C., the capital of the United States, the mayor decided to paint "Black Lives Matter" on the plaza in front of the White House, in response to the 2020 summer of protests against racist police violence. There, mere days later, law enforcement continued to brutalize protestors while the mayor supported a multimillion dollar budget increase to their budget.[5] More important, overinvestment from any level of society into such symbolic reparations *could* detract energy and resources from an alternative, preferable political project: "building broad solidarity across race, gender, and other identities around shared concerns of daily life" like "access to quality health care, the right to a decent and dignified livelihood, affordable housing, quality education for all." Here, Reed sounds the alarm later raised by Hughes—that the call for reparations for some distracts from a more worthy political project that would provide justice for all.

But what if the project for reparations *was* the project for "safer neighborhoods and better schools," for a "less punitive justice system," for "the right to a decent and dignified livelihood"? What if building the just world *was* reparations? Indeed, this book will ask, what other form of reparations could even be meaningful in the context of our reality?

Keeanga-Yamahtta Taylor pointed out, in a discussion with Reed on this subject, that the struggle to build a just social system can't be won through simple "universal" programs addressing "common" problems. Taylor gives the example of the large disparity rate in maternal mortality between Black mothers and white mothers: the accumulated history of disparate and discriminatory treatment and policy means that not all of the relevant social problems are, in fact, common to both.[6] To build a just health care system, we would have to address both lack of access due to unjust economic structures and lack of access due to unfair gender- and race-based discrimination. From the point of view of building a just health care system, then, these goals aren't *substitutes* for each other; they are complementary.

In *Freedom Dreams*, Robin D. G. Kelley takes up a similar perspective. After a historical analysis of many eras of reparations campaigns in

---

[5] Rossi and Táíwò, "What's New about Woke Racial Capitalism (and What Isn't)."
[6] *Dissent Magazine*, "The Reparations Debate."

the United States, he concludes that "it was never entirely, or even primarily, about money. The demand for reparations was about social justice, reconciliation, reconstructing the internal life of black America, and eliminating institutional racism. This is why reparations proposals from black radical movements focus less on individual payments than on securing funds to build autonomous black institutions, improving community life, and in some cases establishing a homeland that will enable African Americans to develop a political economy geared more toward collective needs than toward accumulation."[7]

The goal of *Reconsidering Reparations* is to argue for this perspective: the view that reparation is a construction project. Accordingly, I call this way of thinking about the relationship between justice's past and future the *constructive view* of reparations.

Constructive views used to be more popular. The wave of decolonization movements that crested toward the end of the Second World War forced new political questions onto the world stage. Prominent figures in the growing global anti-colonial movement demanded the institutionalization of self-determination as a political principle of the United Nations, worked to form regional political blocs for mutual aid and uplift, and demanded a New International Economic Order with a different set of rules than the set that had characterized the development of the global racial empire established by capitalism.[8]

Political scientist Adom Getachew's *Worldmaking after Empire* argues that anticolonial nationalist movements, particularly in Africa, began from a recognition of the foundational role of trans-Atlantic slavery in the creation of the world as they found it: one marked by racial hierarchy and domination, both within and across international boundaries.[9] Accordingly, since the anticolonial movement represented a movement for global justice, its realized effects were as global as its conceptual scope. Conflicts over the new shape of the world order—the so called Cold War—would involve pitched diplomatic and military battles between domestic and international actors alike, over the decades following the second World War.

---

[7] Kelley, *Freedom Dreams: The Black Radical Imagination*, 114–115.
[8] Getachew, *Worldmaking after Empire: The Rise and Fall of Self-Determination*, 2.
[9] Getachew, *Worldmaking after Empire*, 5.

Anticolonial activists imagined a New International Economic Order of norms, treaties, and laws providing a global political structure of non-domination. They imagined new institutions, different relationships between countries, and also, crucially, the most recognizable aspect of reparations politics: redistribution of global wealth, from the First World (back) to the Third World.[10] They were joined in this perspective by voices in the First World, including the Republic of New Afrika, who demanded that the US government fund their project of redrawing the North American political map and negotiating with Native peoples to create a Black nation in the South.[11]

These activists weren't just fighting *against* the structures of colonial domination and racial apartheid in each of their separate nation-states: they were also trying to build a more just world on a global scale. Getachew calls their project *worldmaking*, and it is intimately tied to the constructive view of reparations I'm writing this book to advertise. Even today, there remain views of reparations that are committed to the worldmaking project that animated yesterday's figures: in the United States, both the Movement for Black Lives policy platform and the National Coalition of Blacks for Reparations in America provide comprehensive and transformative articulations of commitments to building structural justice; as do the Caribbean nations' CARICOM platform and the International Network of Scholars and Activists for Afrikan Reparations.[12] This book contributes to this long and worthy tradition.

What This Book Is Not

Now to say what this book isn't.

---

[10] Getachew, *Worldmaking after Empire*, 151.
[11] Berger, "The Malcolm X Doctrine: The Republic of New Afrika and National Liberation on US Soil."
[12] Caribbean Community (CARICOM) Secretariat, "Reparations for Native Genocide and Slavery—"; Movement for Black Lives, "Invest-Divest"; Movement for Black Lives, "Economic Justice"; "Porto-Novo," | INOSAAR; Frith, "The Global Push for Reparations"; J. H. Scott, "Reparations, Restitution, Transitional Justice"; National Coalition of Blacks for Reparations in America (N'COBRA). "Reparations Means Full Repair: For 400 Years of Terror, and Other Egregious Crimes."

In a speech given at Portland State University's Black Studies Center, the late, great Black philosopher and writer Toni Morrison gave a powerful address called "The Humanist View." She spent considerable time in this speech carefully explaining how racism feeds and perpetuates ignorance, even in the guise of scholarship. "In spite of improved methods of collecting and storing data, and an increased amount of data available," Morrison said, American scholarship has done almost nothing to erase ignorance manufactured by racist ideology. "On the contrary, studies designed to confirm old prejudices and create new ones are really on the increase."[13]

Morrison spoke in 1974; you can judge for yourself whether or not her words apply equally to today's world. What's important about Morrison's description is her diagnosis of the root problem. Nobody ever *really* thought Black people were inferior, she claims provocatively—after all, "[y]ou don't give your children over to the care of people whom you believe to be inhuman." What's actually going on is something much simpler: "They were only and simply and now interested in acquisition of wealth and the status quo of the poor." The racism is a smokescreen.

What's all the white supremacist talk about, then? Morrison says that racism thrives on distraction and misdirection. "*It keeps you from doing your work.* It keeps you explaining over and over again, your reason for being. Somebody says you have no language and so you spend 20 years proving that you do. Somebody says your head isn't shaped properly so you have scientists working on the fact that it is. Somebody says that you have no art so you dredge that up. Somebody says that you have no kingdoms and so you dredge that up. None of that is necessary."[14]

A version of the phenomenon that Toni Morrison is explaining is this: racism keeps you answering other people's questions. Even when you learn that Africa had history, to borrow part of Morrison's example, you end up spending pages and pages *proving it*—answering the questions of an imagined, skeptical reader—rather than simply treating it as a premise and moving on. Philosopher Rachel McKinney

---

13 Morrison, "A Humanist View," 5.
14 Morrison, "A Humanist View."

characterizes this as "extracted speech"—things we have to say because of a power structure that often lurks in the background, unseen and unexamined.[15]

What is (or would be) scholarly work, then, in a world where our speech is self-determined rather than extracted? The "first job for the scholar," Morrison explains, is "to focus on the hysteria and greed of those whose business it is to manipulate us and to keep us anonymous or peripheral to the events of this country." The second is "to bear down hard on those generalities: the statistics and the charts, and make them give up the life they're hiding." These are the tasks this book takes up— to seriously engage with what we can know about our social structure (even if it requires reference to "the statistics and the charts") and to responsibly communicate what they can tell us about the world we live in—whatever the narratives or preoccupations of those who want to manipulate us.

An entire industry of racial commentary, from think pieces to blogs to academic studies and whole fields of researchers, centers upon convincing imagined skeptical whites or Global Northerners that the social sky is in fact blue. We aim to disrupt, contextualize, or falsify stereotypes and correct how we are perceived, and we try to manipulate how attention to different social problems or populations is parceled out.

Most worrying, we spend so much time and energy responding to others' mistakes that we lose the ability to distinguish *their* questions from *ours*. While we produce constant criticism of aspects of the material or attention economy that we don't like, we systematically underproduce or rush through scholarship on questions that are infinitely more important and worthy of our time and analysis. For example, what forms of social life are compatible with our flourishing? What must our economies look like to respond to our social problems? What are the root causes—in a material and institutional sense, from a rigorous perspective—of our current problems, and which of them are alterable? How can we build algorithms, institutions, rules, laws, social movements, or revolutions that do the altering?

---

[15] McKinney, "Extracted Speech."

The focus on proving that structural racism exists, on answering skeptical Global Northerners and whites, has subtly changed the goal posts—on reparations and a host of other justice issues—from where they stood during the anticolonial movements of the twentieth century. Let's put them back.

Thus, this book is written for a general audience, but not *that* general. I do not structure this book to address other people's questions about reparations (though it may well do so). That is, I am not trying to convince people who oppose the project of racial justice from the outset to support the specific view of reparations I advocate here. There will be occasional responses applicable to the arguments of people who oppose reparations, but they are not the focus of the book. Moreover, the interlocutors I have in mind for such arguments are people like Coleman Hughes and Adolph Reed, not like, say, the conservative US Senator Mitch McConnell. I'm not talking to his ilk.

There's an important difference between being accountable to everyone in principle and in practice trying to answer everyone—the latter can result in centering our analyses and investigations around things white people are insecure about, especially in an academic system that they largely control. But as a person who has rarely read a mainstream book on any political subject that structures itself around the very specific objections of Pan-Africanist materialist thinkers, I can confidently assure skeptical readers that learning from a philosophical text does not require that its author answer the specific questions or objections that match your particular political inclinations.

This book is also not trying to design a particular reparations proposal or dive into the weeds of specific criteria for who does and doesn't deserve reparations. These are among the meaningful questions that deserve answers and merit serious inquiry, and I will have some things to say about them. Chapter 5, in particular, will consider a range of policy choices that are relevant to the view of reparations I develop here—but policy design will not be the focus of the book either.

I am also choosing to practice the intellectual culture of justice that I want to participate in—holding out hope that it will exist one day, and adding my small contribution to the collective effort to make it so. The massive project of global racial justice requires no less a commitment.

What This Book Is

In this book, I am trying to convince people who are committed to racial justice in some way, shape, or form that the *particular* way, shape, and form I defend here is a worthwhile one. This task is urgent, I think, at a time in human history in which the ability of our social systems to respond to climate crisis may increasingly become definitive of what forms of freedom and security are available and who has them.

From an academic perspective, this book is an attempt to give a philosophical articulation of a particular perspective on reparations, and the perspective of justice that it emanates from. I will distinguish this view from other candidate views and give some considerations in its favor and against some of those other candidate views.

From a political perspective, this is an impassioned attempt to change the subject of racial justice *back* to the more relevant form it took in a previous political era. For those who are perhaps not reparations proponents but who support anti-racism generally, my aim is to persuade them to embrace *this* understanding of what it concretely requires. For those who are already concerned with reparations, my hope is that when we look closely into what sort of things reparations want to respond to and what they want to achieve, we will find our conversation changes: we should have different standards of success and progress, and find different things relevant that we currently do.

But any way you slice it, this is a book about justice, at a world scale—about the appropriate response to world-scale problems, past injustice and to future climate crisis. This is, already, notably different from how some people think about reparations and racial injustice more generally. For some, reparations are a national project, as in the United States. For others, it is regional or supranational: examples include the Caribbean nations' CARICOM project, reparations projects formed on the African continent, and demands from Indigenous groups who have collaborated across their nations to push for redress of grievances.[16]

---

[16] Caribbean Community (CARICOM) Secretariat, "Reparations for Native Genocide and Slavery—"; National Coalition of Blacks for Reparations in America (N'COBRA), "The Abuja Proclamation (Pan-African Conference on Reparations—1993 Abuja,

I should say immediately that I support each of these versions of reparations. However, something of broader scope is also needed. For better or for worse, our political communities live within borders that have been produced by war and conquest more often than by fairly negotiated development between communities. As a result, we've produced partially contained political structures with connected but distinct histories, and global justice will require justice at the level of these communities. In the United States, for example, national-level reparatory justice will require special focus on the populations that slavery and colonialism primarily wronged: African-American descendants of US systems of slavery and Indigenous peoples displaced by the settling of what became the United States.

But slavery, colonialism, and the political structure they produced were and are global phenomena. I treat them as such in this book and try to offer a global theoretical perspective on what could (and does) unite these separate political projects.

Where We're Going from Here

This introduction is chapter 1. In chapter 2, "Reconsidering World History," I describe the global scale of the constructive view and explain how we got here. I argue that we now live in a social system that is as large as the globe, and that this system was built by the converging processes of trans-Atlantic slavery and colonialism that I call "global racial empire." We should understand this system as a system of distribution, explaining where social advantages and disadvantages are made and how much of those social advantages and disadvantages different people and places get. Over time, advantages and disadvantages accumulate.

Chapter 3, "The Constructive View," explains the worldmaking view of justice that this book is written to promote. Since the injustice that reparations responds to is global and distributive, the constructive view helps explain what reparations needs to accomplish: building a

Nigeria)"; National Indian Brotherhood, *Indian Control of Indian Education: Policy Paper Presented to the Minister of Indian Affairs and Northern Development*.

just distribution. The view of racial injustice that the previous chapter introduces also helps explain why racial justice requires reparations: we have to respond both to today's injustices in distribution and the accumulated result of history's distributive injustices.

Chapter 4, "What's Missing," defends the constructive view against other common ways of thinking about and defending reparations, which I summarize as harm-repair arguments and relationship-repair arguments. I examine the strengths and weaknesses of each. This chapter also argues for standards that we should use to evaluate different reparations arguments and set priorities.

In chapter 5, "What's Next," I argue that, on the constructive view, a politically serious reparations project must focus on climate justice. As climate impacts accelerate, we can expect them to perversely distribute the costs and burdens of climate change, disproportionately impacting those who have been rendered most vulnerable given the accumulated weight of history. Our political and economic system distributes risk and vulnerability according to the patterns developed by the history of global racial empire: the people who will be most protected tend to be whites in the Global North, and those least protected tend to be Black and Indigenous peoples in the Global South. This threatens not only to present a future racial injustice, but also to effectively roll back gains made toward racial justice in recent decades. The chapter also discusses some policies and forms of organizing we can adopt to advance this project.

Finally, chapter 6, "The Arc of the Moral Universe," concludes the book by discussing a moral perspective we can develop to help us along in the fight for justice. The theoretical perspective of worldmaking and the concrete task of climate justice both force us to contend with the immense scale of injustice and thus the immense scale of the struggle for justice. It may well be outside of any generation's ability to win outright. But if we choose to relate to the world as ancestors, we can prevent this realization from overwhelming us into political paralysis. Many of the things that we do every day link us with countless people who have come before us and—if we succeed at preventing the worst climate outcomes—countless people who will come after us. We can do the spiritual work to act from this knowledge and faith right now. The world depends on it.

***

The 1835 Malê revolt in Brazil was decades in the making.

Years of immense social tensions in the north of the "Bight of Benin" region (in what is now Nigeria) came to a head in 1804. There, Fulani political leader and religious scholar Shehu Uthman dan Fodio led an uprising against the ruling Hausa elite: opposing their perceived heavy taxation, corruption, and intolerance of orthodox Islam.[17] He and many of his powerful followers also opposed the predation on Muslims of the Trans-Saharan and Trans-Atlantic slave trades—trades pursued by Muslims and non-Muslims alike, all in the pursuit of profit.[18]

dan Fodio's revolt did not stop the trade. Instead, the result of the revolution was a united Sokoto Caliphate, which became so large and powerful that it would eventually hold the second largest slave population in all of world history.[19] The Sokoto Caliphate's southward expansion produced conflict between the (now united) Hausa and Fulani militaries on the one hand and the Yoruba states on the other. This expansion combined with civil and intra-ethnic wars throughout Yorubaland as the once powerful Yoruba Oyo Empire declined, generating a flood of fresh Muslim and non-Muslim captives to join the victims of slave raids and other conflicts.[20]

The kingdom of Dahomey had long dominated the regional slave trade. Looking to circumvent them, the Portuguese and other foreign traders cooperated with Oyo to establish a new port for trans-Atlantic slave traffic to the east, to this day referred to by the Portuguese word "Lagos." The captives of the war in the north who weren't sold into

---

[17] Ojo, "Beyond Diversity: Women, Scarification, and Yoruba Identity"; Nmah and Amanambu, "1804 Usman Dan Fodio's Jihad on Inter-Group Relations in the Contemporary Nigerian State"; Barcia, "'An Islamic Atlantic Revolution:' Dan Fodio's Jihād and Slave Rebellion in Bahia and Cuba, 1804–1844."

[18] Salau, *Plantation Slavery in the Sokoto Caliphate: A Historical and Comparative Study*, Vol. 80, 48–49.

[19] By 1900 it would house between 1 and 2.5 million slaves—a historically large slave population worldwide, second only to the United States at its height, which held 4 million people of African descent under the condition of slavery in 1860. McKay et al., *A History of World Societies, Combined Volume*, 755.

[20] Barcia, "'An Islamic Atlantic Revolution:' Dan Fodio's Jihād and Slave Rebellion in Bahia and Cuba, 1804–1844," 7–8; Ojo, "The Organization of the Atlantic Slave Trade in Yorubaland, ca. 1777 to ca. 1856," 79–82.

slavery in Yorubaland were transported to Lagos' Atlantic port for sale to North and South America. The unlucky came from all of the region's ethnic groups, but the Yoruba were especially hard hit: as many as 1.62 million Yoruba were trafficked during the centuries of the trans-Atlantic slave trade.[21]

This mass transfer had speedy effects on the population of Brazil, and Salvador in particular. A 1775 census had found that whites made up 36% of the population of Salvador, and enslaved Black and mixed-race people were 41%.[22] Thanks in part to the wars of West Africa and the swelling currents of the slave trade, Salvador experienced a population boom, and by 1807, Black peoples (free and enslaved) made up nearly three quarters of the city. These numbers put the whole system at risk.

[21] Eltis, "The Diaspora of Yoruba Speakers, 1650–1865: Dimensions and Implications," 25–28.
[22] Reis, Rebelião Escrava No Brasil: A História Do Levante Dos Malês Em 1835, 14–15.

2

Reconsidering World History

"All men are interdependent. Every nation is an heir of a vast treasury of ideas and labor to which both the living and the dead of all nations have contributed. Whether we realize it or not, each of us lives eternally 'in the red.' We are everlasting debtors to known and unknown men and women. When we arise in the morning, we go into the bathroom where we reach for a sponge which is provided for us by a Pacific Islander. We reach for soap that is created for us by a European. Then at the table we drink coffee which is provided for us by a South American, or tea by a Chinese or cocoa by a West African. Before we leave for our jobs we are already beholden to more than half of the world."

—Dr. Martin Luther King, Jr., Where Do We Go from Here: Chaos or Community?

Baldwin and Buckley

In 1965, James Baldwin—luminary African American novelist, essayist, and philosopher—was invited to a historic debate at Cambridge University. The motion on the floor for debate: "This House believes that the American Dream is at the expense of the American Negro." The Buckley–Baldwin debate illustrates how an understanding of what is now the case necessarily encompasses an understanding of the past, and how both these understandings are necessary in order to envision the future.

Baldwin's parents were driven to New York by racial violence and economic necessity. David Baldwin left the South when it descended

Reconsidering Reparations. Olúfẹ́mi O. Táíwò, Oxford University Press. © Oxford University Press 2022. DOI: 10.1093/oso/9780197508893.003.0002

into an outbreak of lynchings and pogroms following the conclusion of the First World War.[1] Emma Berdis Jones was born in a small town in Maryland. Her mother died when she was young, and she decided to leave the house when her father re-married, moving in with her sister Beulah, the aunt that James once described as "the only mother I ever knew." After brief stints in other eastern cities, Berdis made her way to New York, where she found a job as a live-in domestic worker for a wealthy family. Soon after, in 1924, James Baldwin was born in Harlem, then the country's largest ghetto.[2]

When James was two, Berdis met and married David Baldwin, James's stepfather (whom he regarded as a father).[3] David worked as a day laborer and a Pentecostal preacher. Both Berdis and David were paid less than comparably employed whites. David and Berdis frequently appealed to the Home Relief Bureau for economic relief when they couldn't make ends meet but were frequently unsuccessful—as tended to be true for Blacks, at rates much higher than white applicants.[4] Along with the many children they were supporting on their meagre and inadequate earnings was David's mother, Barbara, a formerly enslaved woman. Barbara knew this struggle well, being the mother of fourteen children—some of whom had a white father.[5] James's relationship with his grandmother Barbara and the slavery in her living memory, as well as his understanding of the forces that put his family in the city in the first place, likely greatly influenced his understanding of the ongoing legacy of slavery in the racial domination he experienced in New York.

Opposite the Black son of a Harlem preacher on the Cambridge debate stage was the white, Irish Catholic son of an oil magnate.[6] Buckley senior made his money in the interlocking businesses of oil and authoritarianism throughout Latin America. He got his start defending American oil interests as a corporate lawyer in Mexico City and

---

[1] Baldwin, "The Black Scholar Interviews: James Baldwin."

[2] Buccola, *The Fire Is upon Us: James Baldwin, William F. Buckley Jr., and the Debate over Race in America*, 8–9.

[3] Leeming, *James Baldwin: A Biography*, chap. 1.

[4] Buccola, *The Fire Is upon Us*, 10.

[5] Leeming, *James Baldwin: A Biography*, chap. 1.

[6] Bridges and Coyne Jr., *Strictly Right: William F. Buckley Jr. and the American Conservative Movement*, 4–9.

eventually owned a Venezuelan oil company.[7] After growing up in a mansion on a forty-seven acre estate with an extensive staff of domestic workers, coaches, and tutors, William Jr. ended up an infamous rabble-rouser at Yale University. After graduation, he made his way to Mexico City to work for the CIA.[8] Spanish was his first language, and in fact he hadn't even begun learning to speak English until he was six years old, such was his father's investment in the Latin American oil business.[9]

In the biographical sense, it is difficult to imagine a much starker contrast of figures. Baldwin, on the one hand, rose from the nation's largest center of concentrated urban poverty, from its most exploited racial group of people. Buckley, on the other hand, hailed from an elite family of colonial managers. Though they saw themselves on opposite sides, the two men conceived the stakes of their political commitments in essentially the same way: as a battle over the soul of the American Republic. They were both intensely popular figures who had expanded the popular reach of the political cultures to which they belonged: Black liberationism and American conservatism, respectively.[10] In this sense, they were the ideal interlocutors to embody the nation's struggle over how to imagine a just version of itself.

Baldwin developed his political views among some of the leading Black radical political actors and artists of his day, including luminary figures like Eartha Kitt, C. L. R. James, and Alain Locke.[11] He even spent some time in the Young People's Socialist League.[12] Buckley, meanwhile, having returned from his role with the CIA in Mexico, founded the *National Review*, a publication widely considered to have played a key role in the renewed popularity of intellectual conservatism that followed the Second World War.[13] Among the many articles that Buckley penned himself for the publication, one in particular stands out: his 1957 article "Why the South Must Prevail," in which he argued that "[t]he white community in the South is entitled to take

---

[7] *Dissent Magazine,* "The Spanish-Speaking William F. Buckley."
[8] Buccola, *The Fire Is upon Us,* 53.
[9] *Dissent Magazine,* "The Spanish-Speaking William F. Buckley."
[10] Buccola, *The Fire Is upon Us,* 3–4.
[11] Buccola, *The Fire Is upon Us,* 24–25.
[12] Buccola, *The Fire Is upon Us,* 25–26.
[13] Nash, *The Conservative Intellectual Movement in America since 1945,* chap. 5.

such measures as are necessary to prevail, politically and culturally," given that it was "for the time being . . . the advanced race."[14] The major thread running through his otherwise inchoate views was a general antagonism toward any threat of cultural or political change that could complicate or challenge his conception of Christian and American values.

Buckley insisted that Baldwin should be "addressing his own people, and urging them to take at least the advantage of those opportunities that exist." For Buckley, incredibly, *not* choosing to tell Blacks that they had to imitate the Jewish and Irish immigrant communities was tantamount to "telling us [whites] that we should renounce our civilization."[15] He ended his remarks with a warning, cautioning Black people that the cost of reaching for a "radical solution" would be a "radical confrontation." He likened this confrontation to the war against imperial Nazi Germany, in which an unspecified "we" would fight "on beaches and on hills, on mountains and on landing grounds" in defense of civilization itself, as embodied in the "American way of life"—which, by the way, Buckley took to be "indistinguishable" from the "European way of life."[16]

When Buckley spoke of "our" civilization he blithely allowed the "we" to be inferred. Baldwin, on the other hand, spoke of civilizations, plural, and the interactions between them. Rather than accepting Buckley's assumption that "the" American version of civilization is singular and is identical with the concept of civilization itself, Baldwin described a more complex and realistic world. The answer to the proposition, Baldwin said, must rest on "the question of whether or not civilizations can be considered as such equal, or whether one civilization has the right to overtake and subjugate, and in fact to destroy, another."

Throughout his speech, Baldwin connected the specific plight of those Indigenous peoples killed so their land could be transformed into white profit to the plight of those people of African descent who were enslaved to wreak the transformation. "It comes as a great shock

---

14 Buckley Jr., "Why the South Must Prevail."
15 Buccola, *The Fire Is upon Us*, 396.
16 Buccola, *The Fire Is upon Us*, 398.

around the age of five or six or seven to discover the flag to which you have pledged allegiance, along with everybody else, has not pledged allegiance to you. It comes as a great shock to discover that Gary Cooper killing off the Indians, when you were rooting for Gary Cooper, that the Indians were you!"[17]

The audience laughed, but I doubt that Baldwin was joking. It was a poignant way to try to illustrate how your individual response to the subject of the American Dream "has to depend in effect" on "where you find yourself in the world."[18] If you live in a world where you believe that under the American flag you cannot be enslaved—that you will have freedom of speech and movement and access to property and the ability to reap profit—if you live in such a world, you might well imagine that the flag and civilization are one. But if you find yourself in a community in which enslavement, violence, and expropriation have been the actual experiences over which the American flag has presided, this point of view is dead on arrival. Ultimately you must find yourself in solidarity with everyone else whose survival is likewise imperiled by the "European system of reality."

The Baldwin–Buckley debate has the same essential shape as the conversation that engulfs us now: Where do we find ourselves in reality? And what steps must we take in the present moment in order to create the future? This book will argue that James Baldwin is still right: slavery and colonialism built the world we know. Seeing this world for what it is will help us think and act our way out of its demise.

The World System

"Wasi'chu is the Lakota (Sioux) word for 'greedy one who takes the fat.' It was used to describe a strange race that not only took what it thought it needed, but also took the rest. It was used to describe the white race. Wasi'chu is also a human condition based on inhumanity, racism, and exploitation. Indians have been victims of war

[17] Buccola, *The Fire Is upon Us*, 381.
[18] Buccola, *The Fire Is upon Us*, 379.

and aggression for most of the past five hundred years. The so-called Indian wars were always fought over the issues of land and resources. We have always had something that the Wasi'chu wanted."

—John Redhouse[19]

The Present

We live in a "world economic order." As Martin Luther King, Jr. told us sixty years ago, you can't go through a basic action in your day without participating in a global interaction. Odds are good that you ordered this book on a device with materials mined in the Democratic Republic of the Congo, assembled in China, and shipped to yet a third continent for sale. This global economic system that we have distributes rewards and even basic economic functions to different parts of the world through networks of trade, exchange, and movement. Some countries specialize in the manufacture of particular physical goods: perhaps petroleum, like Nigeria or Saudi Arabia; coffee and cocoa, like the Ivory Coast. Other countries specialize in being tax havens for the wealth of the world's elite, like Switzerland and Monaco. A range of "internal" political activity organizes and optimizes this activity within the borders of nation states, through means such as taxation, subsidization, and regulation to zoning, housing, and education.

To some extent, then, these sovereign nations control how things go within their borders. But their economic activity relies on what's going on in the rest of the world, often more acutely than on what's going on inside. Apparently "internal" Nigerian or Saudi decisions about producing petroleum actually succeed or fail based on which cars are on the road in China or the United States; how much cocoa to produce in the Ivory Coast depends on how much chocolate is being eaten in Belgium

---

[19] John Redhouse, following, wrote the introduction to *Wasi'chu*. Redhouse is a Diné (Navajo) veteran of the Red Power movement and Indian rights organizations, including Indians Against Exploitation and the Coalition for Navajo Liberation. See Johansen and Maestas, *Wasi'chu: The Continuing Indian Wars*, 11; Estes, "Decolonization and Indigenous Liberation."

or France; the likelihood of which financial incentives will attract foreign licit and illicit capital to Monaco or Atlantic City depends on what the other tax havens are offering.

It's not entirely unsurprising, then, that we also live in a world *political* order: a system of countries that relate to each other, and institutions that work alongside, between, and above these. Alongside the United Nations, International Monetary Fund (IMF), and World Bank are a host of other institutions such as regional development banks that make up the formal and semi-formal politico-economic connections knitting the world together. Nongovernmental organizations add additional sinews, including, at the top end, international heavyweights such as the Gates Foundation and international weapons manufacturers, alongside the more lucrative of the criminal business networks and empires.

These political and economic "orders" describe the same world system. The separation between these two ways of looking at the world order is a matter of emphasis, to the extent that it is not simply imaginary. In many times and places the exercise of power is a fairly holistic matter. Accordingly, even institutions that seem purely focused on global economic relations, like the IMF, in effect and thus in fact operate politically, and vice versa. Understanding this is key to understanding the pressures that built our global social system, and the scope of what it will take to rebuild them in the direction of justice.

Structure and Motion

On the constructive view of reparations, reparations are a worldmaking project. This involves thinking about justice and injustice in distributive terms: that is, as a matter of who gets what. But the relationship of persons to resources is not a static, one-time transaction. Resources flow to and away from people continuously. We can look at the politico-economic system of the world as something like a water management system, a web of aqueducts that spans the globe, channeling, instead of water, advantages and disadvantages from one place to another. The system describes which way future waters will naturally run, and where they will *not* run without novel intervention. If we try to explain modern finance, or philanthropy, or pollution, or medical care, we end up describing their *motion* in the world. The system of the world, then, is not best described by the metaphor of a blueprint, or an organizational chart of political powers, but as a set of inertias, gravities, pressures, and bottlenecks that bound and channel the endless flow of the present: material, money, media, violence, advantage, disadvantage. It is their *motion in time* that makes the system of the world, and we can map the system to the extent that we can predict the direction of motion.

The stones of the aqueducts that contain and discipline the continuous motion of the past into the future were laid in the seventeenth, eighteenth, and nineteenth centuries. This was the period when several European powers vied to create channels of wealth that would link the globe together into a world economic order. For reasons we will explore later, I call the world order resulting from their collective project the Global Racial Empire. And just as the decisions ancient Roman engineers made in building their aqueducts continued to determine who had water long after those engineers, and their original imperial project, were dead, the global distribution system built by the Global Racial Empire continues to function. This fact is easily demonstrated, for the patterns in how advantage and disadvantage flow have changed very little. This perspective on world history helps explain why world historians treat reparations as "less about the transfer of resources . . . as it is about the transformation of *all* social relations . . . re-envisioning and reconstructing a world-system."[20]

Take, for instance, the mines of Potosí in what is now Bolivia. The Spanish empire founded the city in 1545 as a mining town, in search of precious metals—in particular, the silver demanded by China's Ming Dynasty, which faced a monetary crisis.[21] The resources discovered there were of world historical consequence—it is estimated that between the years 1500 and 1800, Latin America produced approximately 150,000 tons of silver, amounting to 80 percent of the world's

---

[20] Murphy et al., "Introduction: World History and the Work of Reparations," 145.
[21] Flynn and Giraldez, "Arbitrage, China, and World Trade in the Early Modern Period."

production in that period, and that in the second half of the sixteenth century 60 percent of that came from Potosí's mines alone.[22]

This monumental production worked for people very far away: it created enormous wealth for the Spanish empire and solved a governance problem for the Ming dynasty. But the wealth extraction and coerced labor system that enabled it powerfully reshaped the region surrounding the mines: within thirty years of the city's construction, it had a larger population than Madrid or Paris.[23] Today, five centuries later, the wealth produced in Potosí seams has all flowed away and accumulated elsewhere: it took significant economic gains over the last decade to move Bolivia from the "low income" to the "lower-middle income" classification by the World Bank.[24] Yet the mines of Potosí are still in operation and still are at the center of economic life there.[25]

Meanwhile, underneath the Salar de Uyuni salt flat in the same area of Potosí is one of the world's largest deposits of lithium, a key material used to make the batteries that power electric vehicles and many other electronics. Green trends in the world economy may position Potosí for a fresh round of world-historic levels of extraction, generating loads of both wealth and toxic byproduct. Where the extracted wealth will ultimately pool will take some time to determine, but its immediate future, absent our intervention, is quite clear: for the global racial empire has been cut out of the rock of political history and all its channels for wealth lead away from Potosí. The formations built to funnel toxins, on the other hand, tend to separate them from wealth and direct them to accumulate where people are poor in both economic and political power.

The Spanish Empire in the sixteenth century wanted to build a global system of wealth and power, into which any advantage they found in any part of the globe could be redirected. They succeeded. *And now we live in that world.* We can tell, because things still fundamentally move in the same directions.

---

[22] Barragán, "Working Silver for the World: Mining Labor and Popular Economy in Colonial Potosí."

[23] Galeano, *Las Venas Abiertas de América Latina*, 38.

[24] "How Evo Morales Made Bolivia a Better Place . . . Before He Fled the Country."

[25] Dickerman and Francescangeli, "Perspective:| What Life Is Like for the Teenage Miners of Potosi, Bolivia."

Aspects of this order have been very intentionally designed by human intelligence in various times and places. However, it is important to note that many of the social conditions this book will analyze cannot be easily attributed to the intention of any particular person, institution, or even empire's artifice. Rather, we live through the slowly unfolding results of decisions made generations ago. The character of today's global social system owes itself not just to active interventions by specific, plotting cabals of conspiring elites (although there are certainly plenty of examples of those), but also to the inertias that describe the patterns of their everyday activities, with or without their conscious action or even perception.

The story of the construction of our world is the story by which the 'Atlantic Order,' what historian Joseph Inikori terms the large but not yet global system of slavery and colonialism, came to encompass the whole globe.[26] Racism and colonialism were the basic structure of the Atlantic Order, and they accompanied and catalyzed the expansion of the Atlantic Order into a fully global economic structure. And the outcome, the global economy, is today managed and directed by global capitalism: so if global racial empire is the *what*, then capitalism is the *how*.

In the beginning, the connection between racism, colonialism, and capitalism was obvious. The latter was built with political and juridical structures that explicitly mentioned race and empire and overtly managed the affairs of business in the context of both. As Karl Marx succinctly explains in *The Poverty of Philosophy:* "Direct slavery is just as much the pivot of bourgeois industry as machinery, credits, etc. Without slavery you have no cotton; without cotton you have no modern industry. It is slavery that gave the colonies their value; it is the colonies that created world trade, and it is world trade that is the precondition of large-scale industry. Thus slavery is an economic category of the greatest importance."[27]

But over time, as the world system has shifted—importantly, in large part because it has been successfully challenged in many ways

---

[26] Inikori, "Slavery and Atlantic Commerce, 1650–1800"; Shilliam, "The Atlantic as a Vector of Uneven and Combined Development."

[27] Marx, "The Poverty of Philosophy," chap. 2, 1.

by generations of people fighting for justice. As a result, forms of domination have become more complex, and power and wealth subtler and harder to understand. Nevertheless, the broad patterns and stratification that explicitly characterized past centuries largely hold today. Across the globe, racism distributes political rights in ways that favor the transfer of material and immaterial advantages toward the colonizers and away from the colonized, and *those* relationships and inertias persist even after the vocabulary of "colony" has given way to newer window-dressings.

History is not merely an interesting point of comparison for our contemporary problems. Everything we experience happens in the flow of time from past to present to future, and so when we struggle to stay afloat in the present—to access health care, to secure food, to form healthy relationships—we are swimming among the currents of history. When we understand the structure of the world as the pattern of its motion, it turns out that history is one of the most powerful ways we can discern where these invisible currents we get caught in are coming from, and where they are going, to perceive where they will pull us under and drown us, and what it would take to avoid that fate. Armed with a global perspective, we can also see how consequences flow from some parts of the world to other parts, often across national borders, and in ways that complicate geographically and politically narrow ways of thinking about reparations.

Throughout this chapter, I will try to show how the things we might label "colonialism" or "neocolonialism" and the things we might label "institutional racism" were produced by the very same historical events and processes, and they are part of the same contemporary structure of injustice. Structurally speaking, the domination of the Global North over the Global South is the domination of white peoples over Indigenous people and other people of color.

In his landmark 1994 book *The Racial Contract*, philosopher Charles Mills borrows the "social contract" language of liberal political thought to make this same claim about the basic organization of the world's social structures. He argues that we live in a world "built by the Racial Contract"; that is, "global white supremacy" is itself a political system, the one resulting from the fact that the world has been "foundationally shaped for the past five hundred years by the . . . gradual consolidation of global white supremacy."[28] Mills characterizes that political system in comprehensive, distributive terms, describing it as "a particular power structure of formal or informal rule, socioeconomic privilege, and norms for the differential distribution of material wealth and opportunities, benefits and burdens, rights and duties."[29] This book contends that he is correct.

As this chapter moves forward to explain the structure of today's world in terms of the historical motions it embodies, it will be helpful to pause first to highlight a key pair of concepts that we will return to throughout the book—cumulative advantage and cumulative disadvantage.

Cumulative Processes

Money, goods, knowledge, and technology can be or can provide social advantages. Debt, pollution, and knowledge gaps are social disadvantages. These are also products, the direct results of intentional human activity. We can ask basic questions about any given moment: Where are these advantages and disadvantages produced, and whose labor is involved in producing them? When they are produced, where do they go, and who gets access to them? More simply, who gets what, and how much of it? These are questions about *distribution*, or how advantages and disadvantages are spread out across people, countries, and social positions. This is a core concept that we can use to analyze many problems of injustice, which can happen when a system directs more or fewer advantages to a place or population than it ought to.

The concept of distribution is intimately related to another important concept: *accumulation*, which marks how advantages and disadvantages build up over time. When we're thinking about advantages, think paychecks. If you get paid more than your bills and expenses cost, you can save up the excess money—an accumulation of advantages. In any given moment of need, money in a bank account

---

28 Mills, *The Racial Contract*, 20, 30.
29 Mills, *The Racial Contract*, 3.

is an advantage. But how much you are able to keep in that account depends on the size of your paychecks over time, that is, your distribution of income. When we're thinking about disadvantages, think about trash collection. If sanitation workers are not available or do not do their essential work, then, like the disposable income in a savings account, the trash accumulates. But in this latter case, the accumulation is adverse, and the amount of trash in an area ultimately represents the distribution of access to sanitation service over time. Since accumulation results from past distributions, this pair of concepts help us understand how past injustice explains present injustice, and how present injustice can explain future injustice.

This also provides a route into a different way of thinking about the political situation, one that animates some reparations arguments. Rather than thinking of racial disparities in wealth or access to public health as evidence of some nefarious undiscovered intentional conspiracy, we can explain disparities in many cases as simply the present accumulated imprint of past racist distributions of resources and infrastructure.

Theories about cumulative advantage and disadvantage were developed by scientists studying a curious aspect of their own social world, the world of science. It's easy to understand the importance of networking, charisma, privilege, and prestige in fields like politics and business. But we might think that science is importantly different from these; that, in principle, anyone with good ideas, sufficient data, and sound analysis should be able to advance themselves and their research.

Nevertheless, researchers found that a small fraction of scientists commanded a greatly outsized share of grant dollars, institutional recognition, and accolades.[30] Moreover, they were put on track to receive the lion's share of these from the beginning of their time in higher education: in the late 1970s, five institutions accounted for more than half of the world's Nobel laureates, and more than half of American Nobel laureates had themselves directly studied under previous winners

[30] Zuckerman, "Accumulation of Advantage and Disadvantage: The Theory and Its Intellectual Biography," 139.

of the prize.[31] None of this is to say that scientists' ideas or research quality had *no* relevance—top institutions made deliberate efforts to seek out and attract top scientific talent, and one of the key predictors of long-term success was the quality and quantity of a scientist's early career research.[32]

But once they *started* winning, they *kept* winning. Early success—say, in college admissions processes—meant respect from and access to the past generation's best researchers. It also meant the best labs, access to similarly situated and connected peers, and training conducted under the most exacting educational and research standards. The early success built out of these favorable conditions also built future success: promising early career research becomes successful future grant applications, resulting in more research resources to repeat and build upon the early success. With each stage of these scientists' careers, the advantages stacked upon each other—that is to say, they accumulated.

All of that is to say that the distribution of rewards, credit, and resources in science were subject to linked cumulative advantage and disadvantage processes: the outcome of all of the previous rounds largely decide in advance the winner of today's round. Sociologist Robert K. Merton offers another description, describing science's social system as a stratified "class structure," where people who have accumulated different levels accordingly have different levels of access to "the means of scientific production."[33] The way you win today's game is by having won yesterday's.

So also with disadvantage. Relative cumulative disadvantage is the easiest to see. Access to advantages like grants or tenure-track positions are often competitive, with many seekers and few opportunities. Every factor that makes the cumulatively advantaged more likely to get scarce opportunities is, mathematically speaking, also a factor that makes the cumulatively disadvantaged less likely to access these opportunities.[34] Sticking with the original example of science's social

---

[31] Zuckerman, "Accumulation of Advantage and Disadvantage," 140; Merton, "The Matthew Effect in Science: The Reward and Communication Systems of Science Are Considered," 61.

[32] Zuckerman, "Accumulation of Advantage and Disadvantage," 141.

[33] Merton, "The Matthew Effect in Science," 57.

[34] Zuckerman, "Accumulation of Advantage and Disadvantage," 144.

system, we could see how early advantages for some scientists could work out poorly for others. Late bloomers, who did their best work later in their careers, and low-status scientists, who did excellent work throughout but started from an institution or social background that was ill positioned to win money or acknowledgment early on, would have to fight an uphill and sometimes unwinnable battle to muscle their way past their better-positioned rivals. And this holds true even if they arrive at an equivalent level of performance or aptitude.

But not all cumulative disadvantage is relative. There are absolute forms of disadvantage, as well, that we don't need comparison or competition to make sense of. Here it helps to leave the social system of science and think about one more obviously related to race: the US criminal justice system. A single event of incarceration, especially as a juvenile, may put a person on a trajectory or "life course" of accumulating disadvantages.[35] This progression of disadvantages is not relative: the damage here doesn't chiefly arrive via competition for scarce opportunities with people who haven't been incarcerated, but in direct and absolute effects upon the person incarcerated. The process starts with the original imposition of punitive disadvantages: incarceration itself and a criminal record. From there, others pile on: the financial burden of incarceration, the lack of access to jobs after release, damage to both self-efficacy and social trust. What's more, as formerly incarcerated people are stigmatized and rejected out of mixed social spaces, they may find themselves relegated to social spaces with higher concentrations of others who have been ostracized for the same reasons. This makes them even more likely to be written off by peers who associate them with criminal, "anti-social" elements, thus increasing their already considerable challenges to reintegration into society.[36] These are absolute disadvantages: the social effects would apply no matter whether the pool of incarcerated persons shrank, grew, or changed composition.

[35] Sampson and Laub, "A Life-Course Theory of Cumulative Disadvantage and the Stability of Delinquency."

[36] For an extended discussion of the way people are policed in high gang-activity areas, see Victor Rios's sociological study. Rios, *Punished: Policing the Lives of Black and Latino Boys*.

The research on cumulative advantage and disadvantage has been used to study topics as varied as the juvenile justice system, racial disparities in aging-related health outcomes, and subprime lending in housing markets.[37] If cumulative advantage and disadvantage help explain how world economic and political structures developed and where they developed, then they help explain why the events that constructed world politics resulted in the world we have now—with wealth, effective institutions, and social advantage concentrated in particular parts of the world and in the hands of particular groups of people within and across those places.

Divide and Conquer

Differences in the cumulative processes in different regions and for different people are patterned by the global racial empire's obsession with hierarchies of various kinds. Sociologist Oliver C. Cox developed a blueprint for this thought over a number of books published throughout the 1950s and 1960s, including *Caste, Class, and Race* and *The Foundations of Capitalism*. Cox's work regarded the capitalist system as an entire global social system, not simply a system of production. That system was "constituted of the whole network of its territorial units and their interrelationships" and the hierarchically arranged interactions between "nations, colonies, and dependent communities."[38] Imperialism, the characterization he gives between the relationships of those at the top of the hierarchy with those below them, has "gone hand in hand with the rise of the capitalist system as a necessary component."[39]

Cox's works and their importance have been largely ignored by his contemporaries and successors for a variety of reasons: a Trinidadian

[37] Rugh, Albright, and Massey, "Race, Space, and Cumulative Disadvantage: A Case Study of the Subprime Lending Collapse"; Sampson and Laub, "A Life-Course Theory of Cumulative Disadvantage and the Stability of Delinquency"; Shuey and Willson, "Cumulative Disadvantage and Black-White Disparities in Life-Course Health Trajectories."

[38] Hunter and Abraham, *Race, Class, and the World System: The Sociology of Oliver C. Cox*, 265.

[39] Hunter and Abraham, *Race, Class, and the World System*, 295.

by birth, Cox was not "networked" in powerful circles; outright racial discrimination prevented Black scholars like him from being employed in well-resourced institutions; and his outspoken radicalism during the age of McCarthyism made him a target and allowed others to ignore his work.[40] However, the balance of academic work produced since Cox's original writings vindicates the broad outlines of his view about capitalism and global racial empire.

In the landmark book *Black Marxism* and throughout his subsequent work, political theorist Cedric Robinson followed up on the work Cox began, uniting its global scope with the "racial capitalism" analysis that was being developed by African activists and intellectuals such as Neville Alexander and Bernard Magubane.[41] Robinson argued that capitalism, which spread after European global conquest, came to the rest of the world bundled with cultural mores and tendencies that affected social organization much more broadly than did its labor and production schemes.[42] One important tendency, which Robinson argues is a prominent feature of European history, is the tendency to organize populations into separate groups, organize those groups into a fairly rigid hierarchy, and promote ideologies naturalizing or otherwise legitimating this hierarchy. This tendency could be seen in internal European politics long before 1492 (one prominent example being the relationship between the British and the Irish) but evolved into what we now think of as racism when European political powers (and, thus, their forms of social organization) gained structural influence on a world scale. At that juncture, skin color became a more prominent part of the story about which groups exist in the world and where they ought to be in hierarchal relation to other groups. Hierarchies now pertained not just within countries or even regions of the world, but between the countries and regions of the world.

The phrase "racial capitalism" is somewhat misleading, since it implies that race and capitalism are the only relevant aspects of social structure to consider. Nonetheless this book's view of history largely

---

[40] Hunter and Abraham, *Race, Class, and the World System,* xviii–xlv.
[41] Al-Bulushi, "Thinking Racial Capitalism and Black Radicalism from Africa: An Intellectual Geography of Cedric Robinson's World-System."
[42] Robinson, *Black Marxism: The Making of the Black Radical Tradition.*

agrees and draws from the insights of Robinson, Cox, Alexander, and the many others who used this phrase and framework.[43] The phrase "racial capitalism" is better thought of as a *name* that abbreviates a much broader historical account of our current social system, rather than as a description of a phenomenon fully characterized by the intersection or interaction of race and class. Accordingly, I'll use the term Global Racial Empire to name this fuller picture. Some of Oliver Cox's own work on caste demonstrated that a reductive approach can't account for the vast network of interconnections between the race, capital, and other important aspects of social organization, like gender, settler status, ethnicity, religion, and ability. The name Global Racial Empire shouldn't be taken to imply that these are irrelevant, but instead it marks a particular perspective on these and other aspects of social organization.

The ideologies and even basic forms of social organization of the global ruling class had powerful effects on all forms of social organization of the people absorbed into the developing world system. One critical aspect was the construction or reconstruction of gender among colonized people. Sociologist Raewyn Connell argues that the imperial social order not only created a racial hierarchy between communities and races, but also that this process was itself gendered—that is, the racial hierarchy was bound up with an evaluation of the racial groups' gendered qualities. The colonizers distinguished 'more manly' from 'less manly' groups among their subjects. The British conquerors of India considered Bengali men to be effeminate, while they regarded Pathans and Sikhs as strong and warlike. Similar distinctions were made in South Africa (between Hottentots and Zulus) and North America (between Iroquois, Sioux, and Cheyenne on one side and southern and southwestern tribes on the other).

Philosophers Shelbi Nahwilet Meissner and Kyle Whyte explain that, when societies had more than two genders, many Indigenous peoples were forced into relationship structures that mirrored the patriarchal gender binaries that settlers understood, expected, and enforced. The re-organization of gender relations among colonized

---

[43] For an example of a criticism of the term 'racial capitalism' along these lines, see Parron, "Capital e raça."

people was likely a result of the same pressures that reorganized their social life in economic, geographical, and other ways: the often forgotten slave trade in Indigenous peoples, the economic pressures of the global economy (mediated through trade with settlers), and the dramatic disruptions of various wars of Native elimination and settler conquest, since the resulting displacement made lifeways tied to the previous land difficult to maintain. But there were also more deliberate and direct efforts to reshape Indigenous social life, including the work of missionaries (often in "mission schools") to assimilate and/or eliminate Native culture.

When societies either didn't have gender at all or had a non-patriarchal gender system, as feminist theorists Nkiru Nzegwu and Oyèrónkẹ́ Oyěwùmí argue was the case in some West African societies, a patriarchal gender evolved in response to the forces of political and economic control.[44] Nzegwu argues that the British and "Native" court system helped shift power and incentives among Igbo people to reshape their families and even reconstruct their family histories in patriarchal ways. Sophie Oluwole makes similar claims about the Yoruba people but emphasizes the role of British business owners, who refused to make deals with Yoruba women, thereby upsetting the previous balance of gender power.[45] Though the means varied in these different cases, the results were largely the same: global racial empire substantially restructured how social and cultural life in general was organized for those it colonized.

By controlling the terms of social identity and the incentives that they shape themselves in response to, global racial empire has been able to maintain control of politics and people on many different scales, from the individual family to the regional bloc of countries.

[44] Nzegwu, Family Matters: Feminist Concepts in African Philosophy of Culture; Oyěwùmí, The Invention of Women: Making an African Sense of Western Gender Discourses.
[45] Ojoye and Alagbe, "My Mum Never Believed I Could Become a Professor—Sophie Oluwole."

Nested Scales

So understanding that our present world order is one that was built as a global racial empire helps us explain where advantage and disadvantage accumulates and for whom. Cumulative advantage and disadvantage are potential features of social systems of any size. But it is important to remember that we happen to live in one big global social system, so these patterns occur at massive as well as micro scales.

The system distributes social advantages such as wealth, bargaining power, prestige, and even attention toward certain parts of the world and certain populations within those regions. At a global scale, these forces shift advantages across countries and continents, toward the so called Global North. Disadvantages are shunted toward the developing nations, the Global South. At a lower scale, viewed within countries or regions, the order of things tends to shift advantages toward people racialized as white and disadvantages toward Indigenous peoples and those racialized as Black.

The global and the national scales are deeply related in ways that invite more nationally or regionally focused views of reparations. In fact, they often seem to have a sort of fractal structure—the racial realities visible at small scales, in the interactions and distributions of power and vulnerability within nations or communities, re-appear when analyzing relationships between nations or world regions. African American scholar W. E. B. Du Bois expressed this idea powerfully when he used "the Color Line" to explain divides between Black and white individuals in nineteenth century United States, as well as the geopolitical lines of power and conflict. The US Civil War—an internal battle over the institution of slavery in the world's most powerful "slave power"—provides an excellent example of the connections between national and global politics that DuBois described.[46]

The US Civil War was an event that had domestic stakes (whether or not slavery would be legal within US borders) and global stakes (where the global market would get its supply of cotton, and who would profit). The global nature of the battle over slavery was not

---

[46] Karp, *This Vast Southern Empire*, 233–234.

lost on the Southern planter elite. As historian Matthew Karp shows, the Southern elite of the United States were a highly politically literate and cosmopolitan class, responsible for the first citations of lofty intellectuals like G. W. F. Hegel and Auguste Comte in Congressional proceedings.[47] They tracked economic and political developments across the globe and exerted considerable influence over US foreign policy with an eye toward defending slaveholder interests against the mutually supporting forces of enslaved people's rebellions and insurgent abolitionism. Much of the country had been created by recent imperial conquest: the 1846 invasion of Mexico increased the size of the United States by half a million square miles, and wars of Indigenous dispossession and elimination like the Creek War of 1813 had made it possible to settle the lower South and produce commodities for the global market.[48]

One development they tracked with great interest was the British empire's 1833 abolition of the slave trade. The British empire immediately set its unmatched naval power to the purpose of policing the seas and disrupting and preventing trans-Atlantic human trafficking. Its supposed humanitarian rationale sat awkwardly next to the other imperial developments of the same era: expansion of imperial control over swaths of the world as varied as India, Qing China, South Africa, and Burma.[49] Britain's economic and political dominance, US planters knew, was undergirded by the inhuman exploitation of laborers too, with indentured "coolie" workers from Asia replacing chattel slaves of African descent in the Caribbean, and land rent extracted by torture in South Asia.[50] By 1842, Southern elites were already convinced of what scholars argued decades later: that the supposed "humanitarian" project of imperial abolitionism was actually aimed at the empire's material interests. They took it that the empire's real goal was to disadvantage its slavery-reliant competitors and thereby gain an effective monopoly on the global supply of cotton and sugar.[51]

---

[47] Karp, *This Vast Southern Empire*, 4–5.
[48] Karp, *This Vast Southern Empire*, 37, 181.
[49] Karp, *This Vast Southern Empire*, 158.
[50] Karp, *This Vast Southern Empire*, 237.
[51] Karp, *This Vast Southern Empire*, 24–31.

But in the decades to come, "King Cotton" held firm, and the US South was still the world's dominant producer of cotton, one of the most important global export commodities. This fact, and geopolitical calculations built upon it, crucially undergirded the confidence of the Confederate secessionists.[52] The first full paragraph of the Mississippi declaration of secession identifies "the institution of slavery" as the "greatest material interest of the *world*" [emphasis added], not just of the United States. Despite the insurgence of abolitionist thought in the United States and Europe, the US Confederates believed that European powers would intervene to defend their own economic interest in Southern cotton production and their ideological interest in slavery as a social system—one that reflected in dramatic and local interpersonal terms the white supremacy that European empires aimed to embed throughout the entire world.

The Confederate secessionists were in for a surprise, as the economic powers-that-were had other plans. British colonial officials in India pressed Parliament for massive infrastructure investment and made sweeping changes to criminal, contract, and property law to encourage cotton production in the colony, aiming to make up in colonized Indian labor the potential loss of goods extracted from enslaved African labor.[53] In Africa, the Ottoman Empire also got to work, with Viceroy Sa'id Pasha working to convert Nile lands and laborers to the global economic cause of cotton production, helped along by a US federal government eager to break the economic back of the Confederacy.[54] Brazil, another fellow slave economy in the western hemisphere, ratcheted up its cotton production as well. These efforts were extraordinarily successful: before the end of the 1860s, Bombay's cotton exports to Britain and France surged, Brazil's cotton exports had doubled, and 40 percent of the land around the Nile had been committed to cotton production for the world market.[55]

Thus the supposedly national, "internal" dispute of the US Civil War was anything but. It was, from start to finish, a product of global forces,

---

[52] Avalon Project, "Confederate States of America: Mississippi Secession."
[53] Beckert, "Emancipation and Empire: Reconstructing the Worldwide Web of Cotton Production in the Age of the American Civil War," 1411.
[54] Beckert, "Emancipation and Empire," 1418.
[55] Beckert, "Emancipation and Empire."

and it palpably restructured the daily reality of people on as many as five continents. This level of global connectivity would have been unthinkable a few generations prior. Yet from the standpoint of a farmer along the river Nile, in British India or the Belgian Congo, the resultant economic changes might have felt quite local, as whole swaths of land and labor policies affecting their day-to-day lives dramatically shifted.[56]

In other words, although we think of today's world as uniquely interconnected, for the past half millennium many of our daily and all of our most dire challenges have required a global perspective to fully understand. What remains for us now is to truly break free of the misleading hierarchies of empire to attain that perspective.

A Brief Linear History of the System

Christopher Columbus landed first in the New World at the island of San Salvador, and after praising God enquired urgently for gold.
—C. L. R. James, *The Black Jacobins*

Now that we have a sense of the approach, let us take a closer look at how the Global Racial Empire came to be.[57] As we do so, this point is important enough to bear repeating: this history is not simply a point of comparison to the present. It is a way to map the currents that engulf us in the present. With this in mind, let us briefly survey the linear history of the empire to see how our world today was shaped.

The Atlantic Order: First Contact

The basic framework for the Atlantic Order was forged between roughly 1491, when Columbus first enslaved the Taino people to build a channel funneling wealth back to Spain, and 1571, when the Spanish

---

[56] New Internationalist, "Cotton: A History."
[57] James, *The Black Jacobins: Toussaint L'Ouverture and the San Domingo Revolution*, 3.

conquest of Manila linked trans-Pacific trade to the trans-Atlantic and trans-Indian ocean trades. The "discovery" and conquest of the Americas and Manila was a tremendous event in world economic history: it linked nearly all of the world's populated continents in trade (and thus in politics). This map of linkages founded the Atlantic Order. But the fact that this was occasioned by European discoveries did not *immediately* translate into European control. How, then, did European powers turn this new geographic access into economic, social, and political control?

We are all familiar with imagining the initial cross-cultural encounters that forged each of these global linkages as encounters between the more civilized and the less civilized. Given the huge quantity of white supremacist and revisionist histories produced in the intervening centuries, and their often unquestioned pride of place in our education systems, this is hardly surprising. But perhaps even without the explicit guidance of racist historians, there is a tendency to read the past in light of present-day distributions of power, and thus to see the people of the past as being roughly as wealthy, organized, and powerful as their modern-day descendants.

But this is quite untrue. The Aztec empire, for example, was one of the era's wealthiest societies.[58] It had advanced political organization and had already implemented many social reforms that the countries of the Western world would not adopt for centuries: universal education, government-sponsored housing and caretaking for disabled and medically stigmatized populations, and an advanced legal system.[59] The largest works of civil engineering in human history were not anywhere in Europe—the "Great Walls" of Benin (in what is now Nigeria), for example, were four times the size of China's Great Wall and thirty times the size of Manhattan today.[60]

---

[58] I use the term 'Aztec empire' for clarity, but this is neither how they referred to themselves nor how the land they lived on was referred to by the many peoples who lived there. I'm indebted to Elsa Barraza Mendoza for this point. Bayly, *Indigenous and Colonial Origins of Comparative Economic Development: The Case of Colonial India and Africa*, 3.

[59] Restall, *When Montezuma Met Cortés: The True Story of the Meeting That Changed History*, chap. 3.

[60] Pearce, "The African Queen."

When Vasco da Gama arrived in India in 1497, he offered the local ruler gifts including cloth, casks of oil, and honey. He was rebuffed, informed by a local official that even the poorest merchant from any other part of India—or even as far as Mecca—would have presented a more lavish offering.[61] If he wanted to be taken seriously in this economy, the official suggested, perhaps he should try gold.[62] The economic titans on the planet at this time were in Asia, not Europe.[63] The Portuguese were outmatched in the market by the preexisting players in a well-developed, centuries-old network of economy and trade that stretched from China and the region they knew as the "Far East," through the Indian subcontinent, and clear across to Africa's eastern "Swahili coast."

In that moment, it was far from apparent that a would-be player from a tiny, far-off land had some insurmountable civilizational advantage. The considerable challenges of competing with the highly efficient and organized South Asian economies, particularly the commercial centers of Bengal and Gujarat, was actually one of the key pressures that propelled Europe to begin accumulating power in a struggle for global advantage.[64] Like the Spanish and their fleet of conquistadores, Europeans in the Indian subcontinent aimed to accomplish by conquest and imperial control what they could not by pure participation in trade: control over markets, lands, and seas.[65]

The key to understanding this period is to realize that European colonial powers did not start out with the commanding lead over other societies that have come to define global politics as we know them now—this is not the racist and inaccurate story of an inherently and altogether advanced civilization coming to rule over helpless primitives. They encountered a number of worlds—in many of which they found themselves on *disadvantageous* terms with local powers. The actions

---

[61] Wolff, "Da Gama's Blundering: Trade Encounters in Africa and Asia during the European 'Age of Discovery,' 1450–1520," 1–2.

[62] Williams, *Capitalism and Slavery*, 2–4.

[63] Flynn and Giráldez, "Cycles of Silver: Global Economic Unity through the Mid-Eighteenth Century," 391.

[64] Parthasarathi, *Why Europe Grew Rich and Asia Did Not: Global Economic Divergence, 1600–1850*, 12–14.

[65] Wolff, "Da Gama's Blundering: Trade Encounters in Africa and Asia during the European 'Age of Discovery,' 1450–1520."

of all of the actors involved over the centuries that followed *resulted in a global politics* tilted in Europe's favor. This remarkable imperial success has yet to be overturned, because of the compounding inertia of the unequal and uneven trajectories of accumulation it initiated.

It began with precious metals. The most important commodity traded during the initial centuries of European colonization was silver. The early European conquests of the New World gave the Spanish king strong leverage on the supply side of the silver market: by "conservative estimates," 80 percent of the world's silver was produced in Latin America, mostly by enslaved Africans and coerced Indigenous labor in what is now Mexico and Peru.[66] Nevertheless, the Europeans were middle men in the transoceanic silver trade, exploiting political developments and direction from elsewhere. Decades earlier, a monetary crisis in China had resulted in the devaluation of their paper money system. The policy response of the Ming dynasty followed the preferences of its private sector: to reshape its payment system around silver. This contributed significantly to the economic demand that launched the European ships.[67]

Hernán Cortés, Spain's conquistador of Mexico, arrived in the Aztec empire in 1519 with some important military advantages (most notably horses and firearms) over local armed forces.[68] But these almost certainly could not have been decisive on their own, and his victory involved some fair measure of chance as well as the skillful manipulation of the political complexities of the region—the armed forces of Tlaxcalteca, Tetzcoca, and other indigenous communities were already hostile to Aztec domination and helped lead the fight against them. Plausible explanations for Cortés's ultimate military success also must take into account the demographic collapse of the region: by one estimate, as much half of the populations of towns surrounding Tenochtitlan were killed within two months of the Spanish arrival to the region—neither by Cortes's genocidal rage nor his military prowess

[66] Flynn and Giraldez, "Arbitrage, China, and World Trade in the Early Modern Period"; Brading and Cross, "Colonial Silver Mining: Mexico and Peru."
[67] Flynn and Giraldez, "Arbitrage, China, and World Trade in the Early Modern Period."
[68] Restall, *When Montezuma Met Cortés*, chap. 7.

and ruthlessness but simply by the epidemics the Spanish brought with them, likely smallpox.[69]

This was no quirk of Cortés's expedition: the Spanish empire's later colonial dominion over California likewise resulted in mass deaths from disease, with some populations losing up to 90 percent of their members. The death rates were not solely caused by a lack of immunity to European diseases, but were greatly magnified by the displacement of local hygienic and medicinal practices with less effective ones imposed by the imperial Spanish powers.[70] A sober analysis of the evidence, then, would give a much larger role to substandard European hygiene practices in the early centuries of global racial empire than to any supposed unchallengeable superiority in overall rationality, science, or military prowess.

Politically speaking, the centuries of human history initiated by voyages like Columbus and da Gama's were perhaps equal parts gold rush and arms race. Despite the limitations of his initial bid to enter the market, de Gama did give the Portuguese a fast and direct sea route to India, and that gave them, among the European nations, an effective monopoly over trade in the East Indies, while the rest of the European powers had to trade with the east via the perilous, slow, and middleman-managed land route of the Silk Road. Europeans, steeped in centuries of arcane internecine relationships, entered global expansion in the mindset of competition among themselves. The Vatican attempted to forestall future conflict by brokering the split of the New World between European empires, granting much of what is now North America to the Spanish and what is now Brazil to the Portuguese, but this approach had a limited half-life. England, France, and Holland quickly entered the race with expeditions of their own. Over the next century, the French landed in Brazil, encroaching on

[69] Restall, *When Montezuma Met Cortés*, chap. 8.
[70] Meissner, "Reclaiming Rainmaking from Damming Epistemologies: Indigenous Resistance to Settler Colonial Contributory Injustice"; Anderson, *Tending the Wild: Native American Knowledge and the Management of California's Natural Resources*; Preston, "Serpent in Eden: Dispersal of Foreign Diseases into Pre-Mission California"; Preston, "Serpent in the Garden: Environmental Change in Colonial California."

Portugal's supposedly Vatican-guaranteed territory; the English sailed for North America, founding Jamestown.[71]

Global Colonialism Takes Shape: Territory, Plunder, and Markets

For the European powers, there were several important strategic advantages to acquiring new territory far from the bloodily contested borders of their own continent. Colonies meant an opportunity to geographically extend military, political, and economic presence. Growth in any one of these areas presented an opportunity to increase the other two.

A typical first step of colonialism involves control over territory. Land holdings on distant continents meant a safe environment for militaries and traders alike to rest, restock, and recuperate. Sea voyages took time and energy; safe stopping places were necessary to make long-term trade possible. Some colonial acquisitions were made almost entirely for this purpose, including Manila, which extended the Atlantic Order across the Pacific Ocean, and the Dutch Cape Colony (in what is now South Africa), which was near the southern tip of Africa and thus strategically located to facilitate Indian Ocean trade.[72] Meanwhile, the islands of Cape Verde, which served as an early stopover point in the trans-Atlantic slave trade, soon developed a prototype for the slave plantations that would come to define the early American and Caribbean colonial economies, in which the game was not only trade, but also production.[73]

Historian Vine Deloria, Jr. and Indigenous Studies scholar Glen Coulthard argue that the theft of land is a key aspect of "colonial-capital accumulation." This takes on even more significance among American Indian groups, many of whom take land to be intensely

---

[71] Beeman, "Labor Forces and Race Relations: A Comparative View of the Colonization of Brazil and Virginia," 614–615.

[72] Flynn and Giráldez, "Born with a" Silver Spoon": The Origin of World Trade in 1571"; Fourie, "The Remarkable Wealth of the Dutch Cape Colony: Measurements from Eighteenth-Century Probate Inventories 1," 420.

[73] Mendy, *Amílcar Cabral: A Nationalist and Pan-Africanist Revolutionary*, 19.

meaningful and an important basis for understanding and navigating other relationships.[74] This type of theft was the central aspect of settler colonialism, which involved empires attempting to move large swaths of their European populations off the continent and to the colonies: a strategy trotted out in what became the United States, South Africa, Australia, and Zimbabwe.

With access to land and sea, a new colony provided a second opportunity: plunder. With enough control of a subject population, the colonizer could levy taxes, redirect material resources and ship them across the sea, and control local economies in a variety of self-serving ways. They could reorganize social institutions and (therefore) the patterns of individual lives so that nearly every action of the economy ultimately fed into the channels of wealth flowing back to the colonizers, just as the Spanish empire created fantastic amounts of wealth in Potosí while leaving Bolivia one of the world's poorest countries. The strategies used to construct these pipelines included both brutal and subtle methods of coercion. The subtler forms contribute to the obfuscating social relations of the present day, strategies such as naming and claiming favored ethnic groups to serve as the extortionist middlemen over other groups, or utilizing missionaries to enforce order and create links to the global economy through psychological, religious, and directly economic forms of influence.[75]

There was plenty of naked extortion as well. Districts in nineteenth century British colonial India provide a particularly striking example: administrative divisions were literally called "collectorates," and researcher Sandip Hazareesingh describes the "entire structure of colonial rule in India at the local rural level" as "organised around the levy and collection of land revenue."[76] Economist Javier Cuenca-Esteban describes the transfer of Indian wealth to the British empire

---

[74] Coulthard, "Place against Empire: Understanding Indigenous Anti-Colonialism."

[75] Amin, "Underdevelopment and Dependence in Black Africa—Origins and Contemporary Forms"; McCracken, "Underdevelopment in Malawi: The Missionary Contribution."

[76] Hazareesingh, "Cotton, Climate and Colonialism in Dharwar, Western India, 1840–1880."

as the "least dispensable" contribution to Britain's balance of imports and exports.[77]

But as we've mentioned, this era also saw the growth of capitalism, in which elites seek value not only by directly extorting it, but increasingly through the creation of markets. Control over more land and natural resources meant support for larger and larger populations on both the mainland and colonial territory. Colonial populations were not self-sufficient, and looked to trade for their clothes, food, and luxury goods. Thus, every new colony occasioned the possibility for enlarging the potential customer base for the companies of the mainland. This was doubly important during the first centuries of European colonialism, since mercantilism and protectionism were the ruling economic strategies of the day: each empire viewed itself as in competition with the other empires to maximize its exports.[78] European empires tried to win this zero-sum game by protecting their mainland businesses: levying taxes on goods from rival countries, strategically granting monopolies to homegrown businesses, and regulating the trade to and from their colonies to force their colonists to make economic decisions that played well into their overall strategies. Control over their colonies' economic policies gave empires control over the terms of trade back and forth, which they used to build up not only the coffers of their crowns but also the economic power of the homeland's businesses.

For example: say you're an official in the British empire and you want to build up the British East India Company's global tea business. An easy way to do it is to tax the tea from its competitors, like the French or Spanish. This makes a British company's tea cheaper than its competitors' and more likely to be bought. The more ports you can tax and control, the more purchasers you can control with this policy, and the likelier it is that this pays off for the company. That means you exercise this kind of control over every population who shops at a market where your government can enforce tax collection: in England's case,

[77] Cuenca-Esteban, "India's Contribution to the British Balance of Payments, 1757–1812," 167.
[78] Irwin, "Mercantilism as Strategic Trade Policy: The Anglo-Dutch Rivalry for the East India Trade."

that would include English ports such as London and Liverpool, but also those of its colonial possessions, such as Dublin in Ireland and Boston in colonial America. The Boston Tea Party and the American Revolution it helped ignite demonstrate how this strategy eventually became problematic for many of Europe's empires, but for a couple of centuries it worked to accumulate fantastic amounts of wealth in geographically tiny corners of the overall global trade network.

So exploiting the first advantage, territory, requires the ability to effectively regulate portions of land and sea, which is achieved initially through militarism and settlement (in the Americas, substantively aided by the spread of disease in Indigenous populations). Exploiting the second and third advantages, plunder and captive markets, requires control over the social institutions that govern production and consumption. And when it came to governing production and consumption, the Atlantic slave trade proved to be the key innovation that gave the colonial powers their lasting advantage, and sparked a psychological innovation that transformed the way Europeans justified the extreme violence of their quest for limitless fountains of wealth.

Racialization and Slavery as Stages of Colonialism

When Oxford-educated historian (and eventual Prime Minister of Trinidad and Tobago) Eric Williams published *Capitalism and Slavery* in 1944, scholars reacted intensely. The book's claims were explosive. Williams claimed that slavery had led to the Industrial Revolution, and that the resultant changes in the world economy, rather than the moral enlightenment of the British empire, accounted for the success of abolitionist movements.[79] Where humanists might see an evolving human soul, Williams sees the cold, mechanical motion of a historical cart pushed downhill by the progressive logic of the global racial empire.

Many decades after *Capitalism and Slavery*, a careful look at the available evidence suggests that, if anything, Williams's claim was too modest. Social scientists Daron Acemoglu, Simon Johnson, and James

---

[79] Williams, *Capitalism and Slavery*, chap. 1.

Robinson published a quantitative study of the causes of Western Europe's historically unprecedented growth. They found that the rise of Western Europe was *"almost entirely"* explained by access to the Atlantic economy: which was, in turn, dominated and enabled by the trafficking of enslaved Africans and participation in markets sustained by colonial conquest and exploitation.[80]

Following Williams, we can gain insight by taking careful stock of what is and is *not* historically unprecedented about trans-Atlantic slavery. Slavery, of course, has many precedents in world history: it was the basis of many a Greek economy, and also of the Roman empire.[81] Chattel slavery specifically, in which the enslaved are rendered the legal property of their owners, sits under a wider umbrella of variants of social formations by which coerced labor and expropriation of the lowest class allows other classes to enjoy the economic and social benefits of their oppression. Other historical examples under this umbrella include serfdom, indentured servitude, nineteenth and twentieth century "company towns" in the United States, and aspects of the caste system in South Asia. Contemporary examples include the prison-industrial complex and the economic entrapment schemes that drive people into sweatshop labor.

But *race* as we know it today did not exist during most of those centuries. A Roman or a medieval slave market would often include people of diverse backgrounds, who wound up there through a variety of bad circumstances—usually because they were captured as prisoners of war or sold by family members to pay off debts. In the main, enslavement was an undesirable outcome of individual or group misfortune.

During the colonial period, the emptying of the Americas through plague and displacement created explosive demand for coercible labor, and the volume of the trans-Atlantic slave trade that rose to meet that demand created a radically new demographic situation. The volume of the trans-Atlantic slave trade was double that of all other African slave trades combined.[82] It was, as are all slave trades, a moral atrocity. But

---

[80] Emphasis added. Acemoglu, Johnson, and Robinson, "The Rise of Europe: Atlantic Trade, Institutional Change, and Economic Growth," 3–4.

[81] Williams, *Capitalism and Slavery*, 7.

[82] Nunn, "The Long-Term Effects of Africa's Slave Trades," 142.

to a much greater extent than other slave trades, it was also a massive transfer of population: twelve million people over the centuries from 1400 to 1900 as European colonialism (and, eventually capitalism) was creating the global world order.[83] As Williams says in incendiary fashion: "A racial twist has thereby been given to what is basically an economic phenomenon. Slavery was not born of racism: rather, racism was the consequence of slavery."[84]

In some cases, European empires were able to build colonies primarily out of the cheap labor of European emigrants, as was the case for some of the Northern American colonies. But much more often, European empires faced considerable problems attracting the population levels necessary to secure control of territory and maximally exploit its resources. Politically free European labor was hard to come by: people were unlikely to willingly make the voyage in exchange for the kind of back-breaking working conditions that (for example) sugar cultivation involves. They were also unlikely to leave behind everything they owned, however little it might be, only to land in an even more subservient position with even lower political standing. To illustrate this point, Williams recounts the story of a capitalist who arrived to the Swan River Colony of Australia with 300 laborers, only to find that the abundance of land allowed all of them to become self-employed subsistence farmers and they left him by his lonesome.[85]

The European empires faced a particularly severe labor shortage in the Americas: for over the century following Columbus's voyage, the combination of war, genocide, and disease that followed the Europeans into the American continents killed 56 million people.[86] That figure represents 90 percent of the inhabitants of the western hemisphere, a demographic collapse so severe that it literally lowered the earth's temperature.[87] At several points in colonial history, colonists enslaved Indigenous peoples, but the combination of the Indigenous

---

[83] Nunn, "The Long-Term Effects of Africa's Slave Trades," 142.
[84] Williams, *Capitalism and Slavery*, 7.
[85] Williams, *Capitalism and Slavery*, 4.
[86] Koch et al., "Earth System Impacts of the European Arrival and Great Dying in the Americas after 1492."
[87] Koch et al., "Earth System Impacts of the European Arrival and Great Dying in the Americas after 1492."

demographic collapse and potential military consequences of abduction imposed hard limits on the scale of those plans.[88]

Where else to find the necessary hands to build their empire? For elites trying to build fortunes abroad, enslaving within their existing political network was risky. This is the sort of moral atrocity people tend to remember, and it can breed and spread destabilizing anger. Plato predicted as much in *The Republic*, counseling the hypothetical rulers of a just city to "make a habit of sparing the Greek race" from enslavement and advise fellow Greeks to do the same. This, he imagined, would permit a level of conflict between Greeks but also a level of solidarity as inherently free peoples which would protect them from "barbarian" non-Greeks.[89] As Williams notes, the Irish and Scottish peoples spent centuries providing the British empire an instructive example of the political problems that domination causes. The Irish "hated the English" and "were always ready to aid England's enemies."[90] Disaffected Irish and Scottish peoples routinely provided military intelligence and direct combat support to England's enemies—and, crucially, they were nearby enough to do so.[91]

So the fortune-hunters looked to the African continent—a place with long established slave trades, and much further from the intrigues of European politics. The Spanish and Portuguese were first and worst: they had been trading cloth and horses for enslaved Africans for the better part of the 1400s; a million enslaved people had been sailed to Portugal and Spain's American colonies before the first twenty colonists landed in British Virginia.[92] In the years immediately preceding and following the American Revolution, Africans were enslaved and exploited in every American colony and state, north to south.

Colonies tried coerced labor of other kinds as well: homeless Europeans, convicts, and kidnapping victims were forced onto ships bound for the New World and sold into indentured labor.[93] However,

---

[88]   Engerman, Sutch, and Wright, "Slavery."
[89]   Plato, *Republic*, trans. C. D. C. Reeve, Sec. 469.
[90]   Williams, *Capitalism and Slavery*, 13.
[91]   Williams, *Capitalism and Slavery*, 13.
[92]   Beeman, "Labor Forces and Race Relations: A Comparative View of the Colonization of Brazil and Virginia"; Engerman, Sutch, and Wright, "Slavery."
[93]   Williams, *Capitalism and Slavery*, 9–10.

in the American and Caribbean colonies, the pipeline of Africans created by the entrepreneurs of the Atlantic trade eclipsed other options in sheer volume. This led to distinctive populations of multiethnic enslaved laborers from Africa's many ethnicities and nations. All of these had to build local expertise, social bonds, and an adaptive culture in the pressure cooker of captivity, while their consistent arrival in the hundreds on the same ships often led buyers to perceive them, with wild inaccuracy, as coming from the same place.

Trans-Atlantic slavery clearly solved economic problems for colonizers. Economist Barbara Solow argues that British use of African enslaved labor contributed to British economic growth by providing an efficient and elastic labor supply that secured constant returns on colonial investment.[94] Enslaved labor was also a source of market size: more enslaved people meant more need for clothes, food, and shelter, needs which could be at least partially met by exports from the home country and thus served as a stimulus for business there. By Solow's calculations, profits from the slave trade alone—that is, not accounting for the profits from the colonial ventures it propped up—could account for up to 8 percent of total British investment and 39 percent of all its commercial and industrial investment in a given year at the slave trade's height.[95]

The racial aspect of slavery evolved as the empires and colonizer populations scrambled to respond strategically to conditions in the colonies as they found them after the initial stage of settling. Racializing slavery—associating the condition of enslavement with an imaginary concept of race for which skin color was the convenient proxy, and re-envisioning the concept of free labor on the same principle—solved important political problems.

Historian Barbara J. Fields points out that Europeans had, in fact, held other Europeans in slavery and serfdom, that the law in Tudor England provided for the enslavement of vagabonds, and English brutality against Irish resistance to English domination was of comparable violence to their colonial ventures elsewhere in the world.

---

[94] Solow, "Capitalism and Slavery in the Exceedingly Long Run," 734.
[95] Solow, "Caribbean Slavery and British Growth: The Eric Williams Hypothesis," 105–106.

She concludes that whatever freedoms English citizens had enjoyed were not the result of any *moral* limitations genuinely felt by the English elite, but a ceiling of exploitation set by the political outcome of constant and often violent contest between the classes.[96] Enslaving Europeans, then, could conceivably have provided similar economic advantages to enslaving Africans if it weren't for the fact that it would have saddled colonizers with the political costs of this form of domination. Enslaving Indigenous Americans and African peoples exported the political costs to *their* social networks, setting off disastrous processes of cumulative disadvantage.

The Limits of Slavery and the Renewed Promise of Racialization

However, chattel slavery was never likely to be the end stage of colonialism. Williams treats it as a stage of colonial development, an on-ramp for empire. A key reason has to do with the numbers: even from the coldest productivity standpoint, coerced labor is far from ideal. It takes constant and costly campaigns of terrorism to keep coerced people working at all, much less at a desired level of effort. Hence Williams explains that "[w]hen slavery is adopted, it is not adopted as the choice over free labor; there is no choice at all."[97] To Williams, a slave system serves a sort of stopgap measure, building a colony up to the point of development where it can attract free labor at a competitive level of cost.

But the relationship between slavery and colonialism goes both ways. "Expansion is a necessity of slave societies; the slave power requires ever fresh conquests."[98] These conquests *presume* the lack of rights of Indigenous peoples to the land, resources, and political control of vast swaths of the earth, and then aim to create an actual social structure that matches that presumption. The logical conclusion of this impulse is genocidal: a drive to either exterminate Native peoples

---

[96] Fields, "Slavery, Race and Ideology in the United States of America," 102–103.
[97] Williams, *Capitalism and Slavery*, 6–7.
[98] Williams, *Capitalism and Slavery*, 7.

entirely or to curtail the social and political effects of their existence, which scholars such as anthropologist Patrick Wolfe term "Native elimination."[99]

In the United States, for example, thanks to the accumulated realities of generations of reservation life, including low access to either traditional or federally overseen obstetric services, child mortality rates among Indigenous Americans in 1900 were as high as 60 percent.[100] And even after this, in 1970 the US government took action to limit Indigenous reproduction still further: Family Planning Services and Population Research Act of 1970 resulted in the sterilization of a quarter of American Indian women—by the *lower* estimates.

Williams argues that slavery and colonialism, particularly in the British empire, provided the economic and political conditions for the Industrial Revolution, which revolutionized economic production and helped usher in the global era of capitalism. The balance of power between the economic interests advanced by the imperial British economy began to line up in favor of free trade, and for the proponents of free trade, the idea of "free labor" seemed increasingly ideologically attractive, thus leading to the development of wage work, a different form of labor coercion than chattel slavery. At the same time many British titans of industry liked their chances in free market interactions with other businesses within and beyond the British empire—and combatting the protectionist tax and tariff structures that protected non-industrialized businesses from them meant vastly increasing the markets they could access and thus the profits they could make.[101] So in order to maintain the same overall advantages, the early industrialists shifted the paradigm. As Williams puts it: "The very vested interests which had been built up by the slave system now turned and destroyed that system."[102]

[99] Wolfe, "Settler Colonialism and the Elimination of the Native."
[100] Theobald, "A 1970 Law Led to the Mass Sterilization of Native American Women. That History Still Matters."
[101] Williams, *Capitalism and Slavery*, chap. 8.
[102] Williams, *Capitalism and Slavery*, 136.

Empire at Any Scale

In his landmark 1994 book *The Racial Contract*, philosopher Charles Mills borrows the "social contract" language of liberal political thought to argue that we live in a world "built by the Racial Contract"; that is, "foundationally shaped for the past five hundred years by the .. gradual consolidation of global white supremacy."[103]

White supremacy maintains the Global North (where the world's white population is concentrated) as the location of accumulations of advantage—economic, political, environmental—and the Global South as the location where disadvantages tend to accumulate. White supremacy also distributes power locally away from people of color and Indigenous peoples to people racialized as white, which dictates patterns of accumulation within these zones of opportunity. These two things are, structurally, the same. In the following examples I will try to show how the things we usually label "colonialism" or "neocolonialism" and the things we like to label "institutional racism" are outcomes of the same historical processes, and how together they continuously reproduce the unequal distribution system of the Global Racial Empire.

The Distribution of Tasks and Wealth

Cotton Markets, Land Theft, Brain Drain

To begin with, one thing the world system distributes is *tasks and roles*. This is especially important to understanding economic production, a fundamental pillar of social order. Uneven distribution of tasks and roles creates uneven distributions of knowledge that can persist for generations.

We have already explored how the US South in the nineteenth century specialized in cotton production.[104] But this is just one step of the

---

[103] Mills, *The Racial Contract*, 20, 30.
[104] Beckert, "Emancipation and Empire: Reconstructing the Worldwide Web of Cotton Production in the Age of the American Civil War."

overall production process for consumer goods, such as clothing, made with cotton. Much of the cotton grown in the US South was exported to Europe, where it was spun into yarn or thread, and then knitted or woven into cloth, and finally tailored into particular clothing items, many of which would then be exported.[105] This cycle was most intense in rapidly industrializing England: by one set of estimates, up to 25 percent of all English people's livelihoods were based on the cotton industry, nearly half of its exports consisted of products made of cotton, and a full tenth of all its investment capital was committed to cotton or derivative industries.[106] This was a "local" economy revolving around a raw material produced almost exclusively around a resource from a different continent. In 1857, British economist J. T. Danson summed up the global relationships simply: "cotton must be grown, almost entirely, out of Europe, and manufactured cheaply in Europe" and "[t]hat cotton has hitherto been grown . . . chiefly by slave labour."[107] As Karl Marx put it in *Capital*: "In fact, the veiled slavery of the wage workers in Europe needed, for its pedestal, slavery pure and simple in the new world."[108]

Britain flooded African and Indian markets with cheap English cloth made from slave-grown cotton and English factory labor. It kept those prices decisively low using the protectionist economic regulations of a mercantilist and colonial British Parliament, whose decisions were enforced by the state navy and the mercenary forces of the British East India Company.[109] Thus, with a tight combination of commercial, political, and military power, Britain designated these regions of the world as the cloth consumers of the Atlantic Order, and within a generation, the considerable knowledge and skill of previous generations of clothing makers had disappeared. Elders were too busy trying to survive today's version of the market to teach children skills that only would have been relevant to yesterday's versions (or tomorrow's).[110]

[105] Beckert, "Emancipation and Empire."
[106] Beckert, "Emancipation and Empire," 1408.
[107] Danson, "On the Existing Connection between American Slavery and the British Cotton Manufacture," 1–2.
[108] Marx, "Capital, Volume I," chap. 31.
[109] Parthasarathi, *Why Europe Grew Rich and Asia Did Not: Global Economic Divergence, 1600–1850*, 12–13; Rodney, "How Europe Underdeveloped Africa," sec. 4.2.
[110] Rodney, "How Europe Underdeveloped Africa," sec. 4.2.

Thus, the roles assigned by the Atlantic Order determined what knowledge and skills colonial populations would have access to many generations down the line.

To this day, developing economies face a "brain drain" as yesterday's decisions concerning where the world's universities and research funding would be located become today's decision-making environment for those would-be medical professionals, engineers, researchers, and intellectuals in the Global South. The Global North's accumulated advantages prove an irresistible draw for at least some of these skilled professionals, whose expertise is then put to the service of the already-advantaged Global North.[111]

We can see the same process occurring at the scale of the nation in the United States. In 1920, there were nearly a million Black farmers, but by 2017 there were fewer than fifty thousand.[112] The explanation for why takes twists and turns and involves many complicated intersections that can be summarized in a simple word . . . theft.

A staggering 98 percent of the Black landowners in the United States were dispossessed of 12 million acres of land, through the operations of a racially stratified system of federal investment managed initially by the Farm Security Administration, created by President Franklin D. Roosevelt's New Deal, and eventually by the US Department of Agriculture. The combination of political and commercial domination was backed by para-military violence, in this case performed by white supremacist organizations. Financial and legal advantages helped along by the federalization of US agriculture were steered toward its white landowners, including investment dollars, access to credit, and eventually landownership.[113] The disadvantages of farming, principally debt—for which land often served as collateral—accumulated for Black farmers. The fallout is not only dispossession, though that would

---

[111] According to Docquier, Lohest, and Marfouk, not all developing countries lose out overall, since there are some positive aspects to emigration of highly skilled professionals (they can send money back home and serve as a success story to inspire their neighbors to educate their children more). But as they concede, there are more developing countries that are harmed by this pattern of emigration overall than countries that are advantaged. Docquier, Lohest, and Marfouk, "Brain Drain in Developing Countries."

[112] Sewell, "There Were Nearly a Million Black Farmers in 1920. Why Have They Disappeared?"

[113] Newkirk II, "The Great Land Robbery."

be bad enough. As with African and Indian clothing industries, fewer Black farmers means fewer opportunities to pass along agricultural knowledge and skills between generations.

The Distribution of Citizenship

Infrastructure, Subjects, and Political Rights

Colonial economies developed under the influence of both colonial administrators and the mother countries that sent them. This often precluded strong investment in retentive infrastructure, such as industrial capacity, roads, and bridges that would allow wealth to grow and to circulate. Since the point was to enrich the mother country, infrastructure investments followed a more extractive pattern: roads were built primarily to link sites of production to ports for trade on the world market, and mechanization was applied only to the processes for producing raw material (refinement and manufacture would happen only in the industrialized North). For many former colonies, yesterday's colonially mandated specialization in cotton or sugar became today's reliance on that same kind of commodity in the world market. Why? Because it represented the only aspect of the economy with sufficient infrastructure to support the postcolonial population.[114]

What is true about physical and economic infrastructure is also true of political infrastructure. Institutions also get built over time, and today's decisions about how to navigate them likewise depend on yesterday's decisions about how to structure them in the first place. In the negotiations forced by the anti-colonial movements of the 1950s and 1960s, former colonial powers urged the newly independent states to adopt democratic policies. It was perhaps the first time they had even pretended to encourage democracy in the colonies. Given the political realities of colonial domination, the "natives" rarely had anything approaching a Bill of Rights, much less taxation paired with

---

[114] Galeano, *Las Venas Abiertas de América Latina*, chap. 2.

representation. Colonial political institutions, like their economic ones, were built to benefit colonizers.

Colonial governments wielded broadly autocratic and repressive powers. These included powers to censor media and jail political dissidents without serious charges.[115] Some colonial production systems were buttressed by the authoritarian technology of the coerced labor, most dramatically of prisoners—economists Belinda Archibong and Nonso Obikili find that the rate of incarceration in colonial Nigeria would have placed it third-highest in incarceration rate among large countries in 2020, just behind the United States and Thailand.[116]

As political scientist Ken Ochieng' Opalo explains, colonial governors were imbued with a variety of powers that cut across the distinctions between the judicial, legislative, and executive functions of government that the colonial powers considered so essential for their own home governments.[117] The result is that many of the newly independent states inherited an already autocratic political structure, as well as generations of autocratic political culture and institutional knowledge. As if to match, they inherited an underdeveloped legislature ill-equipped to restrain would-be dictators, much less meet the considerable challenges of equitably legislating for populations whose national borders were crafted by the competing interests of Europeans in the 1880s rather than by their own histories of group identification.[118]

A short while after the wave of liberation movements in the mid-twentieth century, think tanks casually introduced the concept of "development" into global discourse to describe the differences in economic and political organization between imperial centers and recently de-colonized nations, as though they were all students in a class

---

[115] Cheeseman and Fisher, *Authoritarian Africa: Repression, Resistance, and the Power of Ideas*, 4–5.

[116] Archibong and Obikili, "Prison Labor: The Price of Prisons and the Lasting Effects of Incarceration"; Archibong and Obikili, "Convict Labor and the Costs of Colonial Infrastructure: Evidence from Prisons in British Nigeria, 1920–1938"; Pro Market, "Prison Labor Can Create Perverse Incentives for Incarceration and Reduce Trust in Legal Institutions."

[117] Ochieng'Opalo, *Legislative Development in Africa: Politics and Postcolonial Legacies*, 5.

[118] Ochieng'Opalo, *Legislative Development in Africa: Politics and Postcolonial Legacies*, 5.

who could be evaluated in comparison to each other based on their study habits. This provides a convenient, but misleading story about global politics. In reality, the extraction of wealth from the "former" colonies for the benefit of ruling elites has continued unabated, this time facilitated through one-sided "development agreements" between governments and multinational institutions, rather than explicit colonial management. For one telling example: 101 (mostly British) companies listed on the London Stock Exchange collectively control more than $1 trillion worth of Africa's most valuable resources, most of which are concentrated in mining.[119] But the lack of infrastructure, wealth, and democratic political systems that determine the negotiating positions of sides in such agreements were the result of explicit policies actively and directly managed by colonizers a mere decade before. In fact both sorts of countries have continued to function much as they did under the formal colonial system.

Kwame Nkrumah, Ghana's first Prime Minister, made prominent use of the term "neocolonialism" in 1965. He described a possible future world politics that would indirectly maintain the distributions of social advantages put in place by colonial rule, and his words have proved prescient. Nkrumah regarded neocolonialism—at that moment a specter, today a reality—as the "worst form of imperialism" rather than as an improvement, since the lack of formal control over the fate of the exploited people means "power without responsibility" for those in charge and "exploitation without redress" for the ruled.[120]

The decades since Nkrumah's prophecy seem to have confirmed his worst fears. Sometimes the control is overt: the World Bank, the IMF, and private banks have used the financial leverage caused by Third World poverty and indebtedness to control economic policies. Their "structural adjustment" policy demands have included wage freezes, increased privatization, and currency devaluation.[121] Other times, leverage is somewhat more subtle: in 2003, the World Bank adopted the

---

[119] Moore, "A New Cold War Is Coming. Africa Should Not Pick Sides"; Curtis, "The New Colonialism: Britain's Scramble for Africa's Energy and Mineral Resources War on Want."

[120] Nkrumah, "Neo-Colonialism: The Last Stage of Imperialism," i, xi.

[121] Bradshaw and Huang, "Intensifying Global Dependency: Foreign Debt, Structural Adjustment, and Third World Underdevelopment."

"Doing Business Index," a measuring and ranking system comparing the countries of the world on "ease of doing business," thus helping to decide where wealth moved on the planet. The concept of "ease" served as a mechanism by which to penalize governments whose regulations made life difficult for business owners, even where they protected the living standards and collective wealth of the local population—the very kind of self-protecting strategy the colonial powers had spent the last few centuries using to retain wealth in their parts of the world. The annual survey has been described by some as the "World Cup" or "Olympics" given its stakes, and has inspired more than 3,500 reforms across 190 economies since 2003.[122] In 2020, the World Bank was forced to suspend publication of the data, citing "irregularities," which included "inappropriately altered" data for four countries (Azerbaijan, China, Saudi Arabia, and the United Arab Emirates) and suspicions of deliberate manipulation of the ranking of countries with left-wing governments such as Chile's.[123]

At the local level, historian Destin Jenkins follows the political trails of city and county-level finance to draw out connections between violence and racial capitalism, focusing on municipal bond markets. Historically, African Americans and immigrant populations have been at high risk of predation by a variety of illegal and legal exploitative practices, ranging from slumlords renting overpriced and undermaintained housing to predatory lending practices. Abigail Higgins reports that corporate control of real estate has exploded in the US housing market in recent years, in direct response to the profit opportunities that the vulnerability of tenants affords anyone on the globe with sufficient capital.[124] But their *ability* to profit off of Black tenants in this way is owed to the special vulnerability of these populations created by the combination of residential segregation, intergenerational poverty, legal structures that protect profits over people, and job discrimination.[125] These concentrated the worst disadvantages

---

[122] Chakravorti and Chaturvedi, "Ranking 42 Countries by Ease of Doing Digital Business"; Ghosh, "Stop Doing Business."
[123] Ghosh, "Stop Doing Business."
[124] Higgins, "How Corporate Landlords Helped Drive the Covid Evictions Crisis."
[125] Higgins and Táíwò, "Enforcing Eviction"; Desmond, "Eviction and the Reproduction of Urban Poverty."

of housing in Black communities: families were often crammed into attics or living above commercial and industrial businesses, exposing them to noise and worse forms of pollution.[126] These places of concentrated and racialized poverty have been referred to with the term 'ghettos.'

Drawing from historian Arnold Hirsch's influential case study of racial violence, finance, and segregation in Chicago, Jenkins argues that "champions of private enterprise" helped dismantle—and profit—off the destruction of these blighted neighborhoods by the forces of gentrification. Today, cities in the United States increasingly are home to tech firms and workers who already command high salaries, while working class people of color are pushed out toward suburbs. This process of "negro removal" was facilitated by the intervention of public redevelopment agencies, funded by capital supplied by private investors in bond markets and secured with the help of the federal government.

This securitization was federalized: the federal Housing and Home Finance Agency made contracts with local agencies, which created security for the public agencies to borrow against. Insured by the full faith and credit of the United States government against losses, private funds provided a higher class of credit to the agencies at favorable interest rates, which allowed them to buy up land occupied by working class Black families, displace them, and repurpose the land for new, whiter, and higher-class residents.[127] The advantage of financial security for a small class of investors was built atop housing and community insecurity for the Black residents who were targeted by the subsequent campaigns of eviction and other methods of displacement.

This state of affairs recalls broad swaths of colonial history: historian Madeline Woker explains how the French empire secured its metropolitan taxpayers and its settlers via a racialized system of tax collection in its colonies. That system was nakedly violent at its inception in colonial holdings like Algeria and the Ivory Coast: when "taxation" often meant literal expropriation at gunpoint. It was only professionalized and sanitized over decades of institutional development. The decolonization movements of the 1950s and 1960s in Africa and Asia

---

[126] Jenkins, "Money and the Ghetto, Money in the Ghetto."
[127] Jenkins, "Money and the Ghetto, Money in the Ghetto."

prompted massive changes to the system. The European settler elite, dethroned from political power, took their plundered capital with them: sending money fleeing into tax havens in Switzerland, all while eroding the corporate tax base of the newly independent African and Asian countries.[128]

In the present day, it is often said that Global South countries are corrupt, implying by this fact that they themselves are to blame for the continent's problems. There is truth in the assertion, but not in the implication. Problems with corruption in some countries are indeed real and consequential, and Global South political elites are often wholly complicit in schemes that exploit the populations they supposedly serve. But as we will discuss at length in chapter 3, this snapshot view of corruption neglects the role of colonialism in explaining the strengths and weaknesses of the institutional structures that post-colonial societies have in place to manage corruption.[129] The complicity of 'locals' in schemes of domination is a *continuity* of the present reality with past formations of colonialism, not a difference of the present tense. But reflecting on the structure of international financial regulation reveals another, critical point: the *ongoing* role of the Global North corporate and political elite in aiding and abetting corruption in the Global South.

A bribery scandal in Nigeria provides a particularly instructive example. An international group of multinational corporations, including Halliburton, used a shadowy network of banks and offshore tax havens to funnel $182 million worth of bribes to Nigerian elected officials, which netted them $6 billion in government contracts—an amount equivalent to nearly a sixth of the nation's entire federal budget.[130] The London-based global bank HSBC played a pivotal role

---

[128] Ogle, "'Funk Money': The End of Empires, the Expansion of Tax Havens, and Decolonization as an Economic and Financial Event"; Ogle, "Tax Havens: Legal Recoding of Colonial Plunder."

[129] Ochieng'Opalo, *Legislative Development in Africa: Politics and Postcolonial Legacies*; Cheeseman and Fisher, *Authoritarian Africa: Repression, Resistance, and the Power of Ideas*; Schmidt, *Foreign Intervention in Africa after the Cold War: Sovereignty, Responsibility, and the War on Terror*.

[130] Nigeria's federal budget for the year was N4.6 billion, the average exchange rate for the year was around 122 Naira to the dollar, yielding a budget of around $37 billion USD. Abubakar, Yahaya, and Hassan, "Nigeria"; "US Dollar to Nigerian Naira Spot Exchange Rates for 2010."

in funneling the illicit funds. After discovering the bribes, Nigeria indicted the corporation's CEO—Dick Cheney, former vice president of the United States. The matter was settled for a paltry $35 million dollars.

The legacy of the global racial empire shapes today's politics as strongly as it shaped yesterday—indeed, if Nkrumah was right, perhaps even more so. Regular people elect neither the technocrats who write "Doing Business" reports nor the bankers who design structural adjustment programs.

The Distribution of Violence

Cold War, Police State

It took an initial wave of violence for colonizers to gain control of the land and resources that they then organized into exploitable markets and sources of plunder by controlling civil, political, and economic infrastructure. The current relations between post-colonial nations and their former imperial centers show that the currents of material and power keep flowing in the same directions. These systems have considerable inertia, but it is also true that world powers continue throughout history to intervene with active violence to maintain the system that directs where and how advantage and disadvantage will accumulate. At a global scale, developed nations install puppet governments, fight proxy wars in the Global South, or interfere with elections to drive their preferred outcomes. This sort of active interference was a major part of the Cold War, for example: the Soviet Union, the United States, and an emergent China all sought to control the pace and political direction of African decolonization,[131] and the US CIA supported autocratic regimes that were hostile to Communism, particularly (but by no means exclusively) in the Middle East.[132] The horrors of war and the worst aspects of global political conflict are dumped in the Global

[131] Schmidt, *Foreign Intervention in Africa after the Cold War: Sovereignty, Responsibility, and the War on Terror*, 3.
[132] Schmidt, *Foreign Intervention in Africa after the Cold War*, 6.

South, while the social advantages of this scheme of political control accumulate and are relished elsewhere.

This distribution can happen within and across countries. Vincent Bevins's book *The Jakarta Method* provides an illustrative case study of geopolitical conflict during the Cold War. According to the political geography of the era, the "First World" consisted of wealthy colonial powers allied in defense of capitalism: Western Europe, Canada, the United States, Australia, and Japan. The "Second World" was made up of the Soviet Union and the European territories where its Red Army held power or sway, working together in defense of communism. The vast majority of the world's countries and population belonged to neither of these groups, including many of the new states that had won independence after World War Two—countries predominantly populated by non-white, recently formally colonized peoples—constituted the "Third World."[133] This part of the world was the site of much of the "hot" violence of this supposedly "cold" war.

Bevins's book focused on Indonesia in the 1960s, now the world's fourth most populated country, and then home to the largest Communist Party in the world outside of the Soviet Union and China.[134] This latter fact explains why it was one of twenty-two Third World countries over the years from 1945 to 1990 where the United States facilitated systematic mass murder of communists, labor organizers, and others deemed likely to ally with Second World forces. After the failure of US secret attacks and murders of civilians to curb the power and influence of the Indonesian Communist Party, US government officials instead helped develop an autocratic military culture, to which it provided weapons and kill lists. By 1966, up to a million Indonesian civilians were murdered in support of the US anticommunist crusade—a guess that is an estimate because, to this day, there has been concerted resistance from both the US and Indonesian governments to an exhaustive official investigation.[135] Their lives and

---

[133] Bevins, *The Jakarta Method: Washington's Anticommunist Crusade and the Mass Murder Program That Shaped Our World*, chap. 1.
[134] Bevins, *The Jakarta Method*, 2.
[135] Bevins, *The Jakarta Method*, chap. 7.

62   RECONSIDERING REPARATIONS

violent deaths, Bevins explains, seem to call for less accountability than those of others.

Meanwhile, the United States waged bloody campaigns in the socially isolable parts of the mother country, likewise populated by people whose deaths were deemed acceptable to the elites of the era. In 1973, members of the American Indian Movement congregated on the Pine Ridge Indian Reservation at Wounded Knee, South Dakota. Their initial goal was to help ouster then tribal chairman Dick Wilson—whom AIM activists like Russell Means would later suspect of collaborating with US federal agents who wanted access to the copious uranium and other strategic mineral deposits that had recently been discovered on reservation land.[136] The 71-day armed conflict involved daily exchanges of gunfire between AIM activists and federal marshals, and it also supercharged pre-existing conflicts on the reservation that continued to flare long after the siege was over. The aftermath, all told, was far bloodier than the official body count: "Using only the documented political deaths, the yearly murder rate on Pine Ridge Reservation between March 1, 1973 and March 1, 1976 was 170 per 100,000." By comparison, Detroit, the reputed "murder capital of the United States," had a rate of 20.2 per 100,000 in 1974.[137] But since the violence was largely contained on the reservation and borne by Indigenous peoples, this represented an acceptable state of affairs for the powers that be.

To this day, in any country shaped by global racial empire—including the United States—people racialized as Black or Indigenous can expect exclusion or unequal and unfair inclusion in the formal economy. They can expect the concentration of vice, pollution, and mismanagement in poor neighborhoods of color. They can expect the strata of accumulation to directly relate to the extent that they are socially positioned toward the marginalized pole of the racial spectrum.[138]

---

[136] Chertoff, "Occupy Wounded Knee"; Means and Wolf, *Where White Men Fear to Tread: The Autobiography of Russell Means*, chap. 26
[137] Johansen and Maestas, *Wasi'chu: The Continuing Indian Wars*, 83.
[138] Prominent Black Studies scholar Sylvia Wynter seems to articulate a spectrum view like this in the context of the United States in Wynter, "'No Humans Involved': An Open Letter to My Colleagues."

One result we should expect from an environment where violence and exploitation accumulates is lower levels of social trust. This has proved particularly true of areas on the African continent affected by the slave trade—social scientists still find persistent effects on levels of trust between neighbors (particularly of different ethnic groups), and fractionalization of political institutions, in direct proportion to the extent of the communities' historic involvement with the slave trade.[139] As historian Olatunji Ojo explain, slave trading and violence were mutually reinforcing. Slaving operations intensified regional interstate rivalries; warfare weakened civilian chiefs, boosted soldiering, and pitted soldiers against their political leaders.[140]

The slave trade was particularly damaging when it featured the exchange of enslaved people for weapons of war, especially guns and horses, as it did both in the Americas and on the African continent.[141] This kind of exchange incentivized cycles of violence, since being preyed upon by a better armed group encouraged those who had been raided to arm themselves for self-defense and/or retaliatory violence—and a clear strategy for acquiring the arms was finding people to abduct and exchange for guns. By economist William Whatley's estimate: "A one percent increase in gunpowder set in motion a 5-year gun-slave cycle that increased slave exports by an average of 50%, and the impact continued to grow over time."[142] The social, interpersonal, and political effects of these cycles of radiating violence have lasted for centuries.[143]

But just as certain zones within the United States were not spared from the hyperviolence of the Cold War, the deleterious effects of

---

[139] Obikili, "The Trans-Atlantic Slave Trade and Local Political Fragmentation in Africa"; Nunn and Wantchekon, "The Slave Trade and the Origins of Mistrust in Africa," 2011.

[140] Ojo, "The Organization of the Atlantic Slave Trade in Yorubaland, ca. 1777 to ca. 1856."

[141] Blackhawk, *Violence over the Land: Indians and Empires in the Early American West*; Whatley, "The Gun-Slave Hypothesis and the 18th Century British Slave Trade."

[142] Whatley, "The Gun-Slave Hypothesis and the 18th Century British Slave Trade," 5.

[143] Nunn and Wantchekon, "The Slave Trade and the Origins of Mistrust in Africa," 2011; Ojo, "The Organization of the Atlantic Slave Trade in Yorubaland, ca. 1777 to ca. 1856"; Whatley, "The Gun-Slave Hypothesis and the 18th Century British Slave Trade"; Whatley, "Up the River: The International Slave Trades and the Transformations of Slavery in Africa."

global racial empire on trust cannot be limited to Africa or even to the Global South. As political philosopher Tommie Shelby explains in *Dark Ghettos*, pervasive hyperviolence produces a set of circumstances to which irreverence for the laws and authority of the dominant culture are a rational response.[144] In other words, the fact that the world consolidates disadvantages among certain communities and places doesn't just favor economic strategies such as stealing, scamming, or enacting violence, it also commits the members of those communities to being the kind of people who are adapted to them—whether they individually practice such strategies or are simply used to being surrounded by them.

The US domestic crime policies and policing have long performed this kind of consolidation, with predictable results. Historian Elizabeth Hinton describes the methodical construction of the United States' unprecedented system of mass incarceration in *From the War on Poverty to the War on Crime*. The book follows the development of the United States as a high-incarceration country, beginning with the passage of the Law Enforcement Assistance Administration as part of President Lyndon Johnson's "Great Society" and its rapid and exponential expansion from $10 million in funding in 1965 to $850 million in 1973, less than a decade later.[145] The crime measure intervened into an economic and political context that was already racially stratified. Black unemployment rates were double those of their white counterparts by the 1960s. All workers suffered from the general rise in unemployment as strides in automation competed with workers, but this ratio starkly reflects the ongoing effect of racial stratifications in job security caused by discrimination in both hiring and firing.[146]

Rather than ameliorate these racial stratifications, crime policy acted to exploit and exacerbate them, particularly under the Nixon administration. Federal policy became increasingly punitive in sentencing, and grant dollars for police to patrol and incarcerate spiked. These interventions—and their disadvantages—were concentrated in working-class Black communities, all while creating a small

---

[144] Shelby, *Dark Ghettos: Injustice, Dissent, and Reform*.
[145] Hinton, *From the War on Poverty to the War on Crime*, 2.
[146] Hinton, *From the War on Poverty to the War on Crime*, 28–29.

professional class of social scientists, police, and bureaucrats who had direct financial interests in looking busy enough to court federal funds.[147] The advantages of this massive apparatus were shifted to the comfortably policed suburbs where class-mobile professional types lived, and the disadvantages were dumped in prison cells and in working class Black neighborhoods, whose policing increasingly resembled military counter-insurgency.

The Shape of the World Today

This chapter has attempted to show that in some ways, the categories we frequently use to describe power—social, economic, political, military, ideological—can obfuscate the general unity of the Global Racial Empire. The several European empires that together produced the world order we live in dealt with the issue of control of the world rather holistically. How else should we explain the domination of Europe and the United States (waning though it might be) throughout so much of recent history? An important, related question is: How else should we explain the tendency for those racialized as white to stand atop social hierarchies within *and* across the world's countries?

When people do try to explain these realities, their explanations tend to bottom out in appeals to the superiority of Western people over those cultures that predominate in the Global South, and the closely related notion of the superiority of white people over people of color (especially Black and Indigenous people). For some, the superiority is biological: famed Enlightenment philosopher Immanuel Kant, for instance, wrote and lectured extensively on geography and anthropology, developing a view of the human race that put whites atop a natural racial hierarchy, with Blacks and Native Americans at the bottom.[148] More recently, the 1994 book *The Bell Curve* gave an updated version of this sort of argument, conceding that much of history had sustained inequality in other ways but nevertheless arguing that trends in the twentieth century had created a class structure of intelligence

---

147 Hinton, *From the War on Poverty to the War on Crime*, chap. 4.
148 Mills, "Kant and Race, Redux."

that could track and explain racial stratifications.[149] *The Bell Curve* was subject to scathing academic criticism from pearl-clutching elites. It was also a bestseller, eclipsing 400,000 copies sold within two months of its release.[150]

Alternately, appeals to specific cultural values of Western civilizations are often trotted out to explain the dominance of Western powers over world politics and of white peoples over people of color. While lacking any substantive distinction from general racism, when these are phrased narrowly enough they perhaps sound a little more acceptable in polite conversation. The prominent social theorist Max Weber famously linked the tenets of Protestantism to the "maxims of everyday conduct" that underlie capitalism—and, presumably by extension, those peoples and states relatively advantaged by it.[151] Others prefer to appeal to Western intellectual values to explain the rise of the West. These values were, presumably, built in "Jerusalem and Athens," as famed cultural commentator Ben Shapiro argues in the aptly titled book *The Right Side of History: How Reason and Moral Purpose Made the West Great*.[152]

But both of these sorts of explanations are ultimately the exception to the general rule. Much of political discussion in the world's rich countries—whether about the country's own racial politics or its relationship to the "developing world," simply prefers not to explain *what our present social reality is built to do*. The conversation just maps a simple space onto a narrow present: here's some poverty, there's some wealth, it's a shame that things somehow ended up this way.

It is accepted that some countries are rich and prosperous. Others, as U.S. President Trump famously remarked, are "shitholes."[153] There are "good" and "bad" parts of town, or "good" and "bad" jobs. These are just bare facts. There are countries facing desertification and countries destroying surplus crops to maintain value—and from which tens of

[149] Herrnstein and Murray, *The Bell Curve: Intelligence and Class Structure in American Life*, 26–27.

[150] Staub, "The Mismeasure of Minds."

[151] Weber, *The Protestant Ethic and the Spirit of Capitalism*, chap. 5.

[152] Shapiro, *The Right Side of History: How Reason and Moral Purpose Made the West Great*.

[153] "Trump Derides Protections for Immigrants from 'Shithole' Countries," *The Washington Post*.

millions of people are already facing displacement from climate crisis, which threatens to make one-fifth of the world functionally uninhabitable by 2070.[154] These are also just facts.

It may, depending on when and where you are, be impolite and impolitic to note which color of people tend to live in the bad place or perform the bad job or be likely to starve in bad conditions. Donald Trump provoked quite a bit of criticism—American popular consensus seemed to be that a public figure is not supposed to *call* them "shithole" countries—but there is no popular perception that evil is actually being actively done when politicians legislate in ways that sustain them as such and that treat their residents as simply, ineffably part of the globe's "bad" neighborhood.

What's worse: our discourse about how to change this social reality tends to offer "solutions" that are hopelessly out of scale to the size of the challenge. This includes personal philanthropy from the Gates Foundation on down, just as surely as it includes the new anti-racist or Global South NGO of the week. If slavery and colonialism built the world and its current basic scheme of social injustice, the proper task of social justice is no smaller: it is, quite literally, to remake the world.

***

The 1835 Malê revolt in Brazil was generations in the making.

In Brazil, an important form of resistance to slavery emerged: autonomous alternative societies made up of fugitives, who built their own dwellings and unique social structure outside the zone of colonial control. These were called quilombos or mocambos, and they aspired toward forms of social organization based on solidarity, rejecting the Brazilian society premised on slavery.[155] The quilombos were made up of people born in Africa to different nations, but also Brazilian-born people of African descent, Indigenous peoples – even, in some cases, Portuguese-descended people.[156]

---

[154] Rigaud et al., "Groundswell"; Lustgarten, "Where Will Everyone Go?"
[155] Barbosa, "O Poder de Zeferina No Quilombo do Urubu Uma Reconstrução Histórica Político-Social," sec. 2.3.
[156] Barbosa, "O Poder de Zeferina No Quilombo do Urubu Uma Reconstrução Histórica Político-Social," sec. 2.1.

Urubu was the first quilombo in the Bahia region, built in the woods on the outskirts of Salvador, on land granted to the quilombo by the Indigenous Tupinambás.[157] *There, the Tupinambás joined forces with Bantu, Nagô, other ethnicities who had escaped Salvador. They sustained themselves with the help of a polycultural agricultural approach in a cooperative, fertile environment. From this base, the quilombo mounted constant offensives to free enslaved people.*[158]

Armed with a bow and arrow, a leader named Zeferina led the fighting women and men of the Urubu quilombo against dismal odds in 1824—less than a decade before the Malê revolt. She and her comrades were outnumbered more than four-to-one against a military force equipped with firearms and horses.[159] Militarily, the confrontation ended in a devastating loss for Urubu—many of the surviving quilombolas were arrested and died in prison, including Zeferina herself. But her name was still spoken, and her battle was far from the end of the struggle against Brazilian slavery and colonialism.

[157] Barbosa, "O Poder de Zeferina No Quilombo do Urubu Uma Reconstrução Histórica Político-Social," sec. 2.6.
[158] Barbosa, "O Poder de Zeferina No Quilombo do Urubu do Urubu Uma Reconstrução Histórica Político-Social."
[159] Barbosa, "O Poder De Zeferina No Quilombo Do Urubu Uma Reconstrução Histórica Político-Social," sec. 2.8.

3

The Constructive View

"Men make their own history, but they do not make it as they please; they do not make it under self-selected circumstances, but under circumstances existing already, given and transmitted from the past."
—Karl Marx, 1852, "The Eighteenth Brumaire of Louis Napoleon"

"My only loyalties are to the morally just world; and my happiest and most stunning opportunity for raising hell with corruption and deceit are with other Black people."
—Cedric Robinson, from Kelley 2017, "What Did Cedric Robinson Mean . . . ?"

In the decades following the Second World War, the globe underwent massive transformation. It was possible then to believe that the global colonial system was cracking, and possible to believe it was ready to crumble. Ultimately, however, while some meaningful power changed hands and the globe's political architecture adjusted, the core of the system proved resilient. The channels distributing wealth, political rights, and violence around the globe continued to operate as new enforcement mechanisms arose, ranging from overt and formally acknowledged levers of power and influence (including the International Monetary Fund and World Bank) to the covert tactics of spycraft and propaganda that characterized the political conflict of the Cold War. The mid-twentieth century *started* the remaking of the world but it only got so far. The project of reparations is to finish the job.

Reconsidering Reparations. Olúfẹ́mi O. Táíwò, Oxford University Press. © Oxford University Press 2022.
DOI: 10.1093/oso/9780197508893.003.0003

The Empire's New Clothes

In 1946, the year immediately following the disastrous global conflict, there were only 35 member nations of the United Nations. But the devastation of the World War spelled opportunity for the colonized of the world. The British Empire, which had ruled over a quarter of the world's population and land before the war, was eclipsed in power by the United States and the Soviet Union.[1] Other major imperial powers were in similarly dire economic and political straits, most notably the French and German states. Resistance was immediate and impossible to contain. A wave of movements seized the opportunity and rebelled, with tactics ranging from insider negotiations to open warfare. When the dust settled in 1970, the number of member-states in the United Nations had nearly quadrupled, from 35 to 127.[2]

Resistance often took the immediate form of a struggle for national independence. In the Third World, the colonial overlords were pushed out, time and again: a Vietnamese army defeated the French at Dien Bien Phu, and Algeria outlasted them in a war of attrition; Cape Verde, Guinea-Bissau, Angola, and Mozambique fought successful, linked wars against their Portuguese overlord; in Kenya, the Mau Mau rebellion violently opposed the rule of Britain, which was still smarting from its disastrous 1947 exit from the Indian subcontinent.

The racial social structure spread by European colonialism had penetrated most of the globe. Accordingly, the resistance to it wasn't confined to the Third World. The 1960s and 1970s also saw a surge in anti-racist activism in the First World, especially in the United States.

The anti-colonial and anti-racist movements were linked. According to sociologist Judith Rollins, some Americans of color even referred to themselves during this period as "Third World Americans."[3] Prominent African American activist Paul Robeson wrote an article illustratively named "Ho Chi Minh is the Toussaint L'Ouverture of Indo-China," comparing the Communist leader of the successful

---

[1] Van Wingen and Tillema, "British Military Intervention after World War II: Militance in a Second-Rank Power."

[2] "Milestones: 1945–1952."Office of the Historian, US Department of State.

[3] Rollins, "Part of a Whole: The Interdependence of the Civil Rights Movement and Other Social Movements," 65.

1940s anti-colonial conflict against the French empire to L'Ouverture, a leader in Haiti's late eighteenth century war of independence against the very same empire. The US federal government was acutely aware of the liability that racial discrimination at home posed to their attempts to win newly independent countries in Asia and Africa to their side of the Cold War.[4]

In some cases, they shared more than a sense of solidarity. In 1968, a group of Black activists in Detroit, Michigan decided to pursue the same goal that many former colonies had: national independence. Naming their organization the "Republic of New Afrika," they aimed to become a country, demanding that the United States cede the land occupied by Alabama, Louisiana, Mississippi, Georgia, and South Carolina, along with a payment of $300 billion to get the fledgling nation started.[5] The group featured important figures in the African American political tradition. Among these were "Queen Mother" Audley Moore (founder of the Universal Association of Ethiopian Women and the Committee for Reparations for Descendants of US Slaves, as well as a member of the Communist Party), and NAACP local-chapter president turned radical Robert F. Williams, author of the classic *Negroes with Guns*, a text influential to later Black radical organizations such as the Black Panthers.[6]

A legal scholar associated with the group, Dr. Nkechi Taifa, made an exceptionally clear argument for reparations. She argued that the amount of money given to the Republic of New Afrika should be "at least sufficient to assure the new nation a reasonable chance of success in solving the problems imposed on us by the Americans in our status as a colonized people," since "[t]he concept of reparations is closely tied to that of self-determination and should not be divorced from it."[7] This would require that Black American descendants of slavery be given the opportunity to choose their political destiny via a voting

---

[4] Jones, "A 'Segregated' Asia? Race, the Bandung Conference, and Pan-Asianist Fears in American Thought and Policy, 1954–1955."

[5] Berger, "The Malcolm X Doctrine: The Republic of New Afrika and National Liberation on US Soil," 50.

[6] Darity, Jr. and Mullen, *From Here to Equality: Reparations for Black Americans in the Twenty-First Century*, 12–13; Williams, *Negroes with Guns*; Blain, *Set the World on Fire: Black Nationalist Women and the Global Struggle for Freedom*, 188–189.

[7] Taifa, "Reparations and Self-Determination."

process. Taifa's explanation provides a national-level example of what I'm calling the 'constructive view' of reparations.

The moral impetus for the project is the past and present treatment of enslaved people and their descendants. But the *target* of the project—the difference it wants to make in the world produced by those moral crimes—is neither a project of reconciliation nor redemption. It is a forward-looking target, a future goal to remake the world map, in this case by adding a self-determining country.

Armed with reparations in the form of land cessions and capital transfers, as well as the right to negotiate with Indigenous people directly about the land, the Republic of New Afrika would have the capabilities to forge its own political path—it would have collective self-determination and thus the ability to confer a version of the same onto its residents and communities. The costs of reaching this target, according to Taifa, should be primarily borne by the inheritors of the moral liabilities associated with the atrocities that form and structure the political reality that we're starting from: the US federal government. Taifa demanded that the US government would bear the start-up cost of the new nation, as it were; meanwhile, it would also be pressed to re-form its own national policies so as to safeguard the self-determination of those Black descendants of slavery who did not choose to emigrate.

There were many ideological and tactical differences between the worldwide anti-colonial and anti-racist movements of this era. But a theme that cut across many was a desire to create a thoroughly new political order, one characterized by self-determination, non-domination, and solidarity. As political theorist Adom Getachew explains, many of the most influential activists and thinkers of this time understood that European imperialism had been "world-constituting," and concluded that this history and its consequences must be met by worldmaking resistance on the same scale.[8]

Ghana, Vietnam, and the Republic of New Afrika all wanted to redraw the political map. Making new nations, however, was necessary but insufficient: merely taking down the colonizer's flag would not change the background conditions of uneven integration into

---

[8] Getachew, *Worldmaking after Empire: The Rise and Fall of Self-Determination.*

the international economic and political system.[9] As Julius Nyerere, prominent member of the struggle against British colonialism and Tanzania's first president, put it: "Equality between nations of the modern world is only a legal equality—it is not an economic reality. Tanzania and America are not equal. A man who needs to sell his labor in order to buy bread and the man who controls both his employment and the price of bread are not equal. Their relationship is one of dependence and dominance."[10]

When Ghana's first Prime Minister Kwame Nkrumah warned of the dangers of "neocolonialism," he pointed out that colonial domination at least saddled colonizers with the burdens of administration, which included comparatively more effective routes to demand accountability for how their decisions affected those under their control.[11] Then the real target was the possibility of reshaping the political relationships among and between peoples toward universal self-determination and non-domination, and national independence was simply a first step down that path.

As Getachew explains, the new world that the anti-colonial activists of the 1960s and 1970s envisioned would have national and international legal structures protecting people's right to self-determination and thus give nations broad powers to control investment and political interference by foreign powers. Regional federations in the Third World would provide economic networks based on solidarity rather than exploitation, supporting their mutual development. In the global background of these national and regional entities would be a New International Economic Order of international norms, treaties, and laws providing a global political structure of non-domination.

These ideas wouldn't be implemented for free. Moreover, they would distribute benefits and impose burdens and obligations on various states and regions in markedly different ways than the previous colonial social order had. The New International Economic Order, then, did not simply involve changing laws and norms but also changes

---

[9] Getachew, *Worldmaking after Empire*, 22–23.
[10] Nyerere, "The Plea of The Poor: New Economic Order Needed for the World Community."
[11] Nkrumah, "Neo-Colonialism: The Last Stage of Imperialism."

to the distribution of global wealth.[12] But as anti-colonial activists Michael Manley of Jamaica and Julius Nyerere of Tanzania explained from opposite sides of the Atlantic, this redistribution was distinct in concept and effect from aid or charity. The change they aimed to make in the world, its "forward-looking orientation," was to reshape that world order rather than simply manage its consequences.[13] In this respect, they shared the perspective articulated by Nkechi Taifa and the African Americans who founded the Republic of New Afrika.

This is the constructive view of reparation: a historically informed view of distributive justice, serving a larger and broader worldmaking project. Reparation, like the broader struggle for social justice, is concerned with building the just world to come. But its more specific role concerns *how* we get there. The transition from the unjust status quo to justice in the future will not be costless, and it will come with its share of benefits and burdens. Reparation is concerned with how to distribute these. To make that determination, it looks in part to the past.

Distributive Justice in Real Space-Time

Since the world order is made out of distributive processes, the constructive view is a view about distribution. Because of past and present facts about how advantages and disadvantages have been distributed, they continue to accumulate unevenly and unjustly across different parts of the world, which is visible both at scales as small as individual differences (e.g. differences between white and Black workers) and as large as different political regions of the globe (Global North vs. Global South). The just world we are trying to build is a better distribution system, by apportioning rights, advantages, and burdens in a better manner than the one we've inherited from the global racial empire. It is also a view that looks to justly distribute the benefits and burdens of that transitional process of rebuilding.

The constructive view is not an approach to reparations that fits every instance of atrocity or crime. It is built specifically in response

---

[12] Getachew, *Worldmaking after Empire*, 151.
[13] Getachew, *Worldmaking after Empire*, 159.

to trans-Atlantic slavery and colonialism. The world prior to the global racial empire was also not a just world. But the global racial empire is not a continuation of the order of the world in the thirteenth century, not in the same way that our world today *is* the continuation of the world of the eighteenth century. The global racial empire created new kinds of injustice and linked them into entirely new global systems. The constructive view of reparations I defend here calls for change of equal scope.

Distribution is key to understanding the fundamental workings of society. People working together, broadly construed, is what makes society possible. The surgeon concentrates on medicine rather than also learning engineering, anticipating that metal workers and other builders will make the scalpels and tools that they need. The metal workers focus on how to build with the raw materials, trusting miners to unearth them and truckers and sailors to transport them. And all these people can afford to put in long working hours on the assumptions that the elders and children who depend on them will be taken care of in their absence, relying on paid and unpaid caretakers to do this critical work. Mining, surgery, transport, and caretaking are all very different kinds of work, but they are all work, and each of these supports the others. When all goes well, everybody wins.

But all doesn't always go well, and things go better for some people than others. Among surgeons, metal workers, truck drivers, and caretakers, some are compensated better than others. One kind of difference in compensation is obvious and easy to measure: income, which doctors and metalworkers tend to make lots of and miners and caretakers tend to make less of. But there are other systematic differences in the levels of prestige associated with the kinds of work, and levels of access to social networks that collectively control influential social institutions and important social resources, such as information (often referred to as "cultural capital"). Distributive justice encompasses all these dimensions of how we parcel out the benefits and burdens of social cooperation.

These systematic differences can magnify in importance over time, entrenching or even widening divisions between groups of people as the years go by. This is because distribution systems, over time, are also systems of accumulation. At the scale of two individuals, a story might go something like this:

Two children, Jessica and Betty, grow up in adjacent neighborhoods in the United States, just after the Second World War.

Betty is Black. Betty grows up caring for her siblings and as a young woman finds a way to support herself as a nanny to a wealthier family. She has three children, who must spend long hours without adult supervision while Betty is busy watching her clients' children instead.

Mae, the oldest, follows in her mother's footsteps by caring for her siblings, and she develops the habit of looking out for those around her. She stops doing homework after DeShawn is born so she can free her academically adept younger sister Wanda from household duties in hopes that she can excel in school. The rapid inflation of high school degrees locks Mae out of most formal employment, and by the time she is in her twenties, domestic positions like her mother's are becoming few and far between. Unable to attain economic independence, she manages her mother's home, and later a husband's, providing care and labor to everyone around her.

Wanda makes some money babysitting during high school, which goes toward family necessities, but still gets good grades and applies to nursing school. Unfortunately, she does not get enough scholarship money to be able to afford the relocation and living costs in the more expensive urban area of the campus, and the family lack any connections there who can help, so she ends up doing unlicensed work taking care of adults with developmental disabilities, handling seizures, injuries, medication regimes, and specialized diets for merely a dollar over minimum wage.

DeShawn, Betty's youngest, gets a job at a gas station through a relative who works there, and for a brief while he becomes the family's top earner. He starts saving money to get a CDL license, but because he has the greatest ability to help, a series of health crises in the family repeatedly empty his bank account.

As cost of living rises and wages stagnate, all the members of the family find themselves forced to make difficult tradeoffs to keep the lights on. The consequences of these forced choices reverberate in the opportunities of their children—Betty's grandchildren.

Over years, Mae suffers accelerating levels of spousal abuse and is unable to afford a deposit on her own apartment and unwilling to burden her mother. Her four children grow up primarily concerned about managing the dangers of their domestic situation. Two move out of state as fast as they can. Gloria gets trapped in a series of scam online schools and marketing schemes, while Francois puts himself through community college, only to end up trapped in an industry where the entry-level jobs are unpaid internships. Two siblings stay home, both for unfortunate reasons: Kegan gets caught at the wrong party in high school during the War on Drugs, after which the state becomes the most important and commanding relationship in his life. Alisha ends up back at home after a workplace back injury. Having been classified a "contractor," she is not eligible for any kind of paid leave, and her disability claim is denied. Doctors are unwilling to prescribe her pain medication. She spends hours and hours a week navigating the byzantine social service system, looking for options.

Wanda and her son Mike develop respiratory problems from the extensive black mold in their housing. They try moving to an even cheaper neighborhood when Mike is four, but the tradeoff is proximity to gang violence, and Mike struggles in school after several traumatic experiences. The school has police but no therapists; the class sizes are too large for teachers to pay attention to his quiet struggles.

The changes of the twentieth century economy wreak havoc on the purchasing power of DeShawn's wages as he moves through a series of jobs. But briefly, in his thirties, he finds enough economic stability to do something his father died too young to do, his mother would have been laughed at for doing, and his grandfather could have been lynched for attempting: apply for a home loan. The first homeowner among Betty's descendants, DeShawn decides it is finally time to start his own family. Then comes 2008, leaving him underwater and underemployed.

Betty works until her dying day, well into her seventies. She had always worked hard, but she couldn't possibly outwork the constant financial and social pressures on her own life and her families. At her death the funeral expenses far exceed the small amount Betty had been able to set aside; it might have been enough twenty years earlier, but prices for even the most basic cremation have risen. The children agree to sell her only asset, a thirty-year-old truck, to a sympathetic buyer to help cover the costs.

Now no one in the family has a vehicle, and after decades of planned infrastructural decay, there are no social services or grocery stores accessible by public transit. The family supports each other as much as they can, but partially as a result of the lack of financial accumulation in Betty's estate, their ability to support each other is as constrained as their mother's was.

Jessica, who grew up on the other side of the tracks from Betty, is white.

Jessica experiences the same twentieth century in a much different way than Betty—due in large part to her own hard work, but hard work at opportunities that were categorically denied to Betty. After attending a medical school that would not have admitted Betty, she grows up to be a doctor with financial independence. She has three children: Emmaline, Sarah, and Reggie. Her high income pays for all her children to get an advanced early education in private schools, and she coaches them so that by the time they graduate high school they each understand how to leverage both of these early schooling advantages into admission to high-prestige professional schools.

Between extracurricular programs, babysitters, tutors, and their mother's social circle, the children receive constant adult attention despite their mother's long working hours. They each draw a small allowance throughout their higher education, allowing them to save the money made from their part-time jobs and put it toward their own goals: cars, musical instruments, a trip abroad, long-term savings that eventually provide the basis for a first home loan.

The children's life is not perfect: they, too, have their struggles. But unlike Betty's children, they also have the resources to respond to them. Any time they are sick or injured, they get health care immediately, and their parents can absorb the cost without draining their savings. When Emmaline struggles in school, a child psychiatrist diagnoses her, and once she is given an individualized education plan she thrives. Reggie struggles with depression and addiction; he is stopped by police a couple of times but never arrested. Eventually he enters treatment, using his savings and insurance and calling in some special favors from his mother's extended network.

Moreover, they have the social advantages that ward off many kinds of trouble in the first place. The children meet a variety of lawyers, consultants, real estate agents, and scholars through their mother's social circle, the racially exclusive suburb they grew up in, and the private school they attended—a private school built in response to "white flight" from the very parts of the city that Betty's children grew up in. They use these connections to gain internships and entry-level positions. They don't even need to know how to spot a scam because they already have connections at half a dozen major schools and companies. They are given investment accounts, coached on how to maintain them, and socialized with people with fairly technical knowledge about finance. Those investments that Sarah's mom set up for her as a baby come in handy when Sarah divorces her abusive husband and decides to go back to school, five years after quitting a nursing program in favor of having a child. Jessica loans her some money for living expenses, enough to tide Sarah over until she's able to finish school and make good money in a skilled occupation.

Jessica retires at sixty-four and cares for her grandchildren when they arrive, not only relieving her children of some of the expense of child care, but also purchasing the grandchildren many advantages with her generous retirement income. When one grandchild is injured in a car accident, insurance covers her physical therapy. When another manifests extreme allergies, Jessica researches a specialized diet for him. The family scatters to different states in pursuing their individual careers, but they can all afford to gather together for family holidays twice a year. These family holidays are the highlight of the year for Sarah's son, Jeff—who is about the same age as Betty's grandson Mike. Mike doesn't have a single family member who has been able to afford a plane ticket anywhere in years.

Some will be tempted, no doubt, to try to maintain focus on the individual decisions that contributed to the later family differences. Why did Betty choose such a low-wage occupation instead of selecting a professional career like Jessica did? Since we've imagined Jessica to be white and Betty to be black, the response is crystal clear: choice has little to do with it. When they were young women, Betty was *literally barred* from most jobs. Many other answers follow a similar pattern. Throughout the global racial empire, race has consistently determined access to specific occupations, housing, and services. Variations of this situation have proliferated across the globe over many generations.

This is enough to answer the skeptic about this particular comparison between Jessica and Betty, but we can also point out a deeper problem here with trying to explain the differences between their lives and their families' lives in terms of their individual decisions. Intergenerational forms of accumulation powerfully shape what options are open to individual people, a fact that calls into question to what extent individual "merit" (or lack thereof) explains individuals' achievement (or lack thereof). Even if the original difference between Betty and Jessica was due solely either to Jessica's ingenuity or Betty's lack of initiative, the *consequences* of those differences can't be characterized in individual terms.

Jessica's family was set on a trajectory toward an accumulated hoard of social advantages and Betty's was set on a trajectory toward disadvantages. As a result, Jessica's grandchild Jeff faces a completely different causal environment than Betty's grandchild Mike. Whatever differences in what Jeff and Mike succeed or fail to accomplish over the course of their lives will be partly a matter of this initial difference, if not entirely reducible to it. Then, if Jeff out-achieves Mike in some sense or other—perhaps with higher GPA or standardized test scores when they are younger, or higher compensation on the job when they are older—why should we explain that difference only in terms of differences between Jeff and Mike, rather than also in terms of differences between Jessica and Betty?

The individualist is in even more serious trouble if we also reflect on the fact that our decision to start the story at Betty and Jessica was entirely arbitrary, and differences between their initial social situations were also the products of generations of accumulation. Why not start with *their* grandparents? This long, elaborate story aimed to draw out an insight: because we followed the chains of causality, we were able to see how an individual level difference between Jessica and Betty—a highly compensated job vs. a less compensated job—jumped a level of scale and became a difference between families, between larger and larger networks of people.

We should notice that this is simply the same kind of story told in the previous chapter: a story about how distributive differences that begin at one scale of analysis become effects visible and important at other scales. The main difference is that the story of Betty and Jessica begins from the opposite "social scale." Rather than starting with whole populations and zooming in to their effects on individuals, individual families, and communities, it goes in reverse and shows how putatively individual differences can, over time, accumulate into group level differences.

The story of Jessica and Betty simply dramatizes a fact well known to social scientists: the accumulation of advantages (particularly of wealth) is an intergenerational phenomenon. This is a fact well known to the world's wealthy, who often go to great and explicit lengths to build up wealth for their children and pass it on: including attending family wealth seminars and lobbying in opposition to inheritance taxes. Sociologists Alexandra Killewald, Brielle Bryan, and Fabian Pfeffer have produced a number of articles investigating intergenerational wealth transfer.[14] Their conclusions include the intriguing finding that grandparental wealth is a "unique predictor of grandchildren's wealth, above and beyond the role of parental wealth."[15] Similarly, their fellow sociologist Jennifer Mueller, using college students' research on their family histories to track accumulations across *six* generations, found stark racial differences in "inheritance pathways" for the reported white, Black, Asian, and Latino families.[16]

Combined with the clear and undisputable role of race in structuring who had access to wealth and other key social advantages only two to six generations ago (for example during Jim Crow in the US context, or the colonial era in the Nigerian context), it's difficult to dispute the racialized structure of accumulation. It is no wonder, then, that researchers like William Darity and other "stratification economists" find compelling evidence of a racially stratified economy: that is, of persistent, structural, and racialized differences in wealth and other

[14] Killewald and Bryan, "Falling Behind: The Role of Inter-and Intragenerational Processes in Widening Racial and Ethnic Wealth Gaps through Early and Middle Adulthood"; Pfeffer and Killewald, "Intergenerational Wealth Mobility and Racial Inequality."

[15] Pfeffer and Killewald, "Intergenerational Wealth Mobility and Racial Inequality"; Pfeffer and Killewald, "Generations of Advantage: Multigenerational Correlations in Family Wealth."

[16] Mueller, "The Social Reproduction of Systemic Racial Inequality."

measures of economic and political wellbeing in the United States and elsewhere.[17]

The full significance of unequal distributions of social resources and opportunities requires us to pay attention to distribution across both space and time. Considering distributive justice at multiple scales along both these axes will help explain why the constructive view is the right reparatory response to the history of global racial empire explained in chapter 1.

Space: Why Global Distributive Justice?

This description I have given of the world, as a linked system that distributes advantage and disadvantage, carries deep moral significance from the standpoint of justice. The plight of the world's less well-off is already morally important as such. But this description invites us to go further than a basic opposition to poverty or suffering and see what the least and the most socially advantaged people in the world have to do with each other. This question matters because associations and relationships can lend strength and importance to moral duties, and even create them where they wouldn't otherwise exist.

This approach, modest as it may sound in the abstract, stands in contrast to how many people conceive of social justice, even within my field of political philosophy. Much of contemporary political philosophy gives both focus and priority to questions about justice within individual states, some even explicitly arguing against the idea of global social justice. Perhaps no philosopher has done so more prominently or influentially than John Rawls, the eminent Harvard philosopher and author of the oft-cited book *A Theory of Justice*.

Throughout various works, John Rawls elaborated a "two-tiered" theory of justice. The first, primary topic was "domestic justice," or justice within a society.[18] A society, for Rawls, is a "fair system of

---

[17] Darity Jr. and Mullen, *From Here to Equality: Reparations for Black Americans in the Twenty-First Century*; Darity and Nembhard, "Racial and Ethnic Economic Inequality: The International Record"; Darity, "Stratification Economics: The Role of Intergroup Inequality."

[18] Rawls, *A Theory of Justice*, 1999.

social cooperation," at least ideally.[19] The "first subject" of justice is each society's "basic structure": the "way in which the major social institutions distribute fundamental rights and duties and determine the division of advantages from social cooperation."[20] International or global justice, from this starting point, is just the confederation of peoples who have each achieved this kind of internal justice.[21] Domestic justice takes precedence, and global justice plays second fiddle.

Rawls's focus on domestic justice takes the artificial separation of countries a little too seriously. As a result, he consistently fails to consider what the world system as a whole has to do with justice in any particular one of its countries. Rawls assumes that the major institutions of society are determined and regulated internally, and thus that the justice of those institutions should be evaluated as though they are part of a closed system.

But as we saw in the last chapter, to apply these assumptions (or the insights derived from them) about hypothetical states to the actual ones we find in the real world would go beyond oversimplification. A colonized nation is literally regulated by an external entity, not its internal polity, while what a colonizing nation affords its citizens depends directly on what they extract from the colonies. Nation states didn't come into existence as closed systems, and in fact their relations to each other have been constitutive the whole time. Along the western coast of Africa, the first steps of inclusion in a global state system came the day that foreigners first offered local elites and warlords guns and trading networks for the children of their neighbors. On the Indian subcontinent, the "modern state" came with the British East India Company and their gargantuan, region-dominating mercenary army. It is the openness of the vast majority of the world to external conquest, domination, and other machinations that explains why there *are* countries in the first place; and some are built to succeed, some to fail at Rawlsian "internal" justice.[22]

---

[19] Rawls, *A Theory of Justice*, 6–7.
[20] Rawls, "The Basic Structure as Subject," 159.
[21] Rawls, *The Law of Peoples: With, the Idea of Public Reason Revisited.*
[22] Táíwò, "States Are Not Basic Structures."

An organizing principle of Rawls's thought is the idea that distributive justice concerns arrangements of people or associations. Justice is bound up with the idea of fairness, and fairness is bound up with the idea of being co-members of some kind of scheme of cooperation—for Rawls, the society. Rawls then develops a view of distributive justice that focuses on idealized closed societies because he believes this is the form of association between people that could explain duties to redistribute. In my view, among the mistakes Rawls and other authors made in ignoring the history of global racial empire is a mischaracterization of what states actually are, and in what sense they are separate from each other.[23]

Cosmopolitan approaches to distributive justice advocated by other thinkers aim to remedy the curious generalizations of a Rawlsian view. Some cosmopolitans advocate for global redistribution and intervention on grounds that ignore institutional separations of people altogether, preferring universal moral commitments to equality or dignity as the explanation for why the well-off should change things for the benefit of the worse off.[24] But this book argues for a different kind of cosmopolitan view: one that looks at specific global superstructures—institutions, associations, chains of production, and norms—to ground a distributive justice analysis for specific historical reasons.[25] The constructive view of reparations is cosmopolitan in this sense.

Time: Why Historical Distributive Justice?

The global racial empire began with the development of the Atlantic order in the fifteenth century. This history maps where the social advantages and disadvantages of the global economic and political system have accumulated.

---

[23] Táíwò, "States Are Not Basic Structures."

[24] Pogge, "The Role of International Law in Reproducing Massive Poverty"; Pogge, *Realizing Rawls*; Pogge, *World Poverty and Human Rights: Cosmopolitan Responsibilities and Reforms*; Singer, "Famine, Affluence, and Morality."

[25] Moellendorf, "Cosmopolitanism and Compatriot Duties," 2011; Young, "Responsibility and Global Justice: A Social Connection Model"; Cohen and Sabel, "Extra Rempublicam Nulla Justitia?"

In one sense, Rawls and others are looking too narrowly, at individual countries, rather than at the geography of the world system. But this mistake is related to one about time. Rawlsians and many others' thinking about global justice often operate on what I call a 'snapshot view' of distributive justice.

A snapshot view is one that analyzes the appropriateness of the current distribution of wealth, resources, and social goods at any given moment in time—that is, we ask how good today's allocations of these important social advantages are, in abstraction from their relationships to what happened yesterday. There's plenty to learn from this kind of view of distributive justice, and any good view of distributive justice ought to pay attention to considerations of this sort. Surely the fact that there is suffering, deprivation, or structural injustice somewhere *right now* is already sufficient grounds to do something about it.[26]

But our views on distributive justice shouldn't stop at problems visible from a snapshot of our present circumstances, otherwise important as they may be. Our social systems are processual—that is, they are the way that they are because of many different activities, all of which take place over time.[27] Taking a snapshot of the world system's distribution today gives us incomplete information: for the nature of the system is that it moves resources from yesterday to today to tomorrow. When we take a snapshot, we are seeing the output of yesterday's processes—of history. We are also viewing a point on a trajectory, a moment in the unfolding of a process, a glimpse of the system becoming what it will be tomorrow. Failing to understand this can lead to serious and consequential distortions of the relevant facts: about today, about yesterday, and about the narrative arc that unites them.

For example, philosopher David Heyd insists that he is staying within the "general Rawlsian view" on global justice when he writes: "Each country leaves to its next generation(s) whatever it

---

[26] For examples of thinkers that argue for global redistribution on the basis of current structural injustice, see Moellendorf, "Cosmopolitanism and Compatriot Duties," 2011; Young, "Responsibility and Global Justice: A Social Connection Model"; Sangiovanni, "Global Justice, Reciprocity, and the State"; Cohen and Sabel, "Extra Rempublicam Nulla Justitia?"; Pogge, "The Role of International Law in Reproducing Massive Poverty"; Pogge, "World Poverty and Human Rights."

[27] For a helpful discussion on the conceptual difficulties here, see Nuti, *Injustice and the Reproduction of History: Structural Inequalities, Gender and Redress*, chap. 2.

chooses to leave or whatever it has at its disposal as a matter of luck. In other words, the fact that some countries had the luck, the initiative, or the intellectual tradition that led to the Industrial Revolution and to the resulting material benefits, does not in itself impose a duty to share its fruits with countries that were 'left behind.' And there is nothing wrong in itself in the African and Asian countries joining the industrial stage at a later point in history."[28]

Heyd takes a snapshot of the present distribution of industrialization between current nation-states and casually projects an entirely fictitious history of parallel development, as though none of these nations ever interacted with each other. The facts determining which countries participated in the Industrial Revolution are not matters of "luck" or "intellectual tradition." Moreover, "initiative" seems an odd description for a moral philosopher to give to the European empires' choices to employ human trafficking, elimination of Indigenous populations, and colonial expropriation and domination on a global scale to fuel their local development of industry and accumulation of profit. I doubt that Heyd or other thinkers adopting the "general Rawlsian view" really mean to characterize mass enslavement and genocide as "initiative." I suspect, rather, that, focused on the snapshot of the present, they consider these issues only as an afterthought, if at all.

I think we should take a historical view of distributive justice. On a historical view of distributive justice, we are still concerned about the problems with current distributions of justice on purely consequential grounds, based on the differences they make in the lives of the people here and now. But we also understand the nature of the here and now. 'Here' is a place in a global system, and 'now' is a moment in an ongoing global transfer that does not pause just because we took a picture.

We should intervene in distributions of goods, resources, and rights in order to make people's lives better and improve the fairness of institutions in the short run. We should intervene so that the global system distributing advantages and disadvantages to our own children, grandchildren, and great-grandchildren works for them more justly. We should also be concerned with present distributions as the

[28] Heyd, "Climate Ethics, Affirmative Action, and Unjust Enrichment."

moral sediment of unjust processes, or even as the continued moral life of those processes. Global racial empire, and its history of slavery and colonial domination, will be fully conquered only when their effects on the accumulation of advantages and disadvantages are also conquered.

Distribution of What?

Some views of distributive justice focus on how society distributes income or wealth. This is certainly onto something. One's access to wealth serves as proxy for so many other potential kinds of social advantages that it makes it a good candidate for special attention. The significance of financial advantage also increases as more aspects of life are monetized, as has been the trend under global capitalism.

With an eye toward these additional complexities, philosopher John Rawls argued for equality in the initial distribution of what he called "social primary goods": the "things that every rational man is presumed to want," including income and wealth, but also other benefits of social consequence such as rights, duties, and self-respect.[29] These primary goods serve as a sort of base measure of what a person can do, as Rawls later clarifies: "[w]ith more of these goods men can generally be assured of greater success in carrying out their intentions and in advancing their ends, whatever these ends may be."[30] So, for Rawls, your effective freedom depends on having the stuff you need to meet your goals.

Rawls's view, along with many others, sees social justice as operating to distribute *instrumental* goods. A few of these goods, such as self-respect, may have intrinsic value, but by and large they're valuable because of what we can do with them. Broadly speaking, the things we use to meet our goals are called "resources" by theorists, and the theories that focus on the distribution of resources are called "resourcist" views.[31]

[29] Rawls, *A Theory of Justice*, 2009, 54.
[30] Rawls, *A Theory of Justice*, 2009, 79.
[31] Dworkin, "What Is Equality? Part 1: Equality of Welfare"; Dworkin, "What Is Equality? Part 2: Equality of Resources"; Dworkin, *Sovereign Virtue: The Theory and Practice of Equality*.

Nobel prize–winning economist and philosopher Amartya Sen took a different approach, believing that we can and should attempt to measure the intrinsic good we are after more directly. I will address what kind of intrinsic good the constructive view wants to target a little further down the road, but for the moment, following Sen, we will use "freedom" to denote the target intrinsic good for which social justice should strive. So how do we measure someone's freedom? To answer this question, Sen joined forces with fellow philosopher Martha Nussbaum, and together they developed the "capabilities approach."

Broadly speaking, I agree that the capabilities approach is on the right track, and will use it to help us build our constructive approach to reparations. The capabilities approach has the benefit not only of focusing more sharply on the actual outcomes we want than do resourcist approaches, but also of helping us to more effectively deconstruct the interactions of the complex factors that feed into those outcomes.

Those who take the capabilities approach tend to talk about two main categories of things: capabilities and functionings.[32] Functionings comprise "beings and doings": for example, the state of being well-nourished, the action of eating food.[33] Capabilities are the capacities to achieve functionings: in this case, the physical ability to feed one's self and the financial and environmental ability to access nourishing food. We can think of 'advantages' and 'disadvantages' as discussed in the previous chapter in capabilities terms: advantages are things that expand or support a person's capabilities, while disadvantages do the opposite.

Effective and real freedom, for Sen, comes down to your real opportunities: what you have the opportunity to do and become. These are your 'capabilities.' This helps explain why resources are only part of the story: what you can do and become also depends on other factors such as what your body is like, what the natural environment enables and what it forbids, and what the built environment and social interactions enable and forbid.

---

[32] Robeyns, "The Capability Approach."
[33] Sen, *Inequality Reexamined*, 40.

Constructing Ramps: Capabilities and Justice

Theorists of disability have greatly advanced our ability to think through these issues. Consider two working-class kids from households of equivalent income, wealth, citizenship status, and other Rawlsian social primary goods. Royce is able-bodied and Pedro uses a wheelchair to get around. Royce is able to access a host of playgrounds, buildings, and other sites of play and socializing that are inaccessible to Pedro. As a result, there are kinds of lives Royce can build for himself that are inaccessible to Pedro.[34]

Rawls divides primary goods in those that can be controlled by the social structure and which are the subject of his theories and "natural goods." Things like health, intelligence, and physical ability are "natural goods" primarily controlled by genetics and environment and only indirectly, if at all, by social structure.[35] Natural primary goods are distributed by nature, not by society. These goods, then, don't fit into the initial distribution that Rawls recommends, and his theory has essentially nothing to say about the difference between Pedro and Royce. He might say it is an inequality of natural primary goods; he would not call it a matter of equity or justice. Pedro got the better set of natural primary goods, and there's nothing to be done about that. Thus, on a Rawlsian view, social justice might well have already been achieved between Pedro and Royce. Yet despite their similar backgrounds, there seems to be some kind of important difference between Pedro and Royce that doesn't boil down to just the shape of their bodies or the scope of their physical motions, but encompasses the shape and scope of their opportunities, of their entire lives in fact. This should encourage us to question whether the social arrangement they live in is just.

Now consider another classmate of Royce and Pedro's from another similar household in the same neighborhood, Four-Eyed Franklin, so called thanks to his trendy but thick-lensed glasses. Franklin goes everywhere that Royce goes. Their opportunities are indistinguishable. When they graduate, Franklin, having met an important mentor as a

---

[34] Sen, *Inequality Reexamined*, sec. 1.6.
[35] Rawls, *A Theory of Justice*, 1999, 54–55.

student, decides to enlist in the Navy and pursue a career in marine science; Royce is able to use an athletic scholarship to pay for college with the plan of becoming a sportscaster. Pedro does not have either of these options.

In terms of social and career opportunities in the world we live in, Franklin has the same advantages as Royce. But, in a different social structure, being nearsighted or farsighted would be quite debilitating. This can be true even in the Global North, but is more easily apparent in the Global South, where health care and corrective lenses are often significantly harder to come by. Estimates of the number of people who could benefit from corrective lenses run as high as 2.5 billion, roughly a third of the world's population.[36] Researchers have connected uncorrected vision problems to decreased job opportunities, suspected contribution to over half of all car accidents, substantial increases in fall risks for the elderly, and even rates of recidivism for juvenile criminal offenders.[37]

If corrective lenses were to become unavailable in the United States, the number of people able to obtain a driver's license, complete a primary education, or serve in the military would plummet. Without those lenses, Franklin might well be unable to read the whiteboards and projections in school, thus limiting his educational attainment. By one experimental estimate, giving glasses to poor children makes an educational impact equivalent to having an additional half of year of school.[38] Franklin would be unable to drive and ineligible for the Navy program he wants to pursue. Without glasses, Franklin would join Pedro in the category of people at a "natural" disadvantage, with severely limited opportunities in life. But now we can see that *this* fact is bound up with facts about the social structure the three friends inhabit: the disability lies an "an interaction between individual and structural factors," as disability rights activist and theorist Tom Shakespeare might observe.[39]

[36] Jacobs, "A Simple Way to Improve a Billion Lives"; Bureau, "World Population Day."
[37] Vision Impact Institute, "The Social and Economic Impact of Poor Vision."
[38] Glewwe, Park, and Zhao, "A Better Vision for Development: Eyeglasses and Academic Performance in Rural Primary Schools in China," 19.
[39] Shakespeare, *Disability Rights and Wrongs Revisited*, 55.

If we in the Global North don't think of nearsightedness or far-sightedness as disabling, it is at least partially because of how things are distributed and have accumulated. There, centuries of wealth and knowledge accumulated and became the sediment to create a social structure (made up of policies and institutions) that adequately addresses some of the problems of justice associated with having less than 20/20 vision. The possibility of modern ocular medicine evolved because of contributions from discoveries spanning a host of related fields, including medicine (surgery, pharmacology, microbiology), mathematics (statistics), and economics (the development of insurance).[40] Almost all Global North countries have institutionalized vision testing, free or heavily subsidized corrective eyewear for poor populations, and other accommodations that allow a wider range of people to achieve similar capabilities as people with 20/20 vision.[41]

Things are different in the Third World. In 2018, Uganda had just 45 eye doctors covering a country of 41 million people. That is a ratio scarcely better than one doctor per million Ugandans, and in absolute numbers registers several orders of magnitude less than the United Kingdom (which has over 11,000 optometrists) or the United States (with over 30,000).[42] This is no accident: as discussed in chapter 2, the world system has shunted important advantages such as research universities and the ability to attract skilled medical labor toward the First World. Simultaneously, as education scholar Nirmala Erevelles points out, conditions like war and large-scale conflict, environmental pollution, and malnutrition are concentrated in the Global South—and these conditions are all generative of disabilities.[43]

The difference between the conditions that the Global North considers unproblematic or barely acknowledges, such as variations in vision, and the conditions that we think of uncritically as disabilities

[40] Vogel and Berke, *Brief History of Vision and Ocular Medicine*.

[41] Glewwe, Park, and Zhao, "A Better Vision for Development: Eyeglasses and Academic Performance in Rural Primary Schools in China," 28.

[42] Bureau of Labor Statistics, "Optometrists"; Bureau of Labor Statistics; Jacobs, "A Simple Way to Improve a Billion Lives."

[43] Erevelles, *Disability and Difference in Global Contexts: Enabling a Transformative Body Politic*, chap. 4.

pure and simple, such as variations in mobility, should lead us to question what is and is not a "natural good."

Imagine another neighbor of Pedro, Royce, and Franklin. Divina, who was born Deaf, has superb vision and is physically able to go everywhere Franklin and Royce like to play. But she has grown up in a segregated educational system and feels socially ostracized in most of these spaces. Within the Deaf community she can communicate rich and complex thoughts and needs and can build equally rich and complex relationships, take on socially important roles and responsibilities, express herself, and choose from a wide range of personal goals. Outside of that community, she is afforded far more limited opportunities to build a fulfilling identity. Divina is thus far less likely to obtain an athletic scholarship, even though she is a better athlete than Royce, simply because most of the early childhood athletic programs available are not prepared to integrate a Deaf team member. Similarly, the unfriendliness of many social activities early in her life leaves her with a far shallower pool of potential mentors than Franklin.

Farsightedness and nearsightedness—the kinds of differences Franklin has from Pedro, Royce, and Divina—are among the human differences in ability that we can very effectively mitigate via technology. The same is not true for every kind of biological difference: so long as Pedro cannot walk, there are going to be specific kinds of actions that Royce is capable of that Pedro is not, since Pedro uses a wheelchair to get around.

Nonetheless, these limitations are *social* limitations. After all, there are also differences that are possible but not desirable to reduce. It would be wrong to assume that Divina would prefer to be hearing, like Pedro, Royce, and Franklin, if it were possible. These complications led philosopher Elizabeth Barnes to argue that "disability" is not well understood as a sort of body, that there's no common feature uniting disabled bodies themselves into a conceptual category. Instead, she argues that disability is better understood as a way to press for justice based on "group solidarity," or "a social category people have found useful when organizing themselves in a civil rights struggle."[44]

---

[44] Barnes, *The Minority Body: A Theory of Disability*, 41–45.

Deaf scholars like Bauman and Murray have advocated a "reframing" approach to the description of disabilities. They use the term "deaf gain" to describe what others might describe as "hearing loss."[45] They point out that there is a deaf culture that is inherently valuable to the people who are able to participate in it, sign languages that deaf people use increase linguistic diversity, and intellectual and creative perspectives developed through deafness and its study that have made important intellectual and artistic contributions to society writ large.[46] Deafness as a disability is the "old frame," in their view: "[e]very deaf baby born on this planet is a gift to humankind."[47]

Although we can't—and, if "deaf gain" theorists are right, we *shouldn't*—erase all body differences between people, we can and should participate in the process of collectively deciding how these differences relate to people's *capabilities* in life. Does being Deaf mean that you can't thrive in public school? Does using a wheelchair mean that you can't fly a plane? The answers depend not on the individual but on what kind of world we live in, and how we've built it. These kinds of worldmaking decisions constitute a holistic approach to distributive justice.

This helps us shift our perspective in a general way. We no longer need to ask how many resources or goods to distribute to Pedro, who uses a wheelchair, to give him a bundle of "primary goods" equivalent to Royce's, who can walk. Rather than focusing narrowly on evaluating how primary goods are distributed and focusing on those inequalities, we could just as well ask how *stairs and ramps* are distributed—in other words we should focus on what the fact that Pedro uses a wheelchair *means* in terms of his capabilities and functionings, and thus for his freedom. The fact about where the ramps and stairs are and how they are geographically distributed is a fact about our built social environment itself. Thus, a worldmaking perspective endows us with the mission, not simply of distributing "stuff" in order for everyone to have

---

[45] Bauman and Murray, "Reframing: From Hearing Loss to Deaf Gain"; Barnes, "The Social Model of Disability: Valuable or Irrelevant"; Burke, "Bioethics and the Deaf Community."
[46] Bauman and Murray, "Reframing: From Hearing Loss to Deaf Gain."
[47] Bauman and Murray, "Reframing: From Hearing Loss to Deaf Gain," 10.

equal amounts of it, but rather of creating a world where the variations we are born with are all socially translated into lives rich in capabilities. Justice, then, sometimes literally comes down to a construction project. Among the things we need to produce and distribute are practical affordances: parts of the built environment that make it navigable and usable by people with a wide range of abilities. The question of which buildings are accessible to wheelchair users (for example) and which are not depends on design choices in the built environment—choices made by people. This has long been noticed by activists working for disability justice, such as architect Ronald Mace, who was influential in the development of the idea of 'universal design': the "design of products and environments to be usable to the greatest extent possible by people of all ages and abilities."[48] Just like the anti-colonial activists and revolutionaries of the 1960s and 1970s, disability justice activists, too, want to literally remake the world. Both the ethos and the concrete goals of disability justice help direct the constructive view of reparations in response to global racial empire and in the search of justice.

Constructing Norms

What else do we need to build and distribute? Physically constructed environments are one important aspect of justice. A world with more ramps and fewer stairs would distribute capabilities more broadly than the one we have, for example, since strictly more people would be able to access more spaces. Others of the built aspects of the world that we navigate are social and cultural, including formal rules and laws.[49]

But there is still another layer of social and cultural structure to the environment that shapes the capabilities of individual lives. Thinking about disability justice in the African legal context, legal scholar Oche

---

[48] Story, Mueller, and Mace, "The Universal Design File: Designing for People of All Ages and Abilities," 2.
[49] For a discussion of the relationship of the capabilities approach to what Murphy calls the "just pursuit of societal transformation" (equivalent, when thought of globally, to what I call the "constructive view"),– see Murphy, *The Conceptual Foundations of Transitional Justice*, chap. 3.

Onazi argues that we need more than new laws: we also need a totally new public, moral culture built around understanding and acceptance of asymmetrical moral obligations, and the personhood of people with disabilities.[50] Accordingly, worldmaking requires approaching our built environment differently, but also combating stigmas by constructing new sets of norms.[51] The ancient Chinese philosopher Confucius is one of history's most influential theorists of these informal aspects of social structure, referring to them with the term *li*. *Li* is often translated into English as "ritual," but philosopher Amy Olberding argues that we should instead think of it as encompassing what we in the contemporary United States might denote as civility, manners, and etiquette.[52] These features of informal social structure form a sort of "cultural grammar," says philosopher Chenyang Li, that governs whether our behavioral sentences are well formed by the moral norms and rules of the relevant community.

As Olberding explains, *li* habituates us into regulated patterns of behavior, which signal important things to those neighbors and strangers we share the world with. Informal aspects of social structure, like norms of civility and etiquette, turn our abstract commitments to social goods like trust, attention, and respect into specific behaviors. That I say "Please pass the salt," for instance, represents my use of one possible community solution to the problem of how to ask for things, while also signaling that I recognize the other people at the table as having status: they are neither physical objects that I can use nor political subjects that I can command to aid my acquisition of the salt.[53]

Attention to social norms is important for racial justice given that habits of thought and attention have been built up over the same history and under the constraints of the same processes that are responsible for economic and political injustice. As philosopher Bill Lawson argues, the moral and political vocabulary we've inherited

[50] Onazi, "Disability Justice in an African Context: The Human Rights Approach," chap. 6.

[51] Thanks to Elizabeth Barnes for pressing me on this point.

[52] Olberding, *The Wrong of Rudeness: Learning Modern Civility from Ancient Chinese Philosophy*.

[53] Olberding, *The Wrong of Rudeness: Learning Modern Civility from Ancient Chinese Philosophy*, chap. 4.

from history lacks adequate resources to truly explain the depths of American slavery and its ongoing effects in the lives of present day Black descendants of slavery: directing attention and understanding in the right ways is important for securing justice here and elsewhere.[54]

African American polymath W. E. B. DuBois famously described a mundane incident in the beginning of his book *The Souls of Black Folk,* an autobiography and work of philosophy. One day the children in his schoolhouse were exchanging cards, and a white child refused his. He realized immediately that, as the only Black child in the group, he was different from the others. We might say that social grammar enabled this sequence of actions, whereas the meaning of the rebuff would have been completely different had the position of the two children been reversed. He later realizes that the same social structure that made the rebuff of his card acceptable also explained the far more desperate social and economic position of other Black children.

Understanding these kinds of implicit social grammars is essential to grappling with contemporary racism. Reading legal codes alone will fail to capture the everyday interactions in which trust, attention, and respect are distributed. Political theorist Melvin Rogers argues that this observation is key to understanding Du Bois.[55] Du Bois and Rogers, like Olberding and Confucius, both take it that our informal structure habituates us into patterns of care, concern, and attention. But where the latter two thinkers focused on how *li* regulates daily life as a positive, for Du Bois and Rogers, this is the problem. The patterns that actually exist in society may fail to distribute respect, care, and concern to all of its members, resulting in a "cultural grammar" that systematically excludes and victimizes certain people.

The ancient Greek philosopher Plato wrote a classic dialogue called *The Republic,* in which he gives a description of a just social structure. The participants of the dialogue spend much more time and attention discussing how the members of Plato's just city are to be socialized and acculturated than they spend discussing alternative class structures or formal separations of powers. Plato's Socrates goes as

---

[54] Lawson, "Moral Discourse and Slavery."
[55] Rogers, "Introduction: Disposable Lives"; Rogers, "The People, Rhetoric, and Affect: On the Political Force of Du Bois's *The Souls of Black Folk.*"

far as to call formal aspects of the social structure such as laws and regulations "trifles," since a properly socialized population will reliably act lawfully, and clever legal designs cannot redeem a poorly socialized population.[56]

Then, one of the things we need to build and distribute are the right kinds of structures for social interaction. Our habits of thought and action also feed back into our material reality: the patterns of care, concern, and attention that we learn in our mundane interactions ultimately explain which sorts of bodies are taken into account when a building is designed, which people's circumstances are used as benchmarks when a policy is written, what kinds of people are included in medical research that determines what is a normal treatment for a given condition. For example: the recent 2019 Ebola outbreak in the Democratic Republic of Congo was deadly for everyone, men and women alike. But, during some of the worst periods of the outbreak, over a thousand at-risk women were barred from receiving a highly effective trial vaccine—because they were pregnant or breastfeeding. There is scant research on the effects of many medicines and procedures on the health of pregnant or breastfeeding women, and correcting this gap has been consistently deprioritized by the global medical community.[57] The disproportionate risk of pregnant Congolese women in 2019 was thus the result of decades of accumulated neglect of pregnant women's health across the entire world.

The worldmaking perspective on justice, then, is concerned with material and social resources, formal rules and norms, and also with informal patterns of attention and care. A just system should move material resources around to places that can produce wheelchairs and assisted walking devices, and then we should move those wheelchairs to the homes of people who need them. We should also move training for eye doctors to regions with many patients and few doctors, and put in place social incentives to make it feasible for an adequate number

[56] Plato, *Republic*," sec. 425 a–c, trans. C. D. C. Reeve.
[57] Schwartz, "Clinical Trials and Administration of Zika Virus Vaccine in Pregnant Women: Lessons (that Should Have Been) Learned from Excluding Immunization with the Ebola Vaccine during Pregnancy and Lactation"; Lyerly, Little, and Faden, "The Second Wave: Toward Responsible Inclusion of Pregnant Women in Research"; "Pregnant Women in DRC Finally Receive Ebola Vaccine," Devex.com.

of doctors to stay in those communities. We should pay attention to which children are rebuked for which behaviors, and change those patterns where they reveal an unjust difference in the social grammar that applies to one child versus another.

Not all of these aspects of the world we need to build are obviously "resources" in the sense of money or education. But they are all aspects of our environment that we have an active duty to reform in order to improve our world. As such, the constructive view, armed with its worldmaking perspective, aims to achieve justice in all of these. As a view of reparations, it demands that we distribute the costs of making the just world toward those corporations, governments, and people that have inherited the moral liabilities of the worldmaking that preceded us.

The Target: Self-Determination in a Just World

The project of reparations is to learn how to distribute capabilities justly in order to make a new world. Such a just world must by its nature be fundamentally incompatible with the one we are in now: the world of global racial empire, in which laws and norms maintain the unjust distributions of racial capitalism.

I should note why I say 'justly' rather than 'equally.' We can and should recognize the historical importance of social movements' use of the term "equality" in the pursuit of justice, while also recognizing the difficulties of leaning on it too heavily in order to answer tough conceptual questions about what we should do and what arrangements of society we should want. Amartya Sen points out that everyone wants *something* to be equal. Libertarians are egalitarian with respect to a set of basic rights and liberties; welfare-egalitarians want everyone to have the same level of welfare; utilitarians want everyone's individual costs and benefits to be weighed equally when evaluating social policies; and so on.[58] Sen argues that in the face of these kinds of disagreements,

---

[58] Sen, *Inequality Reexamined*, ix.

framing the political battle as though it were between people in favor of equality and people against equality is misleading and unproductive.[59]

Obviously, giving every person a wheelchair would in one sense be treating them equally, but it would not be all that helpful for achieving a just world. More generally, focusing on equality can tend to constrain us to a snapshot view. For example, if you distribute grain equally to one million people, without taking into account the families who already have accumulated grain reserves, who own their own storage and who do not, who already have the knowledge of how to preserve and use this type of grain and who do not, and who are physically able to eat grain and who are not, you won't achieve a just food distribution. A broader historical view would enable to you to focus on the desired *outcome,* which is actually dismantling the historical accumulations of resource and privilege such that everybody *has enough to eat.* That requires paying attention to the causal imprint of yesterday's distribution, not just fitting today's distribution to principles of fairness abstracted from history. Likewise, if you distribute equal citizenship rights to one hundred people, without paying attention to the *li* that patterns their interactions, you will be likely to find that those who previously had citizenship will continue to treat those who previously did not differently in most of the situations that make up our day-to-day lives.

The capabilities approach will carry us much further, because it directs us to look squarely and holistically at outcomes, and in order to make sense of outcomes it directs us to widen our focus to take in all the dynamic interactions that produce them. This necessarily involves understanding the present moment in its place between the historical forces of accumulation and the future that those forces shape.

Earlier we briefly glossed the ideal target of distribution with the term "freedom," which of course has myriad definitions. Returning to legal scholar and activist Nkechi Taifa and political scientist Adom Getachew's intellectual work will guide us more precisely to what this target is: a world where people can relate to each other on terms of non-domination rather than on the terms of domination we've inherited.[60]

---

[59] Sen, *Inequality Reexamined*, chaps. 1–2.
[60] Getachew, *Worldmaking after Empire*, 23.

Taifa's work demonstrates this view in action, in her argument for reparations in a specific part of the global racial empire: the United States. In "Reparations and Self-Determination," Taifa explains that the predicament of Black American descendants of the enslaved is made up of pressing questions, including "how should we govern ourselves?" and "what does freedom mean?" The answer for Taifa involves giving each Black American descendant of slavery the choice between staying in the United States, emigrating to the Republic of New Afrika (as described earlier), or emigrating elsewhere. What ties these otherwise quite different choices together is a belief in what the choice achieves: the capability of self-determination at both an individual and a collective scale.

Philosopher Elizabeth Anderson developed a theory of distributive justice that is close in spirit to the constructive view. She calls her theory "democratic equality." Anderson begins from a very congenial starting point: noting that the point of justice is not to eliminate something—whether it be natural or social difference or the brute effects of luck—but to create instead a community where we all stand on terms of equality with one another. What's required for this equality, in Anderson's view, is the exercise of individual capabilities of three categories: as a human being, as a participant in economy, and as a participant in a political system (which she imagines as a democratic state). To be capable of functioning as a human being, she says, requires effective access to the means of sustaining one's biological existence (food, health care, shelter) and the tools required to effectively exercise agency (knowledge of one's circumstances and options, and the ability to deliberate over them). To be capable of participating in an economy without being dominated requires capabilities such as effective access to the means of production, choice over occupation, and fair recognition for one's work. Finally, to be capable of participating in a democratic state without being dominated requires capabilities that include freedom of speech, rights to vote, and so on. Reparations, then, as political theorist Lawrie Balfour has explained, could be tasked with creating the balance of power and material conditions whereby we can relate to each other in the ways democracy demands.

The target for the constructive view of reparations that I propose will be broadly similar to this proposal of Anderson's. But it will be different in two crucial respects. First, as discussed, I drop the language of equality altogether and go with justice as the moral yardstick. The second disagreement is more substantive. Anderson seems to perceive the state as the important political structure that we live in, and thus she privileges the social relationships within that structure. As I've argued in this book and elsewhere, I think this is a mistake: the realities of colonial conquest and the "post-colonial" world clue us into the fact that the interactions that shape our social world have never respected state borders.

As a generation of Third World anticolonial freedom fighters made clear, the whole division of nation-states and the broader international order we live under are up for revision and evaluation. The export-led growth being planned in Beijing and executed in factories in Guangdong affects the employment and negotiating power of workers in manufacturing-dense areas of the United States such as Alabama or Tennessee.[61] Similarly, the realities of life for the citizens of Iraq and Afghanistan cannot be understood without including their relationship to the United States in the picture. Our political borders obscure the closeness and consequences of the relationships that stretch across them.

Borders are features of the international superstructure through with goods and rights and duties and violence flow; they do have effects on those flows, but they never function as retaining walls isolating micro-systems.[62] Rather, the superstructure directs the production of advantage and disadvantage and directs the traffic of both from their sites of production to their destinations. Many kinds of economic production take place across many different state borders, involving "citizens" of one state in processes with citizens of another state. This situation invites the question of whether our theory of justice ought to preserve 'democratic equality' in these relationships as well.[63]

---

[61] Autor, Dorn, and Hanson, "The China Shock: Learning from Labor-Market Adjustment to Large Changes in Trade," 224; Táíwò, "States Are Not Basic Structures."

[62] Táíwò, "States Are Not Basic Structures."

[63] For arguments linking the economic structure of the world to broader demands of justice, see Moellendorf, "Cosmopolitanism and Compatriot Duties," 2011; Julius, "Nagel's Atlas"; Táíwò, "States Are Not Basic Structures."

Perhaps the world order would be improved by the creation of a state that doesn't yet exist, as the proponents of New Afrika and the colonial liberationists of the twentieth century contended. But as Nkechi Taifa, Julius Nyerere, and Kwame Nkrumah all anticipated from their very different contexts, statehood by itself cannot protect citizens from domination and thus cannot bring about justice without broader changes in the international arena.

As the target for the constructive reparations, then, we need a goal that matches the scope of our global reality. We must globalize Anderson's positive claims about which capabilities must be justly distributed. Everyone in the *world order* should have capabilities that grant effective access to the means of maintaining their biological existence, economic power, and political agency. Our target must be a global community thoroughly structured by non-domination.

***

The defeat of the 1835 Malê revolt in Brazil was mere days in the making.

In 1791 on the French colony of Saint Domingue, revolution blossomed, and the spiritual practice of Vodou paved the way. Boukman was a man of high rank: both a Papaloi or High Priest of Vodou and a headman of a plantation. From this position he kept tabs on political developments among whites and mixed-race Haitian creoles alike, and with this information the enslaved Africans plotted to take the entire colony of Saint Domingue.[64] They set fire to the plantations, destroying the symbolic and actual structures that had cemented their slavery, and began fighting at once, liberating enslaved people as they went. By 1804, they had the island—inspiring similar fights for independence from slavery and colonialism throughout the Western Hemisphere that roared for the remaining century.[65]

---

[64] James, *The Black Jacobins: Toussaint L'Ouverture and the San Domingo Revolution*, 86–87.

[65] James, *The Black Jacobins: Toussaint L'Ouverture and the San Domingo Revolution*.

In 1835, in the Brazilian empire, Islam paved the way for a broad coalition to form.[66] *Since the religion united Africans from a variety of ethnic backgrounds, it was unsurprising that the Malê revolt was organized in a madrassa, hidden in a rented house.*[67]

There, Manoel Calafate and Aprígio, two free Nagôs who were senior religious leaders, along with Ahuna, an enslaved Nagô, and a group of primarily enslaved Muslim students, spearheaded a plan to mount armed resistance during the last ten days of Ramadan.

Following these leaders was a group of 600 Muslim and non-Muslim participants "from virtually every ethnic group of African-born slaves and freedmen in Bahía" who came together to address their common oppression.[68] *Indeed, the Malê revolt was remarkable in the breadth of its coalition, including nearly equal numbers of free and enslaved. But the plan was foiled.*

Sabina da Cruz, a freed Nagô, stumbled upon her husband at Manoel Calafate's iftar, discussing the plan for tomorrow's uprising. She alerted a friend and fellow free Nagô, Guilhermina Rosa de Souza. Rosa de Souza alerted the local government, including Francisco Gonçalves Martins, the chief of police, who put the police on high alert and ordered extra patrols in the parts of town identified by da Cruz. The next day, when the alliance of 600 Africans gathered in makeshift barracks for what they had hoped would be a surprise assault, they found themselves preemptively confronted. The group opposing them included civilians, enslaved people loyal to the Crown, and soldiers.[69] *The revolutionaries overcame this initial opposition and headed for the jail, hoping to free imprisoned comrades, but were repelled, routed, and imprisoned. All told, 600 African revolutionaries went up against 1,500 police, cavalry, national guardsmen, and soldiers, most of whom were equipped with superior arms.*[70]

---

[66] While the group was in fact quite diverse, the Malê revolt is often associated with Islam. "Malê" comes from the Yoruba word *imale*, referring to a Muslim person.

[67] Rosa, "Du'as of the Enslaved."

[68] Rosa; Graden, "An Act 'Even of Public Security': Slave Resistance, Social Tensions, and the End of the International Slave Trade to Brazil, 1835–1856," 256.

[69] Reis, "Slave Resistance in Brazil: Bahia, 1807–1835," 125.

[70] Reis, *Rebelião Escrava No Brasil: A História Do Levante Dos Malês Em 1835*, 89.

4

What's Missing

"Tell no lies. Claim no easy victories."

—Amílcar Cabral

If I was trying to discover myself—on the whole, when examined, a somewhat dubious notion, since I was also trying to avoid myself—there was, certainly, between that self and me, the accumulated rock of ages. This rock scarred the hand, and all tools broke against it. Yet, there was a me, somewhere: I could feel it, stirring within and against captivity. The hope of salvation—identity—depended on whether or not one would be able to decipher and describe the rock.

One song cries, "lead me to the rock that is higher than I," and another cries, "hide me in the rock!" and yet another proclaims, "I got a home in that rock." Or, "I ran to the rock to hide my face: the rock cried out, no hiding place!"

The accumulated rock of ages deciphered itself as a part of my inheritance—a part, mind you, not the totality—but, in order to claim my birthright, of which my inheritance was but a shadow, it was necessary to challenge and claim the rock. Otherwise, the rock claimed me.

Or, to put it another way, my inheritance was particular, specifically limited and limiting: my birthright was vast, connecting me to all that lives, and to everyone, forever. But one cannot claim the birthright without accepting the inheritance. Therefore, when I began, seriously, to write—when I knew I was committed, that this would be my life—I had to try to describe that particular condition which was—is—the living proof of my inheritance. And, at the same time, with that very same description, I had to claim my birthright.

Reconsidering Reparations. Olúfẹ́mi O. Táíwò, Oxford University Press. © Oxford University Press 2022.
DOI: 10.1093/oso/9780197508893.003.0004

I am what time, circumstance, history, have made of me, certainly, but I am, also, much more than that. So are we all. The conundrum of color is the inheritance of every American, be he/she legally or actually Black or White. It is a fearful inheritance, for which untold multitudes, long ago, sold their birthright. Multitudes are doing so, until today. This horror has so welded past and present that it is virtually impossible and certainly meaningless to speak of it as occurring, as it were, in time. It can be, and it has been, suicidal to attempt to speak of this to a multitude, which, assuming it knows that time exists, believes that time can be outwitted.

Something like this, anyway, has something to do with my beginnings.

—James Baldwin, Baldwin, *Notes of a Native Son,*
"Autobiographical Notes"

Georgetown

I teach philosophy at Georgetown University in Washington, D.C., the capital of the United States. Like the United States' capital, and like the nation itself, Georgetown University was built within a global racial empire using racist technologies of oppression: it was physically assembled and maintained by enslaved people upon colonized land taken from Indigenous peoples, in order to be filled with teachers and students who rated them as less than human. An institution in which rivers of finance channeled by the labor, suffering, and exchange of enslaved people were diverted into deep pools (which have yet to be drained), and pumped into florid fountain works of cultural propaganda.

It all started with some risky investments stretched across three continents.

North America, 1609: Captain John Smith sailed around the Chesapeake bay region of North America, surveying lands where the Piscataway, the Mattaponi, the Nanticoke, and the Pamunkey lived, which eventually became the neighboring lands of Delaware, Virginia, Maryland, and Washington, D.C.[1] Undeterred by Sir Walter Raleigh's earlier failure to found a permanent colony at Roanoke, Captain Smith, King James I, and the shareholders of the Virginia Company of London aimed to expand their wealth and control in North America. The marching orders from the shareholders included subjugating the "barbarous" Indigenous peoples and converting them to Christianity—and, of course, returning economic value to the shareholders.[2]

Spain had already sailed this bay a half century before Smith's expedition and laid claim to the entire region of the world, though that claim had not yet materialized in a permanent settlement.[3] Thus, British expeditions to the same territory were no coincidence: the possibility of Spain getting their "ravenous hands upon these gold showing mountains" first was a key selling point. The expeditions aimed to find a sea route to the Pacific Ocean for the British empire to exploit, for their leaders had seen the kind of power that could be gained from long-distance trade. One moment the individual names of da Gama and Columbus became famous, and the next Spain and Portugal were enjoying an early dominance over the affairs of this new, much larger globe than any previous empire had even imagined dominating. Smith's ambition of a permanent settlement succeeded at Jamestown, and for the remainder of the century various colonizers, most prominently the Dutch, French, and English vied for power in this region. The conflict centered on the typical preoccupations of empire: land and trade.[4]

They never found the gold or the desired sea route to the Pacific Ocean, so at first, the vision of trade fell flat. But there was, still, the land.

As the Jamestown colony developed, it produced a variety of goods, but none more influential than tobacco. Tobacco was a reliable cash crop, finding willing markets across the growing Atlantic order's

---

[1] Herman, "A Smithsonian Scholar Revisits the Neglected History of the Chesapeake Bay's Native Tribes."
[2] Asch and Musgrove, *Chocolate City*, 7–8.
[3] Herman, "A Smithsonian Scholar Revisits the Neglected History of the Chesapeake Bay's Native Tribes."
[4] Richter, *Trade, Land, Power: The Struggle for Eastern North America*.

vast trans-oceanic system of trade. The wealth and success of early settlers attracted new settlers and investment capital from merchants in London, which led to a land rush. Captain John Smith and the founding members of Jamestown had initially stumbled into territory controlled by the Powhatan confederacy. Their leadership was, at first, willing to make a deal: if the settlers would relocate from Jamestown to a position closer to the confederacy's capital, the Powhatan confederacy would trade them food for copper and beads, valuable items in the region's economy. The colonists accepted the food but reneged on the deal, instead continuing to explore new territory, claim land, and parcel it out as the colony's population grew.

It was among the first broken agreements between British colonists and Indigenous peoples. It would not be the last.

The settlers eventually explored beyond the boundary of Powhatan territory into what is now Washington, D.C. There, they met groups of people allied under a different banner—the Piscataway confederacy. These groups received the English settlers warmly. likely in the hopes of a military alliance against the Powhatan groups, whom they took to have expansionist intentions toward their territory along the Potomac.[5] Jamestown's diplomatic provocation immediately attracted resistance from the Powhatan confederacy, initiating the "First Powhatan War."[6] The colonists responded with overwhelming violence, destroying entire towns, burning crops, and publicly executing men, women, and children of any age.[7] The violence was indiscriminate: not only would they kill people of any age or gender, but they also destroyed nearby communities even if the town was only loosely affiliated with the Powhatan confederacy, or not at all.[8] These tactics represented the very first importation of English "ad terrorem" warfare onto the American frontier—tactics developed during the guerrilla

---

[5] Asch and Musgrove, *Chocolate City*, 9.
[6] Asch and Musgrove, *Chocolate City*, 6.
[7] Horn, "The Founding of English America: Jamestown."
[8] Fausz, "'An Abundance of Blood Shed on Both Sides': England's First Indian War, 1609–1614," 33–34.

warfare in late sixteenth-century Ireland and here meted out by veterans of those wars.[9]

Through violence, diplomacy, and more violence, Jamestown repeatedly survived Powhatan reprisals and continued to cultivate tobacco. The Jamestown colony, as the first successful British colony in North America, eventually served as something of a prototype for English colonization – not just in the Americas, but worldwide.[10] According to historian James Horn, the new blueprint for settler colonies was simple: profit and security through "the creation of stable political and social institutions" which included "representative government, the church, private property, and establishment of family life," and "the discovery of a lucrative commodity."[11]

Meanwhile, an ocean away, in central Africa, the political situation set a few unsuspecting Africans on a collision course with colonization in the Americas. The Portuguese empire had long had a physical presence on the continent—as early as 1483, when navigator Diogo Cão sailed into a province of the Kingdom of Kongo. King Nzinga Nkuwu, likely hoping for a powerful alliance, converted to Christianity, adopting the name João I of Kongo and sending emissaries to Lisbon in the beginning of what would become a centuries-long cultural exchange. Meanwhile, the Portuguese claimed and settled the uninhabited island of São Tome and spliced themselves into Kongo's lucrative existing system of human trafficking, by offering mercenary soldiers for Kongo's wars and taking payment in enslaved people from surrounding communities.[12]

With the help of these inroads made into local politics, Portugal solidified its strategic position and its colonial ambitions in the region. By the mid 1500s, Portugal had established a physical presence in Angola, helped along by several missions led by fathers of the Jesuit's Society of Jesus and the explorer Pedro Dias de Novias. These

---

[9] Fausz, "'An Abundance of Blood Shed on Both Sides': England's First Indian War, 1609–1614"; Rice, "War and Politics: Powhatan Expansionism and the Problem of Native American Warfare."

[10] Horn, "The Founding of English America: Jamestown."

[11] Horn, "The Founding of English America: Jamestown."

[12] Heywood and Thornton, *Central Africans, Atlantic Creoles, and the Foundation of the Americas, 1585–1660*, 68.

culminated in the founding of the city of São Paolo de Luanda and six Portuguese-controlled prisons along the Kwanza river, further cementing its increasingly lucrative involvement in the slave trade. It also resulted in land and resource grants to the Society of Jesus, including a speculative grant of a mine to the Catholic religious society. Initially, the Portuguese anticipated that they would find silver reserves if they continued to push further inland, a powerful incitement.[13]

They never found the silver. But there were, still, the people.

In subsequent years, Portugal would double down on the slave trade. They enslaved people by direct capture, purchased them in local markets, and received them as compensation for joint military ventures with local powers.[14] They were less than discriminating about their targets for abduction. Historian Linda Heywood explains they regularly preyed on even the citizens of the allied Christian power in the Kingdom of Kongo—even its nobility—despite this practice triggering a series of diplomatic crises.[15] They were also less than discriminating in their choice of local partners, trading and lending military assistance to local terrorist outfits like the Imbangala, who subsisted entirely by pillaging the local communities they lived in alienation from and whose military organization featured some of the earliest systematic use of child soldiers in recorded history.[16]

The Portuguese and the Imbangala even jointly invaded the nearby Ndongo kingdom, capturing thousands of people and selling them into slavery. As a result of this invasion, thirty-six ships full of abducted people set sail, many heading to Brazil, Portugal's South American colony—by far the most common destination for enslaved people throughout the trans-Atlantic slave trade, in part because the Jesuits had raised effective political opposition to the enslavement of

[13] da Silva, "Paulo Dias de Novais e o Desenvolvimento Das Relações Entre Os Portugueses e o Ndongo, Século XVI Paulo Dias de Novais and the Development of Relations between the Portuguese and Ndongo, 16th Century"; Rego, "Portuguese Colonization in the Sixteenth Century: A Study of the Royal Ordinances (Regimentos)," 1–11.
[14] Heywood and Thornton, *Central Africans, Atlantic Creoles, and the Foundation of the Americas, 1585–1660*, 93.
[15] Heywood, "Slavery and Its Transformation in the Kingdom of Kongo: 1491–1800."
[16] XXX

Indigenous peoples.[17] One of these ships was instead bound for the city Vera Cruz of colonial New Spain (now Mexico) when it was set upon by Dutch pirates, who submitted the Africans on board to yet a second kidnapping and diverted them north.[18]

Meanwhile, back in North America, the European colonists of colonial Virginia were anticipating future violence over the land. The Virginia group did not become the first British colonists to survive in North America haphazardly: after conquering tracts of land from the Powhatan confederacy in the First Powhatan War, they did not rest, but enacted careful strategies to shore up their economic and military security. Afterward, from 1618 to 1621, dozens of ships arrived with young men of prime working and military age, immediately put to work expanding plantations and putting down Indigenous resistance. In 1619 alone more than a dozen new plantations were claimed by British settlers.[19] It was the same year, after all, that the Virginia Company established a "headright system" which guaranteed private ownership of land to anyone who could pay their own way over to colonial America from Britain, granting potential colonists a financial stake in settler conquest. This policy from the mother country solved a short-term impediment to colonial ambitions—the winnowing of the colony population by disease and warfare—but in the long run the strategy all but guaranteed continued conflict with the Indigenous peoples whose land the company claimed to have title.[20]

In 1619, a ship arrived: the one that had been diverted from Vera Cruz, carrying abducted African people. Whether the Virginia colonists saw them as natural inferiors is difficult to discern. For much of this century, the conditions of indentured servitude and slavery weren't quite as starkly different as they would later become in the Anglophone world. Many people sold into indentured servitude had been abducted, and indentured servants were sold on auction blocks

---

[17]   Eltis, "The Volume and Structure of the Transatlantic Slave Trade: A Reassessment"; Alexander, "Brazilian and United States Slavery Compared," 350.

[18]   Thornton, "The African Experience of the '20. and Odd Negroes' Arriving in Virginia in 1619"; "400 Years Ago, Enslaved Africans First Arrived in Virginia."

[19]   Rountree, *Pocahontas's People: The Powhatan Indians of Virginia through Four Centuries*, 196: 66.

[20]   Rountree, *Pocahontas's People*, 196: 69–70.

like livestock, used as stakes in card games, and could be awarded as damages in lawsuits.[21] Moreover, slavery was not yet explicitly racialized: Captain John Smith, Jamestown's founder, had himself been a slave for years under the Ottoman empire in Turkey.[22] The system that would eventually congeal into a matured, global network of racial slavery was still amorphous in this period. What is clear is that these Africans were unfree. It's also clear that they and those who came after them were crucial to the development of colonial America.

The Virginia colony fought the Powhatan confederacy yet again in 1622—destroying shelters and raiding the food supply of the surviving population as winter approached.[23] They used the food they took from the Indigenous peoples to sustain the plantation laborers, then predominantly indentured servants and African workers, on the new land, where they established yet more tobacco plantations for the world market. The Virginia colony's successes with tobacco and the regional fur trade attracted new investment capital from London, facilitated by a royal charter for the territory granted by King James I to a Jesuit by the name of Sir George Calvert—perhaps better known as the first Lord Baltimore. After his death, his son Cecilius Calvert (the second Lord Baltimore) was granted proprietorship of a new colony: the colony of Maryland.

Maryland, at first, enjoyed somewhat peaceful relations with the nearby Nacostines and the Piscataway confederacy. The location of the initial settlement was decided a hundred miles south of occupied Piscataway territory in a consultation with Wannas, a Piscataway chief, facilitated by fellow English fur traders from the Virginia Company's colony.[24] But the investors required profit, profit required tobacco, and tobacco required land. Soon, the expanding Maryland colony was at the Piscataway doorstep: by 1670, the colonists had laid claim to all the Nacostine and Piscataway land on which Washington, D.C. now sits.

---

[21] Williams, *Capitalism and Slavery*, 11; Horton, "From Class to Race in Early America: Northern Post-Emancipation Racial Reconstruction"; Fields, "Slavery, Race and Ideology in the United States of America," 102.

[22] Asch and Musgrove, *Chocolate City*, 7.

[23] Asch and Musgrove, *Chocolate City*, 10.

[24] Asch and Musgrove, *Chocolate City*, 11.

This particular land was deeply contested territory: enslaved people and indentured servants were sent out to deforest the area and make room for tobacco plantations despite the constant threat of assault from nearby Piscataway warriors. But the Maryland assembly, newly armed with additional capital and military might from abroad, created a militia and built fortifications around the area, stabilizing the territory for tobacco production. The Nacostines spent the next years fleeing the ever-encroaching lines of European settlement and melding with other groups of Indigenous peoples.[25] Today, the Anacostia River—named after the Latinized version of the word "Nacostine"—divides the city of Washington, D.C., cleaving the prosperous seat of world power from its poorest, Blackest neighborhoods.[26]

In the years shortly thereafter, Catholics would find themselves a small, relatively persecuted minority among European-descended peoples in the American colonies. After the Glorious Revolution at the tail end of the 1600s, colonial American laws doubly taxed Catholics and prevented them from voting, worshiping publicly, owning weapons, or inheriting property (though many of the laws were seldom enforced).[27] Many were current or former indentured servants, as were nearly half of all European immigrants to America in this century. Even a hundred years later, after the boom in the Catholic population of Maryland that followed the Haitian and French Revolutions, Catholics remained a minority at only 12 percent of the local population.[28]

But throughout the eighteenth century, they were an influential minority. Through a bundle of land grants from the colonial governor of Maryland, the Society of Jesus became one of the Maryland's largest landowners, with seven plantation estates spanning thousands of acres of the land the Piscataway and Nacostine peoples had lived on.[29] This small Catholic minority included a middle class of merchants and

[25] Asch and Musgrove, *Chocolate City,* 13.
[26] Asch and Musgrove, *Chocolate City,* 1, 14.
[27] Curran, *The Bicentennial History of Georgetown University: From Academy to University, 1789–1889,* 1:5.
[28] Curran, *The Bicentennial History of Georgetown University: From Academy to University, 1789–1889,* 1:12.
[29] Curran, *The Bicentennial History of Georgetown University: From Academy to University, 1789–1889,* 1:4–5.

small proprietors, and an influential aristocracy of land speculators and early titans of industry. Among these were the Carrolls.

Charles Carroll is known as a leader of the American Revolution, and was reputed to be one of the richest Americans of his generation.[30] His cousin John Carroll initially had different sorts of ambitions: he joined the Society of Jesus, studying Enlightenment thought under Catholic authorities in Austria. But history had other plans for him. In 1773, Pope Clement XIV's suppression of the Jesuit order reached John's school, and he was forced to leave at the point of an Austrian bayonet.[31] After having experienced religious intolerance and violence firsthand, Carroll decided to follow his cousin Charles after all: into politics. John became a fervent supporter of the struggle against the British empire, even going as far as to accompany Charles, Benjamin Franklin, and Samuel Chase on a mission to Montreal to attempt to recruit the Canadians to the revolutionary cause. He was convinced that the post-revolutionary government would be more tolerant than the colonial government had been and open up new and unprecedented opportunities for Catholics. He set his sights on a new goal: nationally organizing Catholic America, with a Catholic college as the centerpiece.

In 1782, Carroll convened a series of meetings of America's ex-Jesuits at the White Marsh plantation in Prince Georges County. Despite the Pope's suppression of the order, the Society of Jesus in the US retained its seven plantations—which, by this year, represented over 12,000 acres of prime real estate.[32] John created a unified body, the "Representative [or Select] Body of the Clergy," to consolidate administration of this land, and the body's trustee-ship over the lands was eventually legally recognized by an act of the Maryland state legislature.[33] It began exploiting these assets,

---

[30] Curran, *The Bicentennial History of Georgetown University: From Academy to University, 1789–1889*, 1:5.

[31] Curran, *The Bicentennial History of Georgetown University: From Academy to University, 1789–1889*, 1:5–6.

[32] Curran, *The Bicentennial History of Georgetown University: From Academy to University, 1789–1889*, 1:9.

[33] Curran, *The Bicentennial History of Georgetown University: From Academy to University, 1789–1889*, 1:15.

selling a small tract of land to allow construction to begin a school building.[34]

But this wouldn't be enough on its own. John recruited and dispatched agents throughout the newly independent American states, and also back in Europe, aiming to raise money for the school. The American public was averse to public funding for institutions, however, and the wealthy Catholics, including John's own cousin Charles, were less than convinced that the enterprise was worth their money. In Ireland, John found that a former appointee of his, Patrick Smyth, was circulating pamphlets accusing American Jesuits of being managed by slave-owning snobs more concerned with their own estates than with the broader Catholic population.[35] It is unclear to what extent these pamphlets were to blame, but what is clear is that the attempt to finance Georgetown by the largesse of fellow Catholics was an abysmal failure. This left Georgetown financially dependent on its lands, and the income derived from their use or sale, for both the startup capital to construct Georgetown in the first place and the liquidity to weather financial shortfalls as they might arise.[36] Their plantation lands were made historically possible and presently profitable by the labor of enslaved Africans.

"That Jesuit priests owned slaves should not come as a surprise," poet and scholar of African independence literature Professor Mukoma wa Ngũgĩ explained at the 2020 Writers Unlimited International Literature Festival. He had learned this from his travels on the African continent, researching the bases along its coasts where abducted Africans would be kept before they were shipped across the Atlantic. After these travels, he realized that "every slave castle I visited had a church in its own compound. In Elmina and Cape Coast the church was built directly above slave dungeons. The pious white Christians would pour water through the cracks in the wooden floor to ease the thirst and

---

[34] Curran, *The Bicentennial History of Georgetown University: From Academy to University, 1789–1889*, 1:14.

[35] Curran, *The Bicentennial History of Georgetown University: From Academy to University, 1789–1889*, 1:18.

[36] Curran, *The Bicentennial History of Georgetown University: From Academy to University, 1789–1889*, 1:19–20.

heat. If there is one institution in dire need of decolonization, it is the church."[37]

The support that plantation income provided was far from sufficient to fund the institutions. As the school got off the ground in the 1790s, tuitions and fees rose to fill the gap, making Georgetown one of the most expensive institutions of learning in the nascent United States, costing more for a single student to attend per academic year than a laborer's annual pay.[38] Historian Robert Curran, professor emeritus of history at Georgetown, has shown that even tuition payments in this period exemplified the wider financial dependence of Georgetown on slavery. Owing to a semi-formal barter economy, some students' parents paid their children's tuition by renting to Georgetown the labor of the enslaved Africans who were regarded as their legal property.[39] In every conceivable sense, Georgetown was financially dependent on the wealth derived from the enslaved and owes its existence to this exploitation.

Even the expansion in tuition-paying students failed to keep pace with the university's expansion in costs (led by new buildings and increases in the number of faculty). The university became deeply in-debted, running large annual deficits.[40] Due to shoddy infrastructure and management, tuition costs contracted in the 1810s despite the fact that Georgetown was surrounded by a rapidly expanding and de-veloping capital city, which one might have expected to sweeten the deal of admission and help drive tuition upward.[41] The university did not fare better in the nationwide economic depression that followed the War of 1812, nor in the following decade.[42] In 1838, it managed its ongoing financial difficulties in dramatic fashion that has rever-berated across the centuries: Georgetown sold 272 enslaved people to

[37] wa Ngugi, "The Pitfalls of Symbolic Decolonization."
[38] Curran, *The Bicentennial History of Georgetown University: From Academy to University, 1789–1889*, 1:36.
[39] Curran, *The Bicentennial History of Georgetown University: From Academy to University, 1789–1889*, 1:36.
[40] Curran, *The Bicentennial History of Georgetown University: From Academy to University, 1789–1889*, 1:66.
[41] Curran, *The Bicentennial History of Georgetown University: From Academy to University, 1789–1889*, 1:63.
[42] Curran, *The Bicentennial History of Georgetown University: From Academy to University, 1789–1889*, 1:79.

manage its debts. Today, the descendants of those enslaved are pushing Georgetown and the Society of Jesus for reparations, armed with the undeniable truth: that it owes its existence to these and other enslaved people.

Georgetown, like the rest of our world, was built by and atop colonial institutions and broader political structures of unfreedom and injustice. These facts are expressed in a particularly stark and dramatic form in the history of this institution, but they are unexceptional. For example: in 2018, the University of Virginia's own presidential commission conceded the inextricable links between slavery and the founding and financing of that school. Historians, following up on this information, uncovered regular violent abuse of enslaved people by the institution's earliest students, many of whom were children of the wealthy and politically connected planter elites of the day, as were Georgetown's.[43] The Morrill Act of 1862, signed into law by President Abraham Lincoln, redistributed 11 million acres of land (the size of Massachusetts and Connecticut combined) appropriated from tribal nations to US universities, including the University of California system of colleges and the Massachusetts Institute of Technology.[44] The same Catholic Church that sustained Georgetown University also operated "mission schools," educational facilities aiming for the "cultural assimilation" of Native children and funded by the treaty and trust funds that were granted to Native Americans who had been forced onto reservations. These schools were rife with sexual and other kinds of abuse, and an *In These Times* investigation revealed that the Catholic schools siphoned a minimum of $30 million from the Native trust funds for most of the twentieth century— until the 1970s, when the funds had been bled dry.[45]

What is exceptional about these institutions is not that they drew their financial lifeblood from the global racial empire, but the fact that the story has actually told rather than obscured.

---

[43] Natanson, "Two Centuries Ago, University of Virginia Students Beat and Raped Enslaved Servants, Historians Say"; University of Virginia. President's Commission on Slavery and the University et al., *President's Commission on Slavery and the University: Report to President Teresa A. Sullivan, 2018.*
[44] Lee and Ahtone, "Land-Grab Universities."
[45] Pember, "The Catholic Church Siphoned Away $30 Million Paid to Native People."

The tale I just recounted is the tale of the part of the world I inhabit as an academic worker: Georgetown University. It is, then, also the institutional story of how this book came to be. My access to Georgetown's financial, social, and intellectual resources explain both why a publisher would take on this book project and also the working conditions under which I was able to complete it. These conditions include sufficiently high compensation to live without constant stress or fear of financial emergency and manageable-sized teaching and administrative responsibilities: both immensely important conditions for serious intellectual work and increasingly rare finds in the crowded academic labor markets.[46]

At the smaller scale of my individual experience, the accumulated advantages that Georgetown has spent a couple of centuries pooling now flow directly into the accumulations of advantage that define my own life. Through my salary, Georgetown contributes to the story of how my bills get paid each month and all the accumulation of privilege that follows from that; through its institutional imprimatur on my standing as a scholar, it contributes to the story of how I accumulate whatever amount of social prestige I have. These, too, are linked to the story of how this book came to be, and also to the story of whatever comes of it. At a wider scale, then, Georgetown's origin story is a major way of explaining the difference between the relative interpersonal, social, and economic security and comfort that I derive from my social position and the comparative lack of security common in the rest of the world.

We Didn't Start the Fire

"You think your pain and your heartbreak are unprecedented in the history of the world, but then you read . . . [T]he things that tormented me most were the very things that connected me with all the people who were alive, or who ever had been alive. Only if we face these open wounds in ourselves can we understand them in other people." (James

---

[46] Xue and Larson, "STEM Crisis or STEM Surplus?"

Baldwin, quoted in Popova, "The Doom and Glory of Knowing Who You Are)

The full truth of how we got here complicates many of the ways that we are used to talking about racial justice, and in turn some of the most common rationales for reparation projects. Some of our stances on reparations are tied to ideas of collective responsibility. Our ideas of responsibility are often bloodless, descriptive notions of how and why things happen (causal responsibility) and more morally-laden ideas like blameworthiness and complicity. Often, we imagine that the people who have inherited responsibility for the crimes of global racial empire and those who have inherited moral claims to reparations map neatly onto contemporary identity binaries: white/Black, settler/Indigenous, colonizer/colonized. We often assume that these binaries that shape our view of the world neatly separate those advantaged by racism from those disadvantaged by racism, those advantaged by the global system of empire and those disadvantaged by it.

So, for example, some appreciable percentage of those who are now racialized as white are descended from those who were directly or indirectly culpable for the atrocities of the global racial empire, and all who are now racialized as white enjoy access to certain accumulations of power and privilege that have flowed from that empire. Some imagine that this helps us explain why white people as such are properly held uniquely responsible for the crimes of global racial empire.[47]

To build a view of reparations on these notions of binary group identity and collective responsibility is to build a house on a sand foundation. I don't see how they can withstand historical or present scrutiny.

To say that the ancestors of some contemporary whites were causally responsible for slavery and colonialism, whether as individuals or as organized groups, is not yet to identify a difference between white people and Black people. To say, for instance, that the labor of Black people built the wealth of colonizing nations is also, after all, to admit

---

[47] Forman, "The Black Manifesto."

that this labor kept the exploitative system going—which is to say that this labor was causally responsible for the system. Perhaps more pressing, Black people were involved in policing enslaved people, preventing escape and rebellion, and securing the slave system from its earliest days. During the 1500s, the *cuadrilleros* patrolling enslaved people in Peru and the *hermandad* militias in Cuba, for example, were drawn from free Blacks, enslaved Africans, Indigenous peoples, and whites alike.[48] The southern American colonies inherited their slave patrols from these early experiments in social control, and these in turn became the modern police departments that today continue to disproportionately kill, incarcerate, and repress Black people.[49]

You may object here to this example—surely if anyone has ever been coerced, it was the Black people pressed into the service of policing other enslaved people. This is a more persuasive point in the case of the enslaved *cuadrilleros* than the free ones, of course, but pointing out the problem with trying to map collective responsibility onto today's racial categories doesn't require contesting this point.

The trans-Atlantic slave trade was possible, after all, because it co-opted an indigenous slave trade with the active complicity of African empires. Linda Heywood gives an instructive example of what this means for us in her history of Kingdom of Kongo. While the ruling elite of the kingdom was complicit in fueling Portuguese slavery in the New World by engaging in regional wars to generate saleable prisoners, they weren't even exempt from abduction *during* collaboration with European empires—which is to say that they likely have living descendants on both sides of the Atlantic. Moreover, in Kongo, as in many other places on the continent, the immensely destructive social pressures caused by slavery led to regime collapse, which in turn made communities of even the freeborn people of the Kongo vulnerable to enslavement by rival powers, likely resentful of the kingdom's complicity in previous cycles of the slave trade.[50]

---

[48] Hadden, *Slave Patrols: Law and Violence in Virginia and the Carolinas*, 10.

[49] Hadden, *Slave Patrols: Law and Violence in Virginia and the Carolinas*, chap. 1; Potter, "The History of Policing in the United States."

[50] Heywood, "Slavery and Its Transformation in the Kingdom of Kongo: 1491–1800," 16–17.

We needn't confine ourselves to the distant past to make this point. According to scholars like Lisa Laakso and Adebayo Olukoshi, "divide and rule" was a tried and true practice of colonial domination. Colonial powers would consolidate ethnic, tribal, or other differences between groups and exploit them to maintain control.[51] Some favored groups could even function as "co-colonizers," as Ernest Wamba-dia-Wamba alleges of the Luba-Kasai in the case of Zaire (now the Democratic Republic of Congo).[52] The social legacy of this uneven relationship to colonial domination survived the transition into statehood. Legal professor Issa Shivji describes African economic elites as "compradorised," that is, the witting or unwitting agents of foreign interest.[53] Divide and conquer tactics continue to be used to this day. Whether as compradores or co-colonizers, there are elites among the (otherwise) dominated who benefit from the power structure as it stands and actively work to maintain it.

What was unprecedented about the practices of trans-Atlantic slavery and colonialism that built the global racial empire was not the criminal nature of the acts that built them, the forms of oppression involved, the moral depravity involved, or the role of greed. What was unprecedented about these practices was exactly one thing: their scale. This global racial empire did not result from the first systems of torture, discrimination, slavery, or apartheid – it resulted from the first system to enact these atrocities at a world scale.

This all combines into a tragic irony for the descendants of the enslaved: the sentiment "we were kings and queens" back in Africa *is* true, in some sense. But that very fact, it turns out, was the problem.

There are important differences between Black people, the Indigenous, and other people marginalized by racial hierarchies. But to

---

[51] Ernest Wamba-dia-Wamba describes this process in the construction of Zaire (now the Democratic Republic of Congo): he claims that the combined institutions of conscripted colonial manual labor and military service helped create the ethnic divisions exploited by the Belgians during the time occupying the territory as the Congo Free State. Laakso and Olukoshi, "The Crisis of the Post-Colonial Nation-State Project in Africa," 12–13; Wamba-dia-Wamba, "The National Question in Zaire: Challenges to the Nation-State Project."

[52] Wamba-dia-Wamba, "The National Question in Zaire: Challenges to the Nation-State Project," 160.

[53] Shivji, "The Rise, the Fall and the Insurrection of Nationalism in Africa."

map these differences onto a simple victim–victimizer binary built around notions of causal responsibility or nearby moral notions like "complicity"—whether we're talking about the present conditions of these peoples or their ancestors' role in the historical events that produced this present—commits us to vast oversimplifications at best. It puts us at serious risk of falsity in the most straightforward sense, and that in turns puts us at risk of losing our grip on how the world works. We will need to maintain that grip if we want to change things.

I don't raise these complications idly, in the service of mere argumentation or point scoring. My goal is not to equate the historical actions of colonizers, whites, or settlers with those of the colonized, Blacks and other people of color, and Indigenous peoples. The political situations that these terms describe are not equivalent, and the things that will liberate the first group will not necessarily liberate the rest of us.

But my goal *is* to equate us with them in one, particular, important way. Baldwin, as usual, put it best, when he said: "One of the great things that the white world does not know, but I think I do know, is that Black people are just like everybody else. One has used the myth of Negro and the myth of color to pretend and to assume that you were dealing with, essentially, with something exotic, bizarre, and practically, according to human laws, unknown. Alas, it is not true. We're also mercenaries, dictators, murderers, liars. We are human too."[54] We have no innate genetic or even cultural moral superiority by virtue of our heritage, much as pretending that there is might serve our psychic and emotional needs, or simplify our moral worlds in ways we find reassuring or helpfully orienting.

There is no way to sugarcoat this. Many of us descended from those who lost out in the creation of the world have retreated to a version of our identity that requires eliding these complications. That sense of pride was a weighty achievement, painstakingly wrested from a media and educational environment that preferred to say nothing about us at

---

[54] Baldwin and Buckley, *Debate: Baldwin vs. Buckley.*

all, or to dismiss us with contempt and bigotry in the few times when our historical presence was acknowledged. Many of our arguments for reparations come from this place as well—we insist that reparation must separate the guilty from the innocent, and adopt a view of history on which this distinction in moral responsibility will map cleanly onto racial categories. But the truth is that we are all morally "in the red," as Dr. Martin Luther King put it; for better or worse, we owe to history the possibilities for our choices and the resources we have to follow through on them.

But we aren't condemned to the (I think) futile effort of rescuing a categorization of responsibility that will vindicate our basic, intuitive convictions about who is owed and who owes. That's because we don't need the notion of responsibility, at all—nor the mistaken accounts of history that it assumes—to make sense of the justice of a reparation project, and to advance the cause of racial justice.

Responsibility is closely tied up with a web of related concepts like fault and cause. It is an important aspect of our moral lives, and the concept to which we often instinctively appeal when we make the case for why someone ought to give something to someone else, particularly in the case where the person or group being asked to give is more powerful or protected than the receiver. In much of our moral lives, responsibility and reparation tend to travel together: my friend is responsible for wrecking my car because he was the one driving it, the collision was his fault, and these help to explain why he is the one who, morally, ought to pay for the damages.

But these common features of our daily moral concepts aren't built to respond to things on the scale of global racial empire. While we can sometimes identify individual culpable parties for individual events or even eras of domination, we are often tracking the impacts of their actions across multiple generations in which complicated legacies often intersect. It's not, in the straightforward sense, the *fault* of present-day descendants of settlers or whites that other people's descendants have a harder time of things. Nor was the world order founded centuries before their birth caused by their actions.

There's a better concept we can use in responsibility's place: liability. Often liability is assigned on the basis of responsibility, such is the strength of the connection between this web of ideas, and the terms are often defined in connection with each other.[55] But it is possible to create some distance between them: for example, on the view that to be liable is simply to be obligated (typically to pay a price or bear a burden). Many legal systems have a version of what legal scholars call "strict liability," which obligates people and corporations to bear the costs of injuries in ways that bypass blame and fault-finding entirely.[56]

For example: in *Vincent vs. Lake Erie Transport. Co*, a ship captain had ordered his men to fast a ship to a dock during a severe storm. The wind repeatedly drove the ship into the dock over the storm, which damaged it. The ship captain was not at fault, nor responsible, nor even in the wrong: he had made the right decision with respect to his ship. The wind and the rain were ultimately to blame. But there was, still, the damage to the company's dock, the question of what should be done about it, and the question of who should bear the costs.[57] Those questions aren't backward looking investigations into who did the wrong thing in the past; they are design choices about our present and future. Rather than trying to punish a wrongdoer, we may instead find ourselves trying to build a world that distributes risk in the right way. And the strict liability rule may be a better fit for that project than alternatives.[58] However we choose to answer the question of how to distribute risk going forward, we should simply notice that it is a different question altogether from one about who to blame for what has already happened—the question lying beneath many conceptions of responsibility.

This sense of liability, rather than responsibility, best fits the distributive principle embodied in the constructive view of reparations. The racially advantaged, the Global North, and institutional repositories of plunder should bear more of the burdens of constructing the just world order, *not* because of the relationship that they, *as responsible moral agents*, hold to the injustices of the past. Those advantaged by global racial empire should bear more burdens because of the relationship

[55] Feinberg, "Collective Responsibility."
[56] Shavell, "The Mistaken Restriction of Strict Liability to Uncommon Activities."
[57] Epstein, "A Theory of Strict Liability," 157–158.
[58] For an extended discussion of risk distribution as a goal of strict liability, see Calabresi, "Some Thoughts on Risk Distribution and the Law of Torts."

that their *advantages* hold to that history. A good reparation argument should survive this distinction.

Introducing the Reparations Views

To date, people arguing in favor of reparations for slavery and racism have tended to use two broad families of argument. I call these harm repair and relationship repair arguments. Both families get something right, and both have limitations, which we will explore below. The approach I advocate, the constructive view, provides a third and more capacious alternative.

Harm repair arguments view reparations as a project in service of restitution or retribution, both aspects of justice. These accounts are often motivated by attention to the living conditions and material realities that Black people today are forced to confront as a result of the history of racial domination. A prominent example of this view includes the recent book *From Here to Equality* by Sandy Darity and A. Kirsten Mullen, who argue that reparations should end racial disparities in wealth, incarceration, and other socially and economically important areas. *Relationship repair* arguments view reparations as a project in the service of reconciliatory justice. According to these arguments, reparations should repair the relationship between the parties that was damaged by past injustice or wrongdoing.

I prefer to think of the constructive view as a third, future-oriented view. Because its systematic scope attends to the consistent and constant interactions between parties in the global whole, it has perhaps more in common with the relationship repair view. But in any given real world instance, these three approaches are not necessarily mutually exclusive. All of these views get something right. What matters most is *what they commit us to*.

Anatomy of a Harm Repair Argument

Harm repair arguments give reparations the role of fixing present harms causally connected to or constituted by past harms. These arguments tend to use a conception of harm (or wrongdoing) that considers the aggrieved party to have harmed the victim by lowering their standard of welfare from some baseline that they would have enjoyed but for the offense. Reparations 'repair' this damage by distributing benefits to the victim that close the gap between their current state of welfare and this baseline, perhaps with some interest for their trouble. These arguments are popular in the legal community, since they make use of legal ways of conceptualizing harm and injury.[59] This view also seems like it is the best representation of the rationale given by N'COBRA (National Council of Blacks for Reparations in America) for why African-Americans are owed reparations, which the organization positions as a response to the "many forms of injury caused by chattel slavery and its continuing vestiges."[60] N'COBRA also emphasizes that reparation is a principle of international human rights law.

This view has a wide uptake beyond organizational politics, in part because of the strong rhetorical appeal and strategic utility of the ready-made legal framework of harm redress that these arguments tend to make intelligent use of. For example, Joel Morse, a professor of finance, and Jetaime Ross, a community organizer, "propose a very preliminary conceptual model that may be useful in addressing the reparations issue" which "relies on a standard forensic economics framework used in US courts. In a typical personal injury litigation situation, an injury (known as a tort) is brought for analysis and possible recompense or 'making the victim whole.' Typically, the first step is to estimate what income would be 'but for' the wrongdoing, and subtract it from actual post-injury income."[61] More recently, William Darity and A. Kirsten Mullen's *From Here to Equality* advocates for a "restitution"-based approach to reparations, which would aim to move the descendants of American slavery toward a "more equitable position

---

[59] See, for examples: Verdun, "If the Shoe Fits, Wear It: An Analysis of Reparations to African Americans"; Levitt, "Black African Reparations: Making a Claim for Enslavement and Systematic De Jure Segregation and Racial Discrimination under American and International Law"; Brophy, "Reparations Talk: Reparations for Slavery and the Tort Law Analogy"; Sherwin, "Reparations and Unjust Enrichment."

[60] N'COBRA, "Reparations."

[61] Morse and Ross, "A Forensic Economics Approach to Reparations."

commensurate with the status they would have attained in the absence of the injustice(s)."[62]

I agree that the harm repair view serves a useful role in some domains of political and legal philosophy—it makes sense as a way to think about justice when someone is injured in a workplace, for example. A major advantage of applying this view to the less discrete case of reparations is that it leads us to focus on "making whole" the descendants of those enslaved. It gets something very important right, in that it focuses on the present-day ramifications of past injustices for people's lives and welfare.[63]

Nevertheless, I'll argue that this strategy is missing something. It runs into serious difficulties in dealing with reparations claims like the ones advanced for trans-Atlantic slavery and colonialism. It invites us to view Black suffering in accounting terms—which political theorist Lawrie Balfour notes is a point of view well suited to process aspects of systematic injustice like the labor stolen from Black peoples under slavery, but isn't obviously up to the task of redressing other systematic aspects of suffering such as systematic sexual violence.[64]

Another, conceptionally related perspective is what Adolph Reed and Merlin Chowkwanyun call the "disparitarian perspective": viewing the differences and disparities between racial groups as the primary or even sole method of diagnosing and responding to racial injustice. Disparities between the disadvantaged and advantaged group come to be how harm is understood, and the elimination of disparity dominates our imagination about solutions. But this involves a dangerously reductive view about racism and injustice, and a counterproductive one. As Reed puts it, the policy recommendations that issue from this perspective tend to "represent détente with rather than commitment to changing capitalist class relations, including those that contribute to intra- and inter-racial disparities in the first place."[65]

---

[62] Darity, Jr. and Mullen, *From Here to Equality: Reparations for Black Americans in the Twenty-First Century*, 3.

[63] Legal professor and critical race studies scholar Vincene Verdun offers a particularly powerful and nuanced version of this argument that offers much for us to learn from: Verdun, "If the Shoe Fits, Wear It: An Analysis of Reparations to African Americans."

[64] Balfour, "Reparations after Identity Politics," 801–802.

[65] Reed and Chowkwanyun, "Race, Class, Crisis: The Discourse of Racial Disparity and Its Analytical Discontents," 165.

Focusing on disparities is an effective rhetorical strategy but a blunt conceptual instrument. We could, after all, resolve racial disparities in criminal justice by judging white defendants more harshly and policing their communities in a more draconian fashion. We could mitigate the environmental racism dramatized in Flint by polluting white neighborhoods' air and poisoning their wells as well. This would mitigate disparities, and perhaps even the stigma and dishonor of being connected to a racially or colonially disadvantaged group (since it would no longer correlate with lower standards of living) but it would not accomplish racial justice. Harm repair views often run afoul of this point; for example, recall that Darity and Mullen's view of reparation treats eliminating "racial disparities" in things like wealth, income, and incarceration as a specification of how reparations would move descendants toward a "more equitable position commensurate with the status they would have attained in the absence of the injustice(s)."[66]

This shows the danger of the politics of incessant comparison, and of an anti-politics that is overfocused on the easy questions about what we are *against*. But justice is about what we're *for*: we don't simply want our children to get as good an education as white children, we want them to get a *good education*, which involves having a view of what a good education is and how it should be made accessible and distributed to people.

A Major Challenge for Harm Repair Arguments: The Existential Worry

One particularly nasty complication with arguments about harm repair concerns what is termed the "non-identity objection" or the "existential worry." The legal, conception of harm based on welfare demands a binary comparison: between the level of welfare enjoyed before the injury and the level of welfare enjoyed afterward, or the level of welfare that the harm otherwise prevented the injured party from maintaining or reaching.

---

[66] Darity, Jr. and Mullen, *From Here to Equality: Reparations for Black Americans in the Twenty-First Century*, 3.

It is very unclear as to what two snapshots of reality to submit to binary comparison. Even had reparation been paid shortly after the abolition of slavery, how could one 'repair' whatever harm was done to a child born into the condition of slavery? Viewed from the vantage point of this individual's life, there is no "before" to return to. Slavery is *constitutive* of this child's social circumstances: of *both* the category into which the child was born and the society that gives that category social meaning, affecting how well the child's life goes. Stated generally, it may be impossible to make sense of an individual 'harm' claim on the repair view if the action or process being charged with harm is also responsible for creating the harmed agent. According to this objection, there is no possible world or relevant counterfactual in which the agent is better off without the harming action, because every world in which the harming action does not exist is a world in which the agent who claims they were harmed does not exist either.[67]
the moral impetus for reparations.

But maybe the problem is that our thinking is being held hostage by individualism. Many argue that this framing is an unnecessary concession to the conceptual habits of the dominant (white) culture in places like the United States, and that this concessionary stance is an ongoing problem with how reparation arguments are framed.[68] Other ways of making out a repair claim might track the welfare of social collectives, perhaps geographical regions, a continent, or nation-states. The question for the repair theorist then shifts from a question about what quality of life an individual would have had if the offense

[67]   Kumar and Silver's own view is an interesting intermediate case between the categories of arguments I've termed "harm repair" and "relationship repair." Like the relationship repair theorists, Kumar and Silver reject a solely or primarily welfare conception of harm as the moral impetus for reparations. They also spend the bulk of their essay on "rectification," which shares argumentative concerns with moral repair theorists, and the inheritance of wrongs (much like the particularly Lockean brand of relationship repair). Nevertheless, they characterize reparations and rectification as responses and remedies to injury (in a non-welfare sense) to African Americans, so I tend to group them with the harm repair theorists. I don't yet see that anything of interest hangs on this categorization. Kumar and Silver, "The Legacy of Injustice. Wronging the Future, Responsibility for the Past."

[68]   Verdun's argument relies on the specific connection of individualism with the dominant ideology of legal scholarship and practice, but also describes individualism as part of dominant culture more generally. Verdun, "If the Shoe Fits, Wear It: An Analysis of Reparations to African Americans."

hadn't happened to a question about what quality of life a collective would have had.

But this strategy does not avoid the existential worry either. Morris' "existential worry" argument was initially applied to individuals but doesn't actually rely on their individuality. If any arbitrarily selected descendant of people enslaved in the United States would not exist but for the particular circumstances engendered by slavery, then the set of such descendants likewise would not exist. It should also be true for a collection or grouping of such descendants—that is, a racial and/or national group like "Black Americans" collectively, perhaps—that the same sort of problem exists.

Even if there is some answer to the observations made so far, it is unclear which counterfactuals to evaluate and how to evaluate them. Let us briefly return to the historic debate between James Baldwin and William Buckley cited in Chapter 1. Buckley invoked a counterfactual comparison in which Blacks' lives in the United States at the time of the debate are compared with those of Black Africans. What if, as Buckley argued to a packed Oxford audience, Blacks in the United States are actually "better off" than their African counterparts?[69] If so, reparations face an even stronger objection than the existential worry: if a Buckley-style objector is right, there is no harm to repair!

Buckley's response looks like an attempt to weaponize the existential uncertainty that haunts any attempt to build a tort-style binary comparison across broad swathes of historical time. But even such weaponization must also fail. If the existential worry is a reason that Blacks could not have been harmed by slavery then it is also a reason that they could not have been benefited by it. Put generally: if the existential worry rules out counterfactuals that establish harm, it in the very same way also rules out those that establish benefit – either for Blacks or whites whose opportunities and life chances (or lack thereof)

---

[69] A closely related style of response is to credit "the West" for any positive developments on the continent (access to modern technology or public health) while blaming African corruption or exogenous environmental and cultural factors for negative developments (war, famine). I'm not sure which argumentative strategy is less philosophically serious, but Mazrui has the stuff of a reply to this concern on pages 8–10 of his MKO Abiola lecture on reparations. Mazrui, "Global Africa: From Abolitionists to Reparationists."

owe themselves to a history fueled by a slave system and global colonial capitalism.

The disparities in quality of life between Black Americans and Black Africans are themselves produced by the historical processes that led to the claims for redress: colonialism and the slave trade. Those processes figure into the economic development of nations like the United States and the relative lack thereof in Africa. Then, they also help explain the very gap in living conditions appealed to by the Buckley-style objector.[70]

There are more existential worries than we initially bargained for. Clearly there's some causal connection between the history of racial oppression and injustice and current living conditions. The tricky part is trying to find a straightforward cause-and-effect story about precisely what effect past injustice has on present conditions, in counterfactual terms. The cost of the insight that racial oppression is baked into the structure of the society is that it shatters the ability to point to any stable level of income, wealth, or overall welfare to blame racism for pushing people below. Neither the United States, nor developed countries, nor African countries, nor formerly colonized countries, nor the various gaps between the life chances of their current inhabitants, would be what they are but for colonialism and the slave trade.[71] This is clear both as an historical and empirical matter and also conceptually speaking.

Historically, the case is massively complicated. But there are some clear, major themes: slave trades in Africa involved transfers of labor power from the African continent so large that, by 1850, the continent's population was half of what it would have been without them.[72] The trans-Atlantic slave trade was, measured by volume of

---

[70] Shiffrin makes this point about the dependence of everyone, not just descendants of slaves, to the historical legacies of slavery and colonialism on pages 334–335. But, for some historical treatments of both sides of the comparison, see: Táíwò, *How Colonialism Preempted Modernity in Africa*; Rodney, "How Europe Underdeveloped Africa"; Williams, *Capitalism and Slavery*; Shiffrin, "Reparations for US Slavery and Justice over Time"; Osabu-Kle, "The African Reparation Cry: Rationale, Estimate, Prospects, and Strategies"; Amin, "Underdevelopment and Dependence in Black Africa—Origins and Contemporary Forms," 334–335.

[71] Shiffrin, "Reparations for US Slavery and Justice over Time."

[72] Nunn, "The Long-Term Effects of Africa's Slave Trades*"; Manning, "Contours of Slavery and Social Change in Africa."

people "exported" from their homes, twice as large as all the other slave trades on the continent combined.[73] The labor power that the abducted people possessed then became an economic input into the macroeconomies of the countries where they were forced to work. That was of considerable economic and strategic importance to colonial powers: for example, the total economic value of enslaved people in the US South was greater than the entire country's combined industrial capital until well into the nineteenth century.[74] The incentive structure generated by the existence of such a lucrative market for kidnapping resulted in the decline of previously stable societies, the creation of sustained financial, political, and military incentives to victimize neighbors and friends alike, and inter-ethnic divisions that continue to measurably undermine political institutions on the continent.[75] These factors powerfully shape the political circumstances and characteristics of African nation-states today.

Conceptually, the explanation is much simpler: the very same racialized system that constituted a person as a chattel slave (or potentially so) also constituted other people as slave owners (or potentially so), and the same colonial social system that constitutes persons as members of the colonized group constitutes other persons as members of the colonizing group. We would explain the status and advantages of ancestry or causal linkage to the colonizing group and the status and disadvantages of ancestry or causal linkage to the enslaved/colonized groups in the same way, and by reference to the same events.

This presents a large conceptual problem for harm repair views like Darity and Mullen's in *From Here to Equality*. In this book, they take moving the descendants of slavery to a "position commensurate with the status they would have attained in the absence of the injustice(s)" to mean the elimination of "racial disparities in wealth, income, education, sentencing and incarceration . . ."[76] To put it another way: Darity

[73] Nunn, "The Long-Term Effects of Africa's Slave Trades," 142.

[74] Piketty and Zucman, "Capital Is Back: Wealth-Income Ratios in Rich Countries 1700–2010"; Williams, *Capitalism and Slavery*.

[75] Rodney, "How Europe Underdeveloped Africa," chap. 4; Nunn, "The Long-Term Effects of Africa's Slave Trades"; Cheeseman and Fisher, *Authoritarian Africa: Repression, Resistance, and the Power of Ideas*.

[76] Darity, Jr. and Mullen, *From Here to Equality: Reparations for Black Americans in the Twenty-First Century*, 3.

and Mullen are appealing to white and/or non-Black Americans as their conceptual "baseline." But taking the world-historic importance of the trans-Atlantic slave trade (particularly the United States' large participation therein) means conceding that these groups would not enjoy their political position, status, or advantages were it not for the power and wealth built out of racial slavery—a point they themselves spend an entire chapter of their book making.[77] Though Darity and Mullen otherwise correctly and meticulously tie to empirically informed explanations of present-day economic and political realities, they don't seem to present an answer to this problem.

Then, *what* point in *whose* history can we appeal to, to establish a baseline of harm without triggering the existential worry? I think the causal entanglements run too deep, and that there likely isn't a satisfying answer to that question on the way.[78]

The stakes of this causal entanglement are not simply conceptual, but also moral and political. As famed reverend, activist, and political philosopher Dr. Martin Luther King Jr. put it in his book *Where Do We Go From Here:* "However deeply American Negroes are caught in the struggle to be at last at home in our homeland of the United States, we cannot ignore the larger world house in which we are also dwellers. Equality with whites will not solve the problems of either whites or Negroes if it means equality in a world society stricken by poverty and in a universe doomed to extinction by war."[79]

This is a consequence of the view of history argued for in the first chapter. The view is that slavery and colonialism built the world order, full stop. That means *everybody's* world order, not just the world order as experienced by the most marginalized.[80] Then, the very arguments

[77] Darity, Jr. and Mullen, *From Here to Equality: Reparations for Black Americans in the Twenty-First Century*, chap. 3.

[78] Daniel Butt offers a noteworthy attempt to do just this in a 2012 article, proposing a "double counterfactual" which invites us to imagine any particular colonized community, not simply without the particular colonial past it has but without having been colonized at all. I suspect this strategy will run into significant hurdles at the calculation stage, and in any event, the constructive view paper obviates the need for it by shifting from "harm" to a more general sort of explanation. Butt, "Repairing Historical Wrongs and the End of Empire."

[79] King. Jr., *Where Do We Go from Here: Chaos or Community?* 2:177.

[80] Lawrie Balfour considers this interpretation of Baldwin's position in the Baldwin-Buckley debate. Balfour, "Reparations after Identity Politics," 801–802.

that establish the central importance of global racial empire, also contribute to the most powerful objection one can make to approaches to reparations that rely on being able to separate the stories of the marginalized from the stories of the privileged.

What Relationship Repair Views Are

Relationship repair views the task of reparations to be fixing damaged relationships: typically between the aggrieved party (and/or those who inherit their identity) and the aggrieving party (and/or those who inherit that identity). Authors making these arguments often frame relationship repair views as a response to the difficulties with harm repair arguments, including the nasty philosophical problem of identifying the right contrast class.

Relationship repair views often assume a different conception of harm than the view based on welfare that harm repair arguments tend to use. Whatever else slavery and colonialism are responsible for, they involved significant moral *wrongdoing*. Wrongdoing involves a violation of justified moral expectations. Wrongdoing can be considered a kind of moral harm, but it doesn't depend on the welfare comparisons that bogged us down in the previous section. If your friend promises to take you to a movie and never shows up, she has wronged you, even if it would've turned out that you didn't like the movie anyway.[81] People can also be harmed by the imposition of conditions that they would not rationally will or are reasonably alienated from.[82] Racial discrimination and disrespect as experienced by much of the Black world, to the extent that these owe their character to slavery and colonialism, qualify as moral harm, even in the case of Black folks whose material standard of welfare is high.

---

[81] Kumar and Silver endorse an explicitly contractualist conception of such moral harm, arguing that imposing conditions on an agent that violate legitimate interpersonal expectations is a way of harming them. Kumar and Silver, "The Legacy of Injustice. Wronging the Future, Responsibility for the Past," 149–151.

[82] Shiffrin, "Wrongful Life, Procreative Responsibility, and the Significance of Harm," 124.

Relationship repair is rooted in this way of thinking about harm; it can include things that would show up as harm on a welfare-based account, but the baseline is a set of absolute moral principles that, unlike a welfare baseline, do not require defining and measuring specific historical phenomena. The various wrongdoings of slavery damaged the moral relations that should sustain political and moral community between differently positioned inheritors of the moral legacy of slavery. Reparation, then, is about fixing these relationships.

Relationship Repair 1: Debt Repayment

One subfamily of relationship repair views reparations as a straightforward payment on a debt. Repayment of debt, while initially transactional, alters the moral relationship between the debtors and those to whom the debt is owed, and may even restore the possibility of peaceful and friendly relations. Many of these kinds of arguments follow a Lockean approach based on a philosophical commitment to reparations as a moral or political right: political philosopher John Locke thought that the right to reparation of harm was a natural right, one that each person would have vis-à-vis every other person whether in a "commonwealth" or even in the state of nature.[83]

Further, on his historical view of reparations, he argued that the children of those dispossessed by war, even where the war is just, retain moral rights to the possessions of their ancestors.[84] Where their rights to those possessions, or any other property, are infringed, the claimants are to be considered "slaves under the force of war" rather than free people.[85] War, then, harms the social relationship between the wronged (and their inheritors) and the broader political community. Reparations do the work of repair by removing one set of barriers

[83] Bernard Boxill points to this passage in "Black Reparations." Locke and Macpherson, *Second Treatise of Government*; Boxill, "Black Reparations." Book II, sec. 6–12.

[84] Locke and Macpherson, *Second Treatise of Government*. Book XVI, "Conquest," sec. 190–196.

[85] Locke and Macpherson. Book XVI, "Conquest," sec. 192, 63.

between the claimants and the broader political community, and thus help create the conditions for non-adversarial political relations.

Finding these sorts of theoretical claims helpful, a number of prominent philosophers have made similar if not explicitly Lockean arguments for Black reparations in the United States. This view is prominently held by philosopher Bernard Boxill. Catherine Lu, J. Angelo Cortlett, and Robert Fullinwider also provide arguments concerning reparations that involve similar elements.[86]

Relationship Repair #2: Communicative Repair

In *Moral Repair*, Margaret Walker argues that reparations construed as restorative justice for anti-Black racism is aimed at the "restoration of relationships" between Black citizens and other citizens, seeing the alienation of Blacks from their (now) fellow citizens and from the government they live under as a primary harm.[87] Similarly, Catherine Lu considers reparation as a reconciliatory task is an intervention upon the victims' alienation from the individuals who harmed them, as well as their alienation from the social and political order that played a causal role in their harm.[88]

Boxill and Shiffrin also consider the communicative effects of refusing to make reparations when they are due. Refusal to take reparative steps when one has injured another can signal that the injured party morally deserved their injury or need not be regarded as a moral equal. Refusal can also be criticized for the culpable failure to signal the opposite commitment.[89] This failure risks tacit endorsement of or at the very least insufficient discontinuity with the morally incorrect attitudes of the past, according to which African, African-descended, and other colonized peoples were deserving of inferior social status

---

[86] Boxill, "A Lockean Argument for Black Reparations"; Fullinwider, "The Case for Reparations"; Corlett, "Race, Racism, and Reparations"; Balfour, "Reparations after Identity Politics."

[87] Walker, *Moral Repair: Reconstructing Moral Relations after Wrongdoing*, 224.

[88] Lu, "Reconciliation and Reparations."

[89] Boxill, "The Morality of Reparation"; Shiffrin, "Reparations for US Slavery and Justice over Time."

and treatment.[90] Then, the value of reparations is to be understood as communicative, an expression of commitment to the moral equality of persons, and a serious and sincere regret of past social arrangements in which this was not true.[91]

A Major Challenge to the Relationship Repair View: Subject Changing

Both versions of the relationship repair view get something important right. The debt payment version acknowledges something important about obligation: both that survivors of the many atrocious events that make up the history of global racial empire (from enslavement and colonial conquest to cultural genocide and racial segregation in education) were themselves owed reparations, at the very least as individuals. The nonpayment of owed reparations is itself an ongoing injustice, and harms the relationships between groups of people and between people and their political and social institutions. This view also acknowledges the importance of informal aspects of social organization, prominently including the moral expectations and trust we have for other people.

But relationship repair views seem vulnerable to the charge that they subtly change the point. They don't explicitly rule out material redress; certainly even the authors who advocate for understanding reparations as a communicative form of repair rather than debt repayment each explicitly support material compensation of some form. However, these views don't treat material redress and the present-day living conditions of the recipients as the point of reparations.

---

[90] Kumar and Silver are speaking about the US context in this section, but I take it that this specific point of theirs generalizes. Kumar and Silver, "The Legacy of Injustice. Wronging the Future, Responsibility for the Past," 152.

[91] Shiffrin, "Reparations for US Slavery and Justice over Time," 335.

A Reminder about the Constructive View

The constructive view, as we saw in the previous chapter, is a view about how to distribute the benefits and burdens of a particular process. That process is the achievement of justice, our transition from our deeply unequal and unethical status quo to the creation of a just world. The constructive view doesn't make direct use of any particular definition of harm or wrongdoing. Instead, the constructive view puts things in terms of justice, which directs us to evaluate social structures and arrangements, and to do so holistically.

A Major Challenge for the Constructive
View: Subject Changing

The constructive view avoids the existential worry that plagued the harm repair view. But it faces its own version of the major challenge that the relationship repair views face: it seems to subtly change the subject. Many people advocating for reparations explicitly have their own group's welfare in mind—their Indigenous nation, their racial group, or their regional federation of states. Moreover, as mentioned earlier in the chapter, they give reasons for the worthiness of their claims that typically are a better fit for other styles of argument. N'COBRA in the United States, for example, appeals to "5 Injury Areas" to explain the harms of the slave trade and subsequent racial injustice, a good fit for the harm repair view. The Caribbean countries' joint reparations program often invokes the language of "crimes against humanity" to describe the impetus for reparations—a better fit, perhaps, for either harm repair or relationship repair rationales for reparations.[92] Coming from the point of view of these specific projects, the global, worldmaking perspective that the constructive view adopts seems like it concerns a different subject.

However, when reparations organizations explain the *target* of ctheir reparations proposals—what they think reparations ought

---

[92] Caribbean Reparations Commission, "10-Point Reparation Plan."

to accomplish, how it should change the world—then the constructive view begins to really fit with the actual practice and discourse of activists. To take just a couple examples: CARICOM demands an "Indigenous Peoples Development Program," a comprehensive response to public health crises on the islands, a demand to facilitate the end of illiteracy, and debt cancellation. In the United States, the African-American Reparations Commission demands no less in their "Preliminary Reparations Program." They call for substantial tracts of land to be transferred to a "National Reparations Trust Authority," for funds to be transferred specifically to "Cooperative Enterprises," and for financing to be provided for the "planning and construction of holistic and sustainable 'villages' with affordable housing and comprehensive cultural-educational, health and wellness, employment and economic services." The sheer breadth of these programs, not to mention their emphasis on both advantage redistribution and the establishment of new institutions and networks, seem well described as a plan to comprehensively reconstruct social life for the people they fight for—exactly what worldmaking is about.

We should recall historian Robin D. G. Kelley's description of reparations activism in the United States from this book's introduction: "it was never entirely, or even primarily, about money. The demand for reparations was about social justice, reconciliation, *reconstructing* the internal life of black America, and eliminating institutional racism (emphasis added). This is why reparations proposals from black radical movements focus less on individual payments than on securing funds to build autonomous black institutions, improving community life, and in some cases establishing a homeland that will enable African Americans to develop a political economy geared more toward collective needs than toward accumulation."[93]

Defending the constructive view against this challenge uses the perspective argued for in the first chapter. The history of global racial empire, properly understood, shows us that different and even distant groups are connected by the global system of production and

---

[93] Kelley, *Freedom Dreams: The Black Radical Imagination*, 114–115.

distribution that powerfully decides all of our fates. It is not an argument built for any particular group, but it will serve each of them.

The global system of racial empire is, ultimately, the terrain on which local and national struggles will be won and lost. Just as the entire global system of cotton production had to shift to accommodate the abolition of slavery in the United States, meaningful change to any national or local scheme of domination affects and is affected by the larger overall global social structure. This has already been understood by those who have made global domination their business: the British empire and the US Southern planter elite both clearly understood their goals as projects of global domination. It was also so understood by those who made global justice their business: anti-imperialist activists of the 1950s, 1960s, and 1970s. It was no coincidence that so much of the African and Asian continents successfully won independence within the same generation—20 years or so. It is also no coincidence that these happened over the same time period as the Stonewall Riots and the March on Washington, D. C. in the United States and the race riots in Nottingham and Notting Hill.[94] The constructive view invites those people who are fighting against injustice to make these connections.

Standards for Reparations Views

So far, we've set one target for a good view of reparations: it should be rooted in, or at least expressible in terms of liability and not just in terms of responsibility. We've also discussed major challenges for each view on its own. But none of the views came out unblemished and each has benefits and drawbacks.

To judge between the different ways of thinking about reparations, it will help to be direct and explicit about what a view about reparations ought to accomplish. Putting the standards in order of priority will also matter here, since it will help us decide between views that do

---

[94] BBC East Midlands, "St Ann's Riot."

well on some standards but not as well on others. I propose these three standards, in this order:

1. Reparations for global racial empire should make tangible differences in the material conditions of people's lives.
2. Reparations for global racial empire should address the core moral wrongs of trans-Atlantic slavery and colonialism, to the extent possible.
3. Reparations for global racial empire should discriminate: should distribute benefits and burdens based on the different relationships of persons and institutions to the core moral wrongs.

The remainder of this chapter will focus on unpacking these standards and exploring how well different approaches to reparations address them.

Standard 1

The first standard is the most important, and also the most complicated. By putting this criterion first, I want to resist treating arguments for reparations on purely intellectual grounds, untethered from the history of activism and political struggle that put the issue on the table in the first place. It's not simply the fact that the moral atrocities happened; it is also the connection of those atrocities to present-day misery, incarceration, poverty, and desperation that explains reparation's importance.

This standard is about what we want reparations to do. It says that reparations for global racial empire should make tangible differences in the material conditions of people's lives—the conditions of their living, working, and relating to each other. It's hard to do better in explaining this priority than Dr. Martin Luther King, Jr. did in his book *Why We Can't Wait*:

> The Negro today is not struggling for some abstract, vague rights, but for concrete and prompt improvement in his way of life. What will

it profit him to be able to send his children to an integrated school if the family income is insufficient to buy them school clothes? What will he gain by being permitted to move to an integrated neighborhood if he cannot afford to do so because he is unemployed or has a low-paying job with no future? During the lunch-counter sit-ins in Greensboro, North Carolina, a nightclub comic observed that, had the demonstrators been served, some of them could not have paid for the meal . . . The struggle for rights is, at bottom, a struggle for opportunities.[95]

In placing material welfare first, I don't presume that cultural or spiritual needs are unimportant. We need recognition, we need acknowledgement, we need good relationships with the people around us. But I do presume that we need to eat and protect ourselves from premature death and suffering, more than we need vindication—whether in cultural narratives, textbooks, or fancy academic journals. I presume that protection against mass displacement is a more fundamental need than the need for reconciliation with our neighbors. While such reconciliation might complement or strengthen such protection, the reverse is not true: without housing security, neighborly reconciliation becomes trivial to meaningless.

So if we prioritize improving the material conditions of people's lives, what approach to reparations best fits the bill?

Relationship repair arguments, particularly the communicative versions, don't seem up to the job. For these views, changing the living conditions of the potential recipients of reparations is more of a *potential outcome* of the main action than a *target*—to the extent that it is considered at all. The focus is on inter-group relations: the possibility of genuine moral community between those who inherit the claim right to reparations and those who inherit a moral liability to pay reparations. Proponents of this view agree that some sort of material and not *merely* symbolic reparations are called for, but this is because of the *communicative* consequences of making serious material concessions – making the attendant apologetic gestures credible as sincere and genuine.[96] The living conditions of the people with the moral claim to reparations thus fades into the background, playing at best an instrumental role in explaining both how we would justify reparations projects and what they would be designed to accomplish.

The harm repair view and the debt repayment version of the relationship repair view seem initially like they are better positioned to meet this first, most important standard. Both share a legalistic reference point that focuses on a concept of welfare. A clear virtue of the harm repair strategy is its preoccupation with the material and political lives of oppressed people. For the harm repair theorists, reparations ought to make a difference in the lives of the descendants of the enslaved and colonized, in concrete terms that make up for the harms they face as a result of their membership in those identity categories.

But harm repair arguments may risk understanding even material welfare *too* narrowly. The danger is something like a resourcist view of racism: that what racial disadvantage comes down to is having less stuff, broadly speaking, than racially advantaged people. After all, those who make harm repair arguments often appeal to the amount of wealth that the racially advantaged. And a close inspection of the debt repayment family of arguments finds that they do not assign direct primary importance to the living conditions of the people who are currently owed reparations. The primary harms and injuries considered in this argument are those that befell the *ancestors* of the people who today are owed reparations. To the extent that harms to people living and breathing today shows up in the argument, it is as whatever particular harm can be contrived into a shape that will attach to non-payment of reparations, rather than in terms of the current living conditions and life chances of these people.

These arguments for reparations, if successful, could at best tell us *that* reparations are owed to today's Black people. These arguments couldn't tell us what current rates of poverty, physical and mental health, or low levels of community institutional power and self-determination have to do with reparations as a project. The social and political conditions that make reparations important fade into the

[96] Shiffrin, "Reparations for US Slavery and Justice over Time," 335.

background, playing at best a rhetorical role in the justification and design of reparations projects designed on this basis.

Proponents of the harm repair view could respond by expanding what they mean by harm, expanding it until the targets for correction include not only income disparities but also the psychological, social-institutional, interpersonal and informal consequences of racism or colonialism. But I've argued that, if they study this carefully, they will find that fewer of the determinants of these aspects of social structure lie in any particular country, church, university, or state government's jurisdiction than they bargained for. If they arrive at a set of reforms that will comprehensively change the social structures that in fact undergird the forms of domination that live on in the current political conditions of their people, they will have arrived at the constructive view: they will be describing a worldmaking project.

Standard 2

Applying the second and third standards is more straightforward, and makes use of the observations we've already made in applying the first standard.

The second standard holds that reparations for global racial empire should respond to the core moral wrongs that these involved. A structural understanding of slavery, colonialism, and their legacy invites us to view the core wrongs of both the *events* (atrocities of slavery and the slave trade, colonial conquest, genocides) and also the social structure built out of these.

The communicative repair view targets our attitudes and normative expectations of ourselves and each other. Some version of this might be required to make meaningful progress in achieving social justice, since our institutions are partly constructed by our attitudes and expectations. But this is an overly narrow view, for the historical processes that we seek to replace set up vastly different schedules of accumulation of social advantages and disadvantages – not just mistrust and lack of camaraderie.

The debt repayment view targets our relationship of obligation, and our ability to inherit moral debts and liabilities. It is certainly true that past generations' nonpayment of individual or collective reparations is *a* wrong. But it hardly seems a compelling construal of the core moral wrong: enslaving and colonizing people are wrong in and of themselves, not just because the slavers and colonizers avoided compensating those they wronged afterward.

The constructive view responds directly to both aspects of the core moral wrongs of global moral empire. It addresses the events with its distributive principle: requiring those who inherited the moral liabilities of the atrocities of the past to take on more of the burdens of building the just world than those who inherit the moral claim rights. It addresses the structural aspect of the core moral wrong by setting a just world order as its practical target.

Standard 3

That brings us to the third standard: that a good reparations view should discriminate, selecting beneficiaries and burdened parties based on their historical relationships to the core moral wrongs under consideration. The constructive view does this, building it in as a distributive principle in a larger social project.

The debt repayment and harm repair views also lend themselves to discrimination, but they are only built to handle a simple binary. This starkness may seem more morally stringent, but it is no advantage. As noted in this chapter's discussion of liability and also of the major challenge for the harm repair view, the relationship of all of us to past oppression is more complicated than such binary accounting allows. The world order determines all of our political circumstances, and all of us are advantaged and disadvantaged by it in various respects. What separates us, largely, is the *extent* to which we are benefitted and the extent to which we are harmed.

In "If the Shoe Fits" Vincene Verdun discusses her past: she discloses that she is descended both from enslaved people of African descent and slave-owning planters of French descent. Similarly, in the present, as an African-American she is someone who is owed reparations, but as a US citizen she is someone who pays taxes and thus would contribute to any scheme of reparations financed by the United States federal government. Rather than explaining this away, she uses it con-structively to argue that it fits squarely into reparation as she envisions it: something that addresses her simultaneously as someone to whom something is owed and someone from whom something is owed. Accepting this complication allows us to decisively reject the specious right-wing objections to reparations projects that sug-gest that rich Black folk like Oprah and Jay-Z are insurmountable complications. Just as the differences in our relationship to history lie in the *extent* to which we are advantaged and disadvantaged by the world order of global racial empire, our relationship to reparations projects should be determined by the extent to which we have inherited moral liabilities versus the extent to which we have inherited claim rights. We don't need a rigid binary between one sort of inherit-ance and the other.

***

The 1835 Malê revolt was defeated. It also succeeded.

From the beginning of Dan Fodio's jihad until the middle of the 19th century, African-led insurrections (typically led by Hausa and/ or Yoruba speaking people) were common throughout the parts of the world that those abducted in the conflict ended up in – predominantly Brazil and Cuba. By 1835, the year of the Malê revolt, nearly two-thirds of the enslaved population were "New Negroes," African-born persons who had experienced freedom in their living memory. A dangerous percentage had intricate knowledge of African warfare and tactics.[97]

This greatly concerned the empire of Brazil. They knew about the Haitian revolution, and knew that those they lorded over were equally aware of it. Some reports indicate that enslaved Brazilians spoke about Haiti boldly in Portuguese—either indifferently or perhaps courting the possibility that passing whites would understand.[98] *The empire tried several measures: expanding the police to deport freed Africans*

---

[97] Graden, "An Act 'Even of Public Security': Slave Resistance, Social Tensions, and the End of the International Slave Trade to Brazil, 1835–1856," 254; Barcia and Paz, *West African Warfare in Bahia and Cuba: Soldier Slaves in the Atlantic World, 1807–1844*, 1–3; Reis, "Slave Resistance in Brazil: Bahia, 1807–1835," 124.
[98] Reis, "Slave Resistance in Brazil: Bahia, 1807–1835," 120–211.

and maintain a curfew, and barring those who remained from participating in specific religious activities and from owning real estate.[99] *But they didn't work: year by year, the number of quilombos increased and "capoeira gangs" (practitioners of an Afro-Brazilian martial art) humiliated the police in the streets of Rio de Janeiro.*[100]

By 1850 the Brazilian government feared the writing was on the wall. They had been fortunate to survive the 1835 revolt. If slavery was maintained in the Empire of Brazil, they could expect to, eventually, meet the fate their French counterparts met in the Haitian revolution. So in 1850 they stopped the importation of Africans, hoping to cut off the flow of insurrectionary sentiment from abroad. But the rebellions kept coming, and the quilombos kept flourishing. In 1888, the Empire of Brazil—the last holdout in the Western hemisphere—finally abolished slavery.[101]

[99] Graden, "An Act 'Even of Public Security': Slave Resistance, Social Tensions, and the End of the International Slave Trade to Brazil," 1835–1856," 264.
[100] Graden, "An Act 'Even of Public Security': Slave Resistance, Social Tensions, and the End of the International Slave Trade to Brazil," 271–272.
[101] Bucciferro, "A Lucrative End: Abolition, Immigration, and the New Occupational Hierarchy in Southeast Brazil."

CLIMATE CRISIS

If slavery and colonialism built the world and its current basic scheme of social injustice, the proper task of social justice is no smaller: it is, quite literally, to remake the world. In our era, climate justice and reparations are the same project: climate crisis arises from the same political history as racial injustice and presents a challenge of the same scale and scope. The transformations we succeed or fail to make in the face of the climate crisis will be decisive for the project of racial justice, and vice versa.

5

What's Next: Why Reparations Require Climate Justice

"The trouble," [Dr.] Martin [Luther King Jr.] went on, "is that we live in a failed system. Capitalism does not permit an even flow of economic resources. With this system, a small privileged few are rich beyond conscience and almost all others are doomed to be poor at some level." Taking a sip from his glass, he continued, "That's the way the system works. And since we know that the system will not change the rules, we're going to have to change the system."

At heart, Martin was a socialist and a revolutionary thinker. He spoke not just in anger, but in anguish. His voice dropped to a more reflective tone as he continued. "We fought hard and long, and I have never doubted that we would prevail in this struggle. Already our reward have begun to reveal themselves. Desegregation . . . the Voting Rights Act . . ." He paused. "But what deeply troubles me now is that for all the steps we've taken toward integration, I've come to believe that we are integrating into a burning house."

We had not heard Martin quite this way before. I felt as if our moorings were unhinging. "Damn, Martin! If that's what you think, what would you have us do?" I asked.

He gave me a look. "I guess we're just going to have to become firemen."

—Harry Belafonte, *My Song*

Reconsidering Reparations. Olúfẹ́mi O. Táíwò, Oxford University Press. © Oxford University Press 2022.
DOI: 10.1093/oso/9780197508893.003.0005

When They Drained the Swamp

On August 29, 2005, Hurricane Katrina made landfall on the Louisiana Coast with devastating results.

In one sense, to say that Hurricane Katrina was intensified by climate change is to make a scientific claim about how our natural systems are responding to global carbon emissions. After all, scientists using sophisticated modelling approaches have made estimates of the contribution of climate change induced sea-level rise to the damage made by the hurricane and found that flood elevations would have been substantially lower under the diminished sea levels of previous years.[1]

But this is just one part of the story. For a more complete picture, we have to include our political systems.

Part of the story of Hurricane Katrina goes by way of canals and marshes; part of it goes by way of developments of corporate and state institutional power and their agendas; part of it goes by way of racial animus embedded in norms, laws, and property. But all of these flow through the aqueduct of history constructed by global racial empire. The accumulated weight of history carved canals of financial power through the political Louisiana terrain just as surely as it carved canals into its literal soil. It built levees that blocked fertile sedimentation of opportunity in Black neighborhoods and neglected to construct or to reinforce the floodgates that would protect them for disaster; for others, it created seawalls of insurance schemes and government protection that would ward off the worst impacts for some and divert that destruction toward others.

Journalists, politicians, and scholars who study Louisiana have given it many revealing monikers and descriptions, including calling it a "petro-state" and an "American Nigeria beset by poverty, illiteracy and ecological devastation while outsiders get fabulously rich extracting its mineral wealth."[2] However you describe Louisiana's evolving political

---

[1] Irish et al., "Simulations of Hurricane Katrina (2005) under Sea Level and Climate Conditions for 1900"; Magill, "Katrina."
[2] Grunwald, "Katrina: A Man-Made Disaster."

situation in the centuries leading to the disastrous hurricane of 2005, it is clear that the path toward disaster was paved by petroleum.

The story of Louisiana and Hurricane Katrina starts with the beginning of global racial empire. Christopher Columbus's fateful 1492 voyage landed him on an island in the Caribbean that he called "Hispaniola." Hispaniola was inhabited by Taíno peoples—whom the conquistadores immediately enslaved in the *encomienda* system in their quest to mine the island for precious metals. Then, they supplemented them with enslaved Africans in response to the population pressures stemming from disease and conflict.[3]

Over the following centuries, the French, British, and Spanish empires fought for control of territory in this region. By 1659, France prevailed and renamed the island "Saint Domingue," importing thousands upon thousands of enslaved Africans and indentured whites to cultivate cash crops on plantations.[4] Saint Domingue generated fantastic amounts of wealth for the French empire and represented a key strategic advantage over its British rival: after the American Revolution, France's plantations in Saint Domingue produced sugar at 20 percent lower cost and exported twice as much volume as Britain's Jamaica colony.[5] But as fate would have it, just years later, enslaved Africans and their comrades-in-arms waged a successful revolutionary struggle against the French empire and the planters, preventing France from decisively overtaking Britain in the long race for world domination. When it was their turn to name the part of the island they controlled—including the spot where Columbus had landed in 1492—they called it "Haiti."

The Haitian Revolution upset the plans of the French Empire. Napoleon Bonaparte aimed to crush the Haitian independence struggle and then project military power from Haiti to tighten up control of Louisiana. Instead, his troops were routed by Haitian military forces. He cut his losses in 1803 by selling his legal claim to the

---

[3] Lowcountry Digital History Initiative, "African Laborers for a New Empire: Iberia, Slavery, and the Atlantic World"; "The Early Trans-Atlantic Slave Trade: Nicolas Ovando."

[4] James, *The Black Jacobins: Toussaint L'Ouverture and the San Domingo Revolution*, 3–5.

[5] Williams, *Capitalism and Slavery*, 122–123.

Louisiana Territory to a nearby regional power: the United States.[6] The 828,000 square mile "Louisiana Purchase" doubled the size of the United States overnight—and included land in the American state now known as "Louisiana" as well as the coastal city of New Orleans.[7]

The United States had already been hard at work removing Indigenous peoples from this region. From 1801 to 1830, successive federal administrations used a combination of strategies involving debt, military alliances, and forced assimilation to get access to the land around the Mississippi river. These actions culminated in the Indian Removal Act of 1830 and the resultant mass deportation of Indigenous peoples by forced marches, known ignobly as the Trail of Tears.[8] Armed now with both de jure and de facto control of the land, the regional power began selling and granting land to private individuals, corporations, and states.

The Swamp Land Act of 1849 transferred ten million acres of wetlands just downriver from New Orleans to the state of Louisiana. The land was seemingly useless for production, and often sold by the state for as little as ten cents per acre. Nevertheless, it had important potential as sites for levees and spillways: strategies to change the land itself in order to protect other parts of the state from flooding.[9]

But then, they discovered oil.

First, it was one salt dome in northwest Louisiana. Soon, hundreds of oil wells were operating throughout the state. In 1927, Louisiana produced around five million barrels of oil and a mere six years later the amount had more than tripled to more than fifteen and a half million barrels. "Worthless marsh" had turned into "liquid wealth."

Oil companies and the federal government went to work remaking this section of the world—literally. They dredged "innumerable" canals through the marsh to drill for, move, and refine oil. Meanwhile, the federal Army Corps of Engineers, tasked with flood control by a monumental act of Congress in 1936, built levees to protect the homes built on the floodplain and the oil infrastructure extracting wealth

---

[6] Dubois, "The Haitian Revolution and the Sale of Louisiana."
[7] Editors, "Louisiana Purchase."
[8] Woods, *Development Arrested: The Blues and Plantation Power in the Mississippi Delta*, chap. 3.
[9] Horowitz, *Katrina: A History, 1915–2015*, chap. 1.

nearby. That is to say, they changed how water was distributed—before, during, and after floods. The point of changing how water flowed was the same motive behind many of the eras of global racial empire: to affect how power and profit flowed.

As far as soil and water were concerned, nature had had its own distribution system. Water and sediment flowed into the Mississippi River from a vast swath of North America, from as far away as the Rockies and Appalachian Mountains, and the sediment was carried by the river to Louisiana. This sediment made Louisiana soil some of the most fertile in the United States, and it also helped add soil to the land itself, stemming the rate of coastal subsidence—the land slowly sinking into the Gulf under its own weight. After a devastating river flood in 1927, Army Corps of Engineers built a massive levee system to protect New Orleans from the river flood. But redistributing the mighty waters of the Mississippi meant redistributing the silt it carried from the rest of the continent, which contributed to subsidence and choked off the coastal marshes in the delta built from that silt. The iron-clad protection the levees provided to oil interests from the river put the city at the mercy of the Gulf.

As the decades wore on, the danger mounted. The devastating 1965 Hurricane Betsy prompted the Army Corps of Engineers to finally take on new, large levee projects like Lake Pontchartrain and Vicinity Hurricane Protection Project in the 1970s and 1980s.[10] The Army Corps of Engineers was tasked with recommending the project that would deliver the most economic benefits compared to the cost to taxpayers. What was conspicuously left out of consideration was what would become of the wetlands themselves, how the benefits of the economic arrangements would be distributed, and any direct, non-economic consideration of the risk of life and home that flooding posed to the residents. Calculating in this way, the Corps decided that building levees that could stand up to Category 4 Hurricanes like Betsy would be "cost-prohibitive," and instead built levees that could stand up to lesser Category 3 storms.

[10] Grunwald and Glasser, "The Slow Drowning of New Orleans."

The new levees expanded the land available for middle class home-ownership. The federal Home Owners Loan Corporation, convened decades earlier as a part of the "New Deal," had put together a "Residential Security Map" identifying which areas of New Orleans were safe for investment and which were risky. Their real estate appraisal map all but ignored flood risks, which the group erroneously took to have been eliminated by the levee system. Instead, the HOLC focused its assessments on other indicators of risk, including the racial composition of the neighborhoods. In New Orleans, just as it had in much of the United States, HOLC helped cement racially stratified distributions and thus accumulation of investment capital—a notorious process that would come to be known as "redlining." A 2020 study finds that the redlining of the HOLC in the 1930s continues to have measurable and large socioeconomic effects on household income, exposure to concentrated poverty, and even credit scores throughout the United States almost a century later.[11]

In New Orleans, the HOLC's Residential Security Map intersected with further class and racial discrimination in subsequent decades to help exclude Black residents from the desirable new neighborhoods built on the newly available, drained land after the Army Corps of Engineers' new levee projects in the 1970s and 1980s. However, ironically, these acts inadvertently protected some Black residents of New Orleans from the worst flooding of Hurricane Katrina, since their racist exclusion from the desirable new neighborhoods meant they were stuck in the older neighborhoods built at higher elevations.

This protection was thin, however, because Louisiana itself began to shrink and sink with the changes made to the natural environment—not at the more typical geological rate of centuries or millennia, but on the timescale of mere years, well observable within a human lifetime. By the end of the twentieth century, the majority of residents of New Orleans lived in homes below sea level.[12]

Five years into the twenty-first century, the disaster struck. Two months before the hurricane, then Louisiana Senator David Vitter

---

[11] Aaronson et al., "The Long-Run Effects of the 1930s HOLC 'Redlining' Maps on Place-Based Measures of Economic Opportunity and Socioeconomic Success."
[12] Horowitz, *Katrina: A History, 1915–2015*, chap. 3.

(R-La.) gave a presentation showing a computer model of a Category 4 hurricane smashing New Orleans and flooding the city. "It's not a question of if," he had said at the time, "but when." The levees built after Betsy had been built for, at worst, a Category 3 hurricane—the considerably more powerful Category 4 hurricane the model was built around would spell doom.

Hurricane Katrina was Category 5.

Vitter had been making a point about responsibility. He accused the federal government of underfunding levees and stalling a plan to restore the coastal marshes that would likewise have protected New Orleans from flooding. Meanwhile, journalists Michael Grunwald and Susan Glasser report, Vitter himself was stalling legislation that would have done both. But he was not wrong: in the years leading up to Katrina, President George W. Bush's administration had converted years of budget surpluses into deficits by passing sweeping tax cuts for the highest tax brackets while launching expensive wars in Afghanistan and Iraq. A coalition of concerned scientists, local politicians, and even Shell Oil (probably looking for a PR victory in defense of their offshore drilling projects in the region) supported an extensive wetland restoration project, which would help defend the city from storms. They were rebuffed by a penny-pinching White House busy concentrating its finances and attention on war.[13]

But the political failure went far beyond the White House: local elites of government and business preferred to advocate for government funds for projects designed to promote commerce, like shipping locks and canals, rather than to protect the local population.[14]

When the storm rolled in in 2005, the levees broke and the floodwalls collapsed—itself a disaster decades or even centuries in the making. But even this tale, stretching as far back as Napoleon, is not the full story. There is also what came next.

In a flash, 80 percent of the city of New Orleans was underwater. The city's football stadium, the Superdome, was full of displaced climate refugees. Though all suffered, not all suffered equally. The previous decisions helped create the crisis. But how the system responds to

---

[13] Grunwald and Glasser, "The Slow Drowning of New Orleans."
[14] Grunwald and Glasser, "The Slow Drowning of New Orleans."

crisis is, itself, determined by accumulated political power and moral importance. These decide what—and who—is deemed expendable in and after extreme situations.

The city issued a mandatory evacuation order hours before the hurricane hit the city. Unsurprisingly, those without the resources or ability to leave their homes at a moment's notice were disproportionately poor, disabled, elderly, and Black.[15] Many took to the streets, looking for dry land, shelter, medical help, and essentials such as food and water. But the media circulated images labeling them as "looters," and they were more likely to do so when they were Black. Law enforcement officials were given orders to shoot "looters" on sight and they were soon joined by impromptu militias of largely white vigilantes, roaming the watery streets and killing Black people with impunity.[16]

Sheriff Marlin Gusman was unusually explicit about adding incarcerated people to the list of those disposable in a crisis: he assured the public that the incarcerated would stay "where they belong" even as the crisis deepened. People incarcerated in the parish prison—disproportionately Black, and including children as young as thirteen—were warehoused in a large gymnasium without food, were left for days in toxic water that rose as high as their chests. As the American Civil Liberties Union explained: "The Louisiana Society for the Prevention of Cruelty to Animals did more for its 263 stray pets than the sheriff did for the more than 6,500 men, women and children left in his care."[17]

At the time, it was among the most destructive natural disasters to ever hit the United States, destroying more than 200,000 homes and causing property damage in excess of $100 billion.[18] In response, the United States launched the largest housing recovery program in its history, "Road Home." But money was distributed to applicants based on

[15] Wade, "Who Didn't Evacuate for Hurricane Katrina?"

[16] Thompson, "Post-Katrina, White Vigilantes Shot African-Americans with Impunity"; Táíwò, "Climate Apartheid Is the Coming Police Violence Crisis," *Dissent Magazine*; "Misleading Reports of Lawlessness after Katrina Worsened Crisis, Officials Say, New Orleans," *The Guardian*.

[17] "ACLU Report Details Horrors Suffered by Orleans Parish Prisoners in Wake of Hurricane Katrina"; Welch, "Hurricane Katrina Was a Nightmare for Inmates in New Orleans."

[18] Deryugina, Kawano, and Levitt, "The Economic Impact of Hurricane Katrina on Its Victims: Evidence from Individual Tax Returns."

the home's appraisal value—and just as under the Home Ownership Loan Corporation decades before, white owned property was valued more highly. As a result, white residents were likelier to get higher government payouts for their lost property, fueling a racially uneven recovery for the city. As of 2020, much of the city has yet to be rebuilt, including many of its historically Black neighborhoods. One in three Black residents have not returned to the city.[19]

New Orleans has new levees now, but only time will tell if they will hold. By January of 2021, the Army Corps of Engineers had turned down a request by state and local officials to increase protection to a 200-year or 500-year level of protection—echoing the decision made after Hurricane Betsy, the deadly Category 4 Hurricane that preceded Katrina. A Corps spokesperson explained: "While the 200-year level of risk reduction alternative was competitive, its net benefits were lower than that of the 100-year level of risk reduction."[20]

How Climate Change Threatens Justice

No mere intellectual or even spiritual appreciation of the weight of history will protect New Orleans from future hurricanes—canals have been dug, levees constructed, seawalls erected. Whether we want to undo what has been done (e.g., destroying or altering levees) or do something else (e.g., "managed retreat" from the waters), we will have to execute either choice with hands, feet, and shovels—not with recognition or symbolism. We will have to change the distribution of wealth, of housing, and of water, not of apologies or memorials. We have to decide what to do from here: where to fortify and what to abandon, whether or not to flee, what to build and rebuild, whom to protect.

There's a larger lesson here. A politically serious reparations project—at least one fitting the goals and ethos of the constructive view—must focus on climate justice. Everywhere is New Orleans.

---

[19] Williams, "Perspective, Katrina Battered Black New Orleans. Then the Recovery Did It Again."; Rivlin, "White New Orleans Has Recovered from Hurricane Katrina. Black New Orleans Has Not."

[20] Schleifstein, "15 Years after Katrina, New Orleans Levees Are in the Best Shape Ever. Experts Say It's Not Enough."

People are usually surprised when I make this argument. The confusion makes sense—after all, they point out, there's hardly an obvious conceptual connection between climate crisis and reparations for trans-Atlantic slavery and colonialism. They're right. The connection is largely contingent: it just so happens, given the particular distributions created by this era of global politics and their ecological consequences, that our response to climate crisis will deeply determine the possibilities for justice (and injustice) in what remains of this century—and if we survive to the next. Had some things gone differently even decades ago—had the countries and corporations of the Global North polluted less, had the fossil fuel interests not worked along with coal and freight rail companies to orchestrate misinformation campaigns, protecting their short term financial gains at the cost of their and our collective future—the relationship between reparations and climate crisis could well have been quite different.[21]

But that's not what happened, and as a result, the possibility of keeping justice alive in our time hinges on our response to the reality of a warming planet. We are going to have to become firefighters.

While the role of European culture and technology is often overstated in explaining this period of human history, it would be difficult to overstate the extent to which their voyages changed the physical, biological world around us. Prior to this period, different regions of the world evolved in a fair degree of ecological isolation: with the exception of birds, insects, and the occasional coconut, much of the natural world only interacted with other flora and fauna nearby, meaning that ecological connections were constrained by the size and scope of human economic trade.[22] The global racial empire stretched that trade across the Atlantic, Indian, and Pacific oceans, which meant what some scholars call the "Columbian exchange": a historically unprecedented

[21] Cook et al., "Exxon Has Misled Americans on Climate Change for Decades. Here's How to Fight Back"; Climate Reality, "The Climate Denial Machine"; Meyer, "A Major but Little-Known Supporter of Climate Denial"; Center for Climate Change Communication, "America Misled: How the Fossil Fuel Industry Deliberately Misled Americans about Climate Change,"
[22] Mann, *1493: Uncovering the New World Columbus Created*, chap. 1; Crosby, "Columbian Exchange."

flow of plants, animals, and pathogens into environments that had never dealt with them before.

The results of this linkage were immediate and of world-historical scale. The introduction of European pathogens alongside forms of colonial domination, especially the extensive slave trade in Indigenous peoples, created public health crises that disrupted lifeways and caused mass death.[23] This toxic combination led to 56 million deaths in the Americas from 1492 to 1600—so many deaths that some Earth System scientists estimate that the "Great Dying" actually cooled the Earth.[24] This would represent the first anthropogenic global climate event—since it preceded and set the political stage for the Industrial Revolution. Its most important impacts, clearly, were the unfathomable suffering and loss of life engendered by diseases and the colonial disruptions that helped spread them. Moreover, the catastrophic depopulation of the Americas probably played more of a role in the success of the European campaigns of imperial conquest than the mythical European cultural superiority.

The Industrial Revolution itself followed some centuries later. For the first time in human history, the "shackles were taken off": "self-sustained growth" in human production was able to outpace the natural constraints of famine and other sources of periodic social breakdown.[25] The British empire, where this process started, was hardly the intellectual center of Europe, much less the world.[26] But it *was* a colonial powerhouse, already dominating key parts of the world, including much of the massive Indian subcontinent, thus linking it to the massive potential riches of competitive advantage at world scale. This combined with a crucial bit of geological luck: it had more available coal on its islands than competitors in Europe or South Asia.[27] British industrialists developed new techniques to extract and use coal energy in order to compete with the Indian producers, which lead to

---

[23] Kelton, *Epidemics and Enslavement: Biological Catastrophe in the Native Southeast, 1492–1715*, xix–xxii.

[24] Koch et al., "Earth System Impacts of the European Arrival and Great Dying in the Americas after 1492."

[25] Hobsbawm, *The Age of Revolution: 1789–1848*, 28.

[26] Hobsbawm, *The Age of Revolution: 1789–1848*, 28–29; Parthasarathi, *Why Europe Grew Rich and Asia Did Not: Global Economic Divergence, 1600–1850.*

[27] Albritton Jonsson, "The Industrial Revolution in the Anthropocene."

new forms of iron production and thus mechanization: crucially, of the textile industry that converted cotton from the American South into clothing for the entire world.[28] Coal-powered, mechanized production revolutionized British manufacture and the economic world, helping to complete the dominance of the colonial powers. And this aspect of the global racial empire, industrialism, also had world-historical ramifications for the ecological world.

Coal would have pride of place for over a century, and is still a major source of global energy. But in the middle of the twentieth century, it would be overtaken by another world-historically important fossil fuel: oil. After the 1950s, oil served as "the principal source of market growth" worldwide. It not only fuels vehicles, but it serves as a needed ingredient in the production of plastics, the use of which are now ubiquitous.[29]

The use of oil, coal, and other fossil fuels since the onset of the Industrial Revolution has sent billions of tons of carbon dioxide and other greenhouse gases into the atmosphere since the nineteenth century. The ecological ramifications of this are tremendous: by as soon as 2070, if present trends continue, an estimated 1 in 3 humans will be pushed out of the climate niche that our species has inhabited for millennia.[30] The main threats include sea level rise, which poses an existential threat to the Pacific islands, Bangladesh, and the Nile delta, while drought and potential agricultural failure leave much of Africa on a knife's edge.[31]

We are finally beginning to collectively understand the fact that climate change is a present-tense ecological crisis, and that the worst is yet to come. How we respond to climate crisis will define the politics of this century—and this success or failure sets the basic political conditions for the world that reparations projects seek to affect. Years of record-breaking heatwaves in Europe and massive wildfires in

---

[28] Parthasarathi, *Why Europe Grew Rich and Asia Did Not: Global Economic Divergence, 1600–1850*, 12.

[29] Baer, "Global Capitalism and Climate Change."

[30] Xu et al., "Future of the Human Climate Niche"; Lustgarten, "Where Will Everyone Go?"

[31] Roberts and Parks, "Ecologically Unequal Exchange, Ecological Debt, and Climate Justice: The History and Implications of Three Related Ideas for a New Social Movement," 393.

the United States and Australia have been tied by scientists to climate change.[32] Accordingly, public opinion about climate change has shifted in parts of the global North, as the percentage of people expressing serious concern in countries like the United States and United Kingdom has risen substantially.[33]

What remains is for all of us, but especially those of us invested in the project of racial justice, is to realize the full implications and urgency of the political crisis that the incoming climate emergency also represents. As climate impacts accelerate, we can expect them to perversely distribute the costs and burdens of climate change, disproportionately impacting those who have been rendered most vulnerable given the accumulated weight of history.

One reason that we can expect the costs of accelerated environmental catastrophe to be distributed in ways echoing the history of global racial empire is that this is already happening. Researchers studying New York City found that heatwave deaths and even the temperature itself was racially distributed: areas with a larger percentage white population had more plants and air conditioners.[34] Similarly: after Hurricane Harvey in Houston, negative financial outcomes like bankruptcy were heavily concentrated among poorer residents.[35] The Isle de Jean Charles Band of Biloxi-Chitimacha-Choctaw won $48 million in relocation funds from the federal government to move further inland, marking them as the first official climate refugees of the United States.[36] It was a landmark in a bleak struggle. Climate change and sea level rise claimed their island, which one local described as the core

---

[32] "Climate Change Affected Australia's Wildfires, Scientists Confirm," *The New York Times*; "Climate Change Is Contributing to California's Fires, *Science*; Cappucci and Freedman, "Europe to See Third Major Heat Wave This Summer, as Temperatures Soar from France to Scandinavia."

[33] Pew Research Center, "U.S. Concern about Climate Change Is Rising, but Mainly among Democrats"; Climate Home News, "Public Opinion on Climate Change Is Up But Let's Not Forget Lessons from the Past"; Climate Outreach, "Engaging the Public on Climate Risks and Adaptation."

[34] Klein Rosenthal, Kinney, and Metzger, "Intra-Urban Vulnerability to Heat-Related Mortality in New York City, 1997–2006."

[35] Billings, Gallagher, and Ricketts, "Let the Rich Be Flooded: The Unequal Impact of Hurricane Harvey on Household Debt."

[36] "Biloxi-Chitimacha-Choctaw Get $48 Million to Move Off of Louisiana Island."

of their culture.[37] Groups without federal recognition of tribal sovereignty have found it difficult to pursue similar claims despite facing similar risks, and as of 2020 the federal government has failed to provide adequate resettlement resources.[38]

Over the very same years of the 2010s, climate change impacts reared their head in the Global South, to much less media fanfare. Decreased rainfall and increasingly frequent droughts in Kenya have already driven pastoralists and farmers to the brink of survival.[39] Researchers link recent violence between neighbors in Mali and Nigeria to resource conflicts exacerbated by climate-related desertification and other impacts.[40] Both small island nations and Indigenous nations in climate-affected areas face existential risks for their nations and lifeways.[41]

Climate crisis is likely to lead to new social divisions between those advantaged enough to buy or coerce security from climate impacts and those who cannot. At a community, local, and national scale, we can expect police to protect the rich and socially well-positioned, often leaving vulnerable those on the business end of nightsticks or behind cell walls.[42] At the scale of geopolitics, we can expect the balance of power between nation states and Indigenous communities to be shaped increasingly by forces of the same kind: the climate crisis is likely to shuffle increasing power and control into the hands of those in command of wealth, coercive force, or strategic resources.[43]

[37] National Geographic News, "The First Official Climate Refugees in the U.S. Race Against Time."

[38] Smith, "Tribal Nations Demand Response to Climate Relocation."

[39] Higgins, "Climate Change Could Devastate Africa. It's Already Hurting This Kenyan Town"; Adow, "The Climate Debt"; GOK, "National Climate Change Response Strategy."

[40] Adigun, "A Critical Analysis of the Relationship Between Climate Change, Land Disputes, and the Patterns of Farmers/Herdsmen's Conflicts in Nigeria"; Egbuta, "Understanding the Herder-Farmer Conflict in Nigeria"; Dörrie, "Europe Has Spent Years Trying to Prevent 'Chaos' in the Sahel. It Failed."

[41] "Faced with Existential Climate Threat, Small Island Nations Sound Climate Alarm at UN"; Smith, "Tribal Nations Demand Response to Climate Relocation."

[42] Táíwò, "Climate Apartheid Is the Coming Police Violence Crisis," *Dissent Magazine*.

[43] Táíwò, "Green New Deal Policies Could Exacerbate a Burgeoning Climate Colonialism"; Martinez, "The Right to Be Free of Fear: Indigeneity and the United Nations."

To be sure, some aspects affecting the distribution of climate impacts are fairly directly ecological: whether or not a family is affected at all by a hurricane or sea-level rise depends on how close they are to a body of water. But, as I argued in the chapter on the constructive view, what matters from the standpoint of justice is how these ecological phenomena affect people's capabilities—what lives they are or are not empowered to live. This is determined not just by what happens to the ecological systems, but by the interaction of those impacts with a host of other factors that are determined by our social and political systems.

Some people who have to, say, retreat from a coastline will have access to money or credit to manage the financial costs of relocation, a passport or citizenship status that will widen the legal possibilities of their relocation, and a social status that will make the receptive communities in the places they are likely to move accepting of their presence. Others will lack some or all of these key advantages. Many will be burdened with some or all of the disastrous mirror image disadvantages: being cash-poor and indebted, having a citizenship status whose immigration is specifically banned or curtailed by other countries, or a social status that attracts stigma and violence.

In short: climate change threatens to turn existing forms of injustice into overdrive at every scale of human life.

If we want insight into how the climate crisis will interact with global racial empire's distribution of advantages and disadvantages, one place to start is an investigation of how global racial empire already distributes environmental risk and vulnerability.

Figure 5.1 is a boxplot, also known as a "box and whiskers plot": a form of data visualization developed by contributions from mathematician Mary Eleanor Spear and (later) John Tukey.[44] They are a quick, powerful way to understand differences between groups: here, between countries that have been colonized and countries that have not. The "whiskers," or the lines extending from the box, extend down to the minimum and up to the maximum value in a group excluding the dots, which represent "outliers," which are cases so different from the majority of the group that statisticians tend to exclude them from

---

[44] Wickham and Stryjewski, "40 Years of Boxplots," 2; Jones, "Credit Where Credit Is Due."

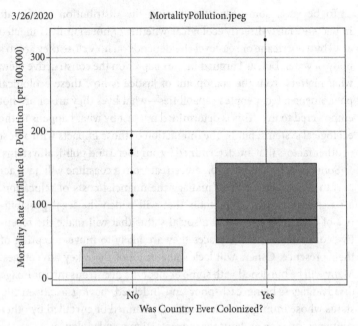

Figure 5.1 How pollution is distributed.

many parts of statistical analyses.[45] The solid black line inside of the 'box' shows the "median," or the "middle" value—in our case here, half the countries in either group have this value or higher and half of them have this value or lower. The top of the box is the median of the higher half, and the bottom of the graph is the median of the lower half. Taken together, the "box" shows you the 50 percent of cases (in this graph, countries) closest to the median, the most representative values of the whole group distribution.

[45] For our purposes, Saez de Tejada Cuenca and I follow what Krzywinski and Altman describe as "well established convention," treating any value outside of 1.5 * IQR as an outlier. In a normal distribution, this would cover 99.3 percent% of the data. For larger discussion of our treatment of these data, see the appendix. For discussion of how outliers have been dealt with in the history of statistics, see Anscombe, "Rejection of Outliers"; Krzywinski and Altman, "Points of Significance: Visualizing Samples with Box Plots."

This boxplot gives us some insight on how global racial empire distributes environmental risk internationally *right now*. Most countries that were not colonized during the last five hundred years have a very low mortality rate due to pollution: fewer than 50 deaths per 100,000, less than half the mortality rate in countries that have been colonized. The boxes for the different groups do not overlap: the entire representative ranges are different—the non-colonized country with the most deadly pollution within the 'box' range has a lower death rate than the colonized country with the least deadly levels of pollution in its box range. The two groups of countries live in different environmental realities.

In environmental economics, the "Ecologically Unequal Exchange theory" gives a specific example of the kind of unequal distribution explained in chapter 2. According to the theory, our world economic system tends to move energy and biophysical resources from poorer to richer countries, and this material distribution has consequences for the distribution of ecological risks.[46] This presents a problem for climate justice that is rooted in the distribution system carved into planetary politics by global racial empire: richer countries like those in the European Union are "draining ecological capacity from extractive regions by importing resource-intensive products and shifting environmental burdens to the South through the export of waste."[47] A recent empirical analysis supports the theory, finding that the net appropriation of resources from the poorer nations to richer ones is "systemic and pervasive in the current structure of the global economy" in every year analyzed.[48]

A group of environmental economists and geographers have proposed a partial explanation of why environmental risk and vulnerability is globally distributed in the way described by those espousing the ecologically unequal exchange theory. The "pollution haven

[46] Hornborg, "Towards an Ecological Theory of Unequal Exchange: Articulating World System Theory and Ecological Economics"; Dorninger et al., "Global Patterns of Ecologically Unequal Exchange: Implications for Sustainability in the 21st Century."

[47] Roberts and Parks, "Ecologically Unequal Exchange, Ecological Debt, and Climate Justice: The History and Implications of Three Related Ideas for a New Social Movement," 391.

[48] Dorninger et al., "Global Patterns of Ecologically Unequal Exchange: Implications for Sustainability in the 21st Century."

hypothesis" predicts that, in our highly globalized economy, companies faced with stringent and costly environmental regulations in one country or region will move production to places with less stringent regulation. Higher income countries, which tend to have more economic leverage against companies and more politically empowered populations, also tend to have more stringent environmental regulations than lower income countries. As a result, the tendency of multinational corporations to seek less regulated productive environments translates into a tendency to move production and pollution to lower income countries—that is, from countries advantaged by the history of global racial empire to those disadvantaged by it.[49] Were this to be the story of our mortality-rate boxplot, it would fit squarely into the very definition of racism offered by geographer Ruth Wilson Gilmore: "the state-sanctioned or extralegal production and exploitation of group-differentiated vulnerability to premature death."[50] A thesis as controversial and politically charged as the pollution haven hypothesis has, of course, been widely contested. Nevertheless, several empirical studies support this hypothesis as well.[51]

Researchers have proposed a similar kind of explanatory mechanism within countries, which they call "green crime havens." Green crime havens are areas of elevated environmental risk, associated with environmental crime violations. Dr. Robert Bullard, pioneering researcher of environmental racism and justice, explains how this kind of thing works: "Many industrial firms especially waste disposal companies and industries that have a long history of pollution violations, came to view the black community as a "pushover lacking community organization, environmental consciousness, and with strong and blind pro-business politics."

These communities were ripe for exploitation. Residents of economically impoverished areas—intimidated by big corporations and deserted by local politicians—were slow to challenge private and

---

[49] Taylor, "Unbundling the Pollution Haven Hypothesis," 2.
[50] Gilmore, *Golden Gulag: Prisons, Surplus, Crisis, and Opposition in Globalizing California*, 21: 18.
[51] Kellenberg, "An Empirical Investigation of the Pollution Haven Effect with Strategic Environment and Trade Policy"; Millimet and Roy, "Empirical Tests of the Pollution Haven Hypothesis When Environmental Regulation Is Endogenous."

governmental polluters of their neighborhoods. Moreover, the strong pro-jobs stance, a kind of "don't bite the hand that feeds you" sentiment, aided in institutionalizing risks at levels that are unacceptable in the larger society.[52] Researchers at Auburn University and the University of Florida found statistical evidence of green crime havens, and contended that these havens predominantly arise "as part of power differences and corresponding zoning decisions," not simply the havens' proximity to natural resources that companies want access to for production.[53]

Both the pollution haven hypothesis and the green crime haven hypothesis share an underlying point: when citizens are empowered to protect themselves against the harmful effects of pollution, they have the power to make their life and health matter. This is equally true within countries, as Flint, Michigan demonstrates.

Using the pollution haven hypothesis to explain the distribution of risk and vulnerability relies heavily on guesses about the deliberate, strategic action of particular actors who own factories and capital. If we want a story about that distribution that sharply splits the world into present day heroes and villains, we need look no further. But, as we recall from the discussion of responsibility and liability, the world is often not so simple as this. Nor do we need it to be: the distribution of environmental risk and vulnerability can be explained simply in terms of the patterns of accumulation described in chapter two.

Accumulation, remember, is the result of distribution over time. If you and I both save ten cents of every dollar we earn over our working lives, we will both end up with accumulated savings by the time we retire. At small scales there is, as always, an element of choice and responsibility in the matter: if we both make around the same amount of money from our jobs and have access to similarly consistent hours, then in the end the person with the most retirement funds will be the thriftiest or hardest working of the two of us. However, if I make minimum wage and you make seven figures a year, there is no point trying to explain the difference between our retirement savings in terms of

[52] Bullard, *Dumping in Dixie: Race, Class, and Environmental Quality*, chap. 2.
[53] Thomson, Espin, and Samuels-Jones, "Green Crime Havens: A Spatial Cluster Analysis of Environmental Crime," 510.

our spending habits or willingness to tack on overtime shifts. The distribution of income in our working years, not our work habits, explains the different levels of accumulation we have when we retire. What we can do in our retirement age, how we are cared for, and what we leave are, likewise, primarily determined by this distribution.

The environmental risk and vulnerability facing countries and populations is much like this: it emerges from several overlapping strands of political, cultural, and economic accumulation, which were largely set in motion generations ago. Climate change researchers at the University of East Anglia created an index of eleven key indicators for vulnerability to climate change impacts, identified through a combination of statistical analysis of a much larger list of potential indicators and consultation with scientific experts of various related disciplines.[54] The indicators: percentage of the population with access to sanitation, three measures of literacy rate (for 15 to 24-year olds, all adults over the age of 15, and the ratio of literate women to literate men), maternal mortality rate, typical caloric intake, civil liberties, political rights, government effectiveness, life expectancy at birth, and a measure of access to justice termed "voice and accountability."[55]

Notably absent from their list are abstract measures of the total economy, such as GDP, or even of economic inequality, such as the Gini coefficient. Present are those aspects of social life that express how material social advantages have been accumulated and distributed throughout a population: access to basic material requirements for flourishing human life, such as sanitation, food, health care, political rights, and literacy. This is right on target from the perspective of the constructive view and its use of the "capabilities" framework: what matters about the economy are the actual lives people are empowered to lead, and we are often better served asking about people's capabilities directly.

Researchers found that climate vulnerability is largely determined by fairly general aspects of how advantages and disadvantages have

[54] Brooks, Adger, and Kelly, "The Determinants of Vulnerability and Adaptive Capacity at the National Level and the Implications for Adaptation."
[55] Brooks, Adger, and Kelly, "The Determinants of Vulnerability and Adaptive Capacity at the National Level and the Implications for Adaptation," 157.

been distributed, and as the global racial empire is responsible for that distribution, the connection between global racial empire and climate vulnerability is clear.

Responding to environmental calamity requires working political infrastructure, the accumulated result of years of development of norms, legal structures, and institutional knowledge. For example: strong legislatures can effectively constrain or altogether prevent excess executive power—even that of dictators.[56] Yet colonized countries, particularly on the African continent, often inherited relatively weak legislatures, deeply autocratic political structures, and the dictatorial institutional memory of colonial management.[57] These initial conditions affected the trajectory of legislative power development even after formal independence was won, since legislative power develops over time and the effects of institutional development survive the rise and fall of particular regimes.[58] This form of accumulation would then directly affect a number of the measures that researchers have found to be key determinants of climate vulnerability, including "government effectiveness," "political rights," "voice and accountability," and "civil liberties."[59]

Responding to environmental calamity and its impacts on public health requires a working epistemic infrastructure: robust networks of knowledge and trust. Substantial empirical and formal evidence suggests that these are the accumulated result of generations-worth of decisions. Some of these distant decisions shape how cultures of trust or distrust are passed down within and across social groups, which affects how knowledge is produced and distributed in a country, community, or region.[60] These factors combine powerfully in institutions, which tend to be built more vulnerably when social trust is low.[61]

[56] Ochieng'Opalo, *Legislative Development in Africa: Politics and Postcolonial Legacies*, 17–18.
[57] Ojwang, "The Residue of Legislative Power in English and French-Speaking Africa: A Comparative Study of Kenya and the Ivory Coast."
[58] Ochieng'Opalo, *Legislative Development in Africa: Politics and Postcolonial Legacies*, 26–27.
[59] Brooks, Adger, and Kelly, "The Determinants of Vulnerability and Adaptive Capacity at the National Level and the Implications for Adaptation," 157.
[60] Tabellini, "Institutions and Culture," 264–266; Algan and Cahuc, "Inherited Trust and Growth"; Francois and Zabojnik, "Trust, Social Capital, and Economic Development"; Nunn and Wantchekon, "The Slave Trade and the Origins of Mistrust in Africa," 2011.
[61] Tabellini, "Institutions and Culture," 264–266.

This kicks off a cycle that is both stable and vicious. Low initial trust within and between groups translates into poor social institutions, whose corruption and ineffectiveness earns the next generation's distrust, thus fueling an atmosphere of distrust that feeds into people's relationships with each other as well. Other generations-spanning decisions are about building knowledge and the capacity to make use of it: these manifest in levels of investment in public education and research capacity, among other things. Neither the colonizers' institutions nor the poor institutions built in the resultant atmosphere of distrust were up to the job: as of 2017, not a single one of the world's top 100 research universities was located in Africa, Central America, or South America.[62]

Because of the confluence of ecological, political, and other postcolonial disadvantages, climate change is likely to further exacerbate and be exacerbated by every kind of international inequality. Another boxplot makes the case dramatically:

This second graph, Figure 5.2, shows the dramatic, structural difference in historically accumulated climate vulnerability between countries with different colonial histories. The colonizing parts of the world are now much less vulnerable to climate change than the regions they colonized, as measured by the aforementioned indicators (percentage of the population with access to sanitation, three measures of literacy rate, maternal mortality rate, caloric intake, voice and accountability, civil liberties, political rights, government effectiveness, and life expectancy at birth).[63] These measures are, again, general indicators of the extent to which people enjoy access to the social advantages and disadvantages that determine their capabilities and empower them to respond to stressors—climate or otherwise.[64] What we've learned here is simply another lesson about how yesterday's distribution affects tomorrow's reality: heightened vulnerability to the incoming aspects

---

[62] Florida, "The World's Knowledge Capitals?"

[63] Brooks, Adger, and Kelly, "The Determinants of Vulnerability and Adaptive Capacity at the National Level and the Implications for Adaptation," 157.

[64] Brida, Owiyo, and Sokona frame climate vulnerability in relation to community ability to respond to climate stressors, which they tie to the global economic context. Brida, Owiyo, and Sokona, "Loss and Damage from the Double Blow of Flood and Drought in Mozambique," 528.

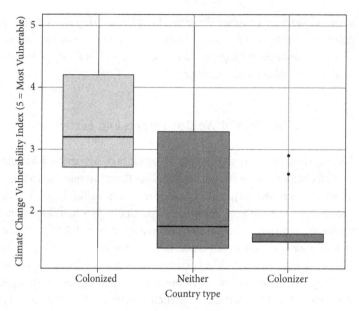

Figure 5.2 How climate vulnerability is distributed.

of climate change just simply is greater deprivation in the status quo. The rich get richer and the poor get poorer.

It is not that every aspect of today's global racial empire is rooted in the impacts of climate change. But every aspect of tomorrow's global racial empire will be. Climate change is set not just to redistribute social advantages, but to do so in a way that compounds and locks in the distributional injustices we've inherited from history. If we don't intervene powerfully, it will reverse the gains toward justice that our ancestors fought so bitterly for, ushering in an era of what the United Nations Special Rappoteur on extreme poverty and human rights calls "climate apartheid."[65]

This represents a double challenge: we need to figure out how to address the ecological and the political disasters. The economic and political systems developed by global racial empire are responsible for the

_____

[65] UN News, "World Faces 'Climate Apartheid' Risk, 120 More Million in Poverty."

accumulations that explain the crisis: both the buildup of greenhouse gases in the atmosphere and the highly uneven buildup of advantages and disadvantages that determine how climate vulnerability is distributed within and between countries.

What Should We Do? Targets and Tactics

It's easy to think, with all this talk of "worldmaking," that we have to make a comprehensive plan in advance. But that's just one way to think about progress toward justice. Another approach to building justice is processual—not centered anywhere in particular, but in a deeply pluralistic recognition of everyone's rights to pursue the political programs that fit their situation, culture, and values. That way of thinking about justice is a good fit for the ideal of self-determination. That recognition has long been part and parcel of the anti-colonial strands of thought and practice that birthed the constructive view. Amílcar Cabral, who played an important role in the revolutionary struggles of Cape Verde and Guinea-Bissau, argued that colonized peoples should return to the "upward paths" of their own cultures. Similar perspectives have been offered by some anti-colonial thinkers in the United States, like Wallace Coffee and Rebecca Tsosie.[66] On this approach, we needn't (and perhaps shouldn't!) be committed a comprehensive program in advance, since different people will come up with different actions and approaches fitting different cultural contexts and strategic situations.

Philosopher Serene Khader explains where this approach goes wrong in her book *Decolonizing Universalism*. Some think that fighting for justice requires having a particular, "one-size-fits-all" view of political principles or a just social structure. This view, which Khader calls "justice monism," has been at the heart of a lot of well-intentioned but ultimately misguided attempts to impose one society's cultural values

---

[66] Cabral, "National Liberation and Culture," 1974; Coffey and Tsosie, "Rethinking the Tribal Sovereignty Doctrine: Cultural Sovereignty and the Collective Future of Indian Nations"; Warrior, "Intellectual Sovereignty and The Struggle for An American Indian Future. Chapter 3 of Tribal Secrets: Vine Deloria, John Joseph Mathews, and the Recovery of American Indian Intellectual Traditions"; Deloria, *God Is Red: A Native View of Religion*.

on another without regard for their context, culture, or political situation. Fortunately, her engagement with the long history of transnational feminism leads her to another approach that she calls "justice enhancement": where the goal is to improve justice rather than reach any particular end-point. Aspects of that struggle could involve a kind of universalism, one that objects to subordinating and oppressive power dynamics everywhere, but would identify these negative power dynamics by analyzing the society in question rather than by uncritically imposing moral reflexes from somewhere else.[67] Similarly, we don't have to agree on every aspect of the new world we're building to agree on ways to improve the justice of our current arrangements.

Political systems are most amenable to progressive change when the interests of the elites align with those negatively affected by the system. Legal scholar Derrick Bell went as far as to name this the "principle of interest convergence," arguing that racial progress for African Americans has only been possible when it coincided with whites' interests. Bell pointed out that, before Brown v. Board provided a Supreme Court ruling and thus a legal basis for ending racial segregation of education, African Americans had spent generations articulating what ended up being the basis for the Court's ruling. What explains the Court finally seeing the light were political facts about the balance of power in a contest of "interest-group politics with a racial configuration."[68] The federal government needed to shore up its strategic position in global politics given the unprecedented anti-colonial movement, much of which was spearheaded by Communists hostile to the racist politics built into global racial empire and its connection to African Americans' political situation. Moreover, white Southerners realized that state-sponsored segregation blocked urban development in the South and thus stood in the path of profit. The interests of white southerners with regional investments, federal government anti-communists, and Black schoolchildren converged, and the powers that be moved accordingly, striking a massive blow against Jim Crow and its scheme of racial apartheid.

---

[67] Khader, *Decolonizing Universalism: A Transnational Feminist Ethic.*
[68] Bell, "Brown v. Board of Education and the Interest-Convergence Dilemma," 523.

We can convert the convergence of interests between elite and op-pressed as an opportunity to construct the just world, or at least to re-build the world in the direction of justice. And if we can distribute the costs and benefits of that construction in the right way—shifting the burdens toward those who've inherited the liabilities of global racial empire and benefits toward those who've inherited claim rights upon it—then we can achieve reparations.

But we shouldn't kid ourselves. Even in times of immense po-litical opportunity, the overlap between the interest of elites and the oppressed is partial, and the possibilities for change are profoundly constrained by the balance of power we've inherited from centuries past. But as Frederick Douglass said, power concedes nothing without a demand: whatever movement toward justice is won will be won with struggle, and struggle is the only way movements toward justice have ever been won.[69]

Specifying a total blueprint for just worldmaking is a much larger undertaking than can be achieved in a mere book by a single author. But that doesn't mean that there aren't places to start. In that spirit, if you are reading this with the intention of engaging in the struggle, here are a set of key targets and tactics this book advocates. "Tactics" are collective actions to join or start up that can meaningfully contribute to change at scale, things you can do right now. "Targets" are places we should hope to get to, by means of these tactics and many others.

Target: Unconditional Cash Transfers

One clear place to start is in the most straightforward form of power transfer possible in a world structured like ours: giving people money. When we imagine reparations, we often imagine people getting a check. It's a fantastic plan—while this book has made some departures from some of the common wisdom about reparations, this is an idea worth its salt.

<hr/>

[69] BlackPast, "(1857) Frederick Douglass, 'If There Is No Struggle, There Is No Progress.'"

In stark contrast to the byzantine social support systems that have come to characterize modern social democracies, social scientists are beginning to embrace "unconditional cash transfers": simply giving people money directly.[70] These kinds of transfers will intervene directly in the patterns of accumulation/ of money, one of our most adaptable forms of social advantages. It also avoids the problems with other welfare programs: the sprawling (and questionably efficacious) overhead, the paternalistic attempts to further shape people's incentives, and the "poverty traps" caused by aid withdrawal once a recipient crosses some threshold of income or welfare.[71] Furthermore, the ethos of the unconditional cash transfer matches self-determination as a goal for reparations policies, which is part and parcel of the constructive view.

Contemporary demands for reparations have rightly kept focus on this tactic. In *From Here to Equality*, Darity and Mullen endorse a strategy rooted in direct payments to African Americans descended from those enslaved in the United States, disbursed over time rather than all at once (to prevent inflation) and via trust funds and endowments. Moreover, it would be governed by a National Reparations Board that enlists its recipients in research about and decisions over the funds—further bolstering a commitment to an outcome of self-determination.[72] Scholar and organizer Dorian Warren of the Economic Security Project has suggested that we adopt a strategy rooted in "targeted universalism": a universal basic income for all, plus an additional amount for African Americans to account for the owed reparations.[73] These proposals have been discussed in the context of US politics, but others have even suggested a global universal basic income, which could be weighted in the targeted way that Warren suggests.[74] These are exactly the kind of demands we should want to win if we want to build a more distributively just society.

---

[70] Handa et al., "Can Unconditional Cash Transfers Raise Long-Term Living Standards? Evidence from Zambia"; Haushofer and Shapiro, "The Short-Term Impact of Unconditional Cash Transfers to the Poor: Experimental Evidence from Kenya."

[71] Wright, "Can the Universal Basic Income Solve Global Inequalities?"

[72] Darity, Jr., and Mullen, *From Here to Equality: Reparations for Black Americans in the Twenty-First Century*, chap. 13.

[73] Warren, "Reparations and Basic Income"; Bidadanure, "The Political Theory of Universal Basic Income."

[74] Wright, "Can the Universal Basic Income Solve Global Inequalities?"

Target: Global Climate Funding

Money is powerful, but cash doesn't rule *everything* around us. We should notice that cash transfers directly redistribute social advantages in a powerful way, but they do not directly redistribute disadvantages: including the kinds of vulnerability to environmental harm and predation by institutions and vigilantes that climate crisis is likely to cause. So simple wealth transfers might give vulnerable folks more options in the ecological crisis of the world to come, but will cash alone suffice where there is no disaster insurance, flood walls, enforced environmental regulations, land rights, or safe housing? From a justice perspective, the benefits and burdens of climate policy are poorly distributed.

What else do we need to do to remake our world, then, in addition to redistributing wealth? Several current initiatives point the way. One, the Equitable and Just Climate Platform, spearheaded by thinkers like Dr. Beverly Wright and organizations in the United States including the Deep South Center for Environmental Justice, is framed around achieving racial and economic justice. It calls for a "new national infrastructure" funded by a "realignment of public dollars at all levels," constructed according to priorities set by "democratic community participation" and aimed at climate targets that advance global climate justice by contributing the US "fair share in the global effort."[75] Another effort, the "Red Black and Green New Deal," is an initiative of the Movement 4 Black Lives aiming to put "Black liberation at the center of the global climate struggle."[76]

Similarly, Mohamed Adow of the climate think tank Power Shift Africa describes the history of climate change as a series of "compounding injustices," calling on the wealthy nations of the West to finally shoulder their fair share of the global burden of climate given their role in the current and incoming immiseration of the world's poorest peoples and nations.[77]

---

[75] A Just Climate.org; Toney, "Opinion | Black Women Are Leaders in the Climate Movement."

[76] Red Black and Green New Deal, "A National Black Climate Agendae."

[77] Adow, "The Climate Debt."

The Climate Equity Reference Framework is an effort-sharing framework that calculates "fair shares" of the global climate transition effort to individual countries based on their "responsibility" (cumulative additions to global emissions from a given target year) and "capacity" (economic ability to mobilize resources, taking into account the stakes of its economic and social development needs). Across a variety of ways of calculating "fair share," poorer countries' pledged emissions reductions greatly exceed their "fair share" of the climate work while richer countries' pledge far less than their fair share. In fact, poor countries have pledged over 50 percent more in reductions than rich countries.[78]

Part of the reason why richer countries' pledged emissions reductions lag behind their fair share is because it would be technologically difficult to make the needed scale of changes in a given country at the needed speed to keep up with fairness. Another approach, then, would be for a richer country to bear the costs of reducing emissions elsewhere, in a place with more opportunities for emissions reduction. The main vehicle in the international system to facilitate the inter-country transfers of money and other support toward this end is the Green Climate Fund.

The Green Climate Fund is a fund managed under the existing United Nations Framework on Climate Change by the United Nations. The rich nations and associated institutions have pledged to raise $100 billion for developing nations' green development, a step in the right direction from the constructive point of view. However, Dr. Mariama Williams of the South Centre, an intergovernmental organization supported and staffed by developing countries claims that this "does not even come close" to what is needed to make significant inroads into the climate crisis. Moreover, the rich countries had failed to follow through and the fund stood at a fraction of its target goal by early 2020.[79] Both the funding target and the follow through by richer countries must increase substantially.

[78] Holz, Kartha, and Athanasiou, "Fairly Sharing 1.5: National Fair Shares of a 1.5 °C-Compliant Global Mitigation Effort."
[79] Adow, "The Climate Debt."

An important point of contention: how we pay for crises and impacts when they arrive? The United Nations and other intergovernmental organization typically refer to crises like those stemming from natural disasters like hurricanes as "loss and damage." Figuring out who should pay for the loss and damage of climate change brings up familiar problems in distributive justice: should rich countries pay because they're richer, because they are more responsible?[80] We can add another: because they've inherited more of the liabilities from global racial empire.

However we settle this issue, the status quo of loss and damage funding shows us what to avoid. Beyond the problem of consistent underfunding, substantial funding going to the Third World is in the form of loans rather than grants—saddling recipients with debt rather than relief.[81] This can take an especially dark turn in cases where political infrastructure is poor. Mozambique, for instance, faces a mounting debt crisis after a devastating cyclone compounds the country's indebtedness after a secret deal made by elites with a Russian bank in clear violation of Mozambican law.[82] Debt jubilee could free up vast amounts of public spending in Third World countries toward increasing climate security.[83] Failing that, debt-relief for climate finance swaps could reverse this: converting sovereign debt into fuel for climate relief for Third World nations whose money is better spent on climate adaptation than debt service.[84]

---

[80] Brida, Owiyo, and Sokona, "Loss and Damage from the Double Blow of Flood and Drought in Mozambique"; Roberts et al., "How Will We Pay for Loss and Damage?"; Morrow, *Values in Climate Policy*.

[81] Fenton et al., "Debt Relief and Financing Climate Change Action"; Khan and Schinn, "Triple Transformation."

[82] "UPDATE 1-IMF"; "Russia's VTB Sues Mozambique over Loan in $2 Billion Debt Scandal"; "Mozambique."

[83] Jubilee Debt Campaign UK, "The Increasing Global South Debt Crisis and Cuts in Public Spending."

[84] Fenton et al., "Debt Relief and Financing Climate Change Action."

Target: Torch the Tax Havens

If we are to be serious about financing all or any of the proposals above, we will have to be serious about preventing elites from hiding and hoarding the world's wealth. In the United States alone, the amount of wealth redistributed to the wealthiest 1 percent over the decades from 1975 to 2018 was estimated at a whopping 50 trillion USD—a figure that could cover every military budget on the planet combined for thirty years.[85] Getting serious about stopping this plunder means fundamentally revamping how the financial system works at local and global scales.

Some countries and other legal jurisdictions act as "tax havens" – sites for the accumulation of wealth, often ill-gotten, which shield wealth holders from taxes. Economist Gabriel Zucman's *The Hidden Wealth of Nations* estimated that at least $7.6 trillion of the world's wealth was held in these offshore accounts.[86] And it is a low-ball estimate, Zucman notes, since his calculation excludes wealth tied up in real assets (e.g., yachts, jewelry) and circulating in cash notes (where much of the wealth from drug and other illegal trades is stored).

To understand the scale of this mammoth figure: in 2019, the budget for United States' *entire* gargantuan military apparatus—including the Department of Defense, all seventeen of its intelligence agencies, its war budget for operations in Iraq and Afghanistan, its nuclear weapons program, and veterans affairs expenses—was estimated at $1.25 trillion, a value less than a fifth of the dollar value of the wealth horded in the world's tax havens.[87]

An iconic example of the tax haven is Switzerland, which exploited its political neutrality in the World Wars to offer secretive banking services to all sides, facilitating tax evaders from all corners of the world.[88] As of 2013, Swiss banks still were the world's premier tax haven, but

---

[85] Hanauer and Rolf, "The Top 1% of Americans Have Taken $50 Trillion from the Bottom 90%—And That's Made the U.S. Less Secure"; Price and Edwards, "Trends in Income From 1975 to 2018"; "Global Military Spending Remains High at $1.7 Trillion, SIPRI.org.

[86] Zucman, *The Hidden Wealth of Nations: The Scourge of Tax Havens*, 36.

[87] Hartung and Smithberger, "America's Defense Budget Is Bigger Than You Think."

[88] Zucman, *The Hidden Wealth of Nations: The Scourge of Tax Havens*, chap. 1.

were joined by a symbiotic network of other tax haven locations in places like Luxembourg, the Cayman Islands, and Ireland.[89]

While tax havens appear in both the Global North and Global South (e.g., Panama), the overall effect of their distribution has worked out to impoverish Global South countries. Zucman estimated that at least 22 percent of Latin American wealth and 30 percent of African wealth is held offshore, representing tens of billions of dollars of lost tax revenue that could be put to the service of crucial green infrastructure development, just housing, or other pivotal worldbuilding uses.[90] Raymond Baker, president of Washington, D.C.-based think tank Global Financial Integrity, reminds us: "For every country losing money illicitly, there is another country absorbing it. These outflows are facilitated by financial opacity in advanced Western economies and offshore tax havens. Implementing transparency measures to curtail tax haven secrecy and anonymous shell companies is crucial to curtailing illicit flows."[91]

One of the targets of a just world must be to access these caches of illicitly hoarded wealth, so they can be used to reshape the world through unconditional cash transfers and global climate funding.

Target: Community Control

Even with the ability to move from a more ecologically dangerous to a less ecologically dangerous area, which unconditional cash transfers might provide, or to improve the infrastructure in a local area via global climate funding, communities remain vulnerable to race-based violence. It was not a Black underclass neighborhood targeted by the Tulsa massacre of 1921: it was "Black Wall Street."[92] Successful businesses and real estate holdings did not save this well-to-do community from an attack that resulted in hundreds

[89] Zucman, *The Hidden Wealth of Nations: The Scourge of Tax Havens*, 22–25.
[90] Zucman, *The Hidden Wealth of Nations: The Scourge of Tax Havens*, 55.
[91] Gascoigne and Fagan, "New AfDB-GFI Joint Report."
[92] Clark, "Tulsa's 'Black Wall Street' Flourished as a Self-Contained Hub in Early 1900s."

of indiscriminate murders; indeed, the community's very success attracted the violence.

Ida B. Wells-Barnett's classic works *The Red Record* and *Southern Horrors* suggest that, for some in the post–Civil War South, any forms of cohabitation on terms of equality could result in murderous violence: whether that was equality in economic competition, sexual competition (Black men in romantic relationships with white women), or social etiquette (Blacks were lynched for being "saucy" or "sassy").[93] We see similar levels of violence and predation in current politics: in the aftermath of Hurricane Katrina, white vigilantes murdered Black people with impunity.[94] It's unclear that increasing individual or household purchasing power, by itself, can secure environmental gains from social backlash.

Nobel Prize–winning economist Amartya Sen's pioneering research on famines helps explain this point more broadly.[95] After reviewing the historical record, Sen discovered that famines had taken place even in times of adequate or even increased food supply. The distribution of deaths in a particularly severe famine in Bengal during the second World War showed the grim logic at work. The city of Kolkata (then Calcutta) was spared the worst because the system reacted to heavily subsidize its food market, allowing residents to survive fluctuations in wages and food supply. Rural Bengal was not simply left to the whims of the market, but had its stocked food supplies taken for the war effort—and here, millions of people died horrifically.[96] We need not just build the resources and stock of social advantages for Black, Indigenous, and other colonized peoples: but also to build a social system that will protect these resources rather than simply expropriate them again when elites feel the pressure from shocks to the system.

93 Wells-Barnett, *The Red Record Tabulated Statistics and Alleged Causes of Lynching in the United States*; Wells-Barnett, *Southern Horrors: Lynch Law in All Its Phases*.
94 Thompson, "Post-Katrina, White Vigilantes Shot African-Americans with Impunity."
95 Sen, "Ingredients of Famine Analysis: Availability and Entitlements"; Sen, "Famines."
96 Táíwò, "Crisis, COVID-19, and Democracy"; Táíwò, "Cops, Climate, COVID."

Tactic: Divest–Invest, from Fossil Fuels to Communities

The view of racial injustice developed in this book has been based on distribution: where and for whom social advantages and disadvantages accumulate. "Divest-invest" strategies, then, respond to racial injustice in the most direct conceivable fashion: by attempting to reroute major channels of accumulation.

The Center for Popular Democracy, Black Youth Project 100, and Law for Black Lives explained what they call the "invest/divest framework" in a report called "Freedom to Thrive."[97] They explain that localities in the United States have "dramatically increased their spending on criminalization, policing, and mass incarceration" all while "drastically cutting investments in basic infrastructure and slowing investment in social safety net programs." These projects aim to reverse that ratio: more infrastructure, more safety, less carceral violence. Similarly, the hundreds of Latin American organizations and individuals who signed the Pacto Ecosocial del Sur (a "Social, Ecological, Economic and Intercultural Pact for Latin America") advocate this kind of approach. Cancelling the sovereign debt of their countries would allow them to reshape their political world: instead of sending resources away for debt service and accumulating pollution and social problems with extractive industries, they could use those same resources to build a regional economy of autonomous communities linked by solidarity. That would mean divesting from debt service and extraction and investing in national and local systems of care, a universal basic income, and food sovereignty for communities.[98]

Similarly, fossil fuel divestment campaigns often aim to move capital from problematic fossil fuel corporations to more "climate responsible investments." On the view of climate justice developed here, green investments in Black and Indigenous communities *are* climate-responsible investments. We ought to think of fossil fuel companies like we think of police, as generators of insecurity, and make similar

---

[97] Hamaji et al., "Freedom to Thrive: Reimagining Safety & Security in Our Communities."
[98] Pacto Ecosocial del Sur, "For a Social, Ecological, Economic and Intercultural Pact for Latin America."

efforts to divert resources from them back into looted communities. The divest–invest framework in both of these divestment campaigns ought to aim for this same pattern of redistribution.

Divestment campaigns don't work until they do: they seem ineffectual until they reach a tipping "threshold," after which they have sudden and dramatic effects. Similarly, the writings of one man, Martin Luther, helped catalyze the establishment of Protestant churches on a global scale. He did not do this alone: his work was made possible by recent technological innovations (namely the printing process) and longstanding grievances with the Catholic church that were not of his making or design. Fellow dissidents might have felt their cause was hopeless in the years before he posted the "95 Theses"—but immediately after his writings appeared, they found themselves in a world bursting with possibility. Tipping points are closely related to the popular concept of the "butterfly effect": a small intervention with huge, system-altering consequences.[99]

Researchers believe that the combination of nature and our responses to it constitute a "social-ecological system" that contains its own tipping points, and they believe that divestment, could bring us to one. Each institution that divests poses limited financial risks for investors, but each additional divesting corporation increases the difficult-to-quantify reputational risks that could trigger wider scale (and more consequential) market movement.[100] A group consisting of fewer than 10 percent of investors, according to simulations, could trigger a systemwide redistribution of social resources away from fossil fuels.[101]

Social movements can also be "tipped" in this way. In 2014, youth runners went on hundred or even thousand mile runs, spreading the news of an incoming pipeline by word of mouth. Hundreds, then thousands, answered the call and camped around the Standing Rock Indian Reservation to defend the Indigenous territory from the

[99] Milkoreit et al., "Defining Tipping Points for Social-Ecological Systems Scholarship—an Interdisciplinary Literature Review"; Otto et al., "Social Tipping Dynamics for Stabilizing Earth's Climate by 2050."

[100] Ayling and Gunningham, "Non-State Governance and Climate Policy: The Fossil Fuel Divestment Movement."

[101] Otto et al., "Social Tipping Dynamics for Stabilizing Earth's Climate by 2050."

construction of the Dakota Access Pipeline being attempted the US
Army Corps of Engineers.[102] The Dallas-based corporation Energy
Transfer Partners aimed to connect North Dakota shale oil fields with
the eastern pipeline networks in Illinois: three hundred Indigenous nations and allied movements aimed to protect the water.[103] The Trump
administration approved construction in the area, but the movement
has won key battles in the courts to limit expansion, including a 2020
court order to halt the flow of oil pending a more thorough environmental impact assessment.[104]

Moreover, the struggle against the combined state and corporate forces drew international attention and mobilized thousands
of activists. Standing Rock was one battle in a larger confrontation: similar campaigns were being waged at the same time and
continue around the world now: from residents in Appalachia opposing Dominion Energy's pipelines through their communities
to the Kenyan environmental activists mobilized against construction of a Chinese-financed coal-fired energy plant on the island of
Lamu.[105]

Anyone reading this within a stone's throw of an institution that is
invested in fossil fuels—a state or national government, a university,
even a company—can start or join a divestment movement, or oppose the construction or expansion of environmentally and socially
harmful production. You can also demand that the divested social resources be invested in and by Black, Indigenous, and other colonized
communities.

[102] Estes and Dhillon, *Standing with Standing Rock: Voices from The# NoDAPL
Movement*, sec. Introduction.

[103] Estes and Dhillon, *Standing with Standing Rock: Voices from The# NoDAPL
Movement*; Elbein, "These Are the Defiant 'Water Protectors' of Standing Rock."

[104] Peischel, "A Judge Handed the Standing Rock Tribes a Big Win in Their Dakota
Access Pipeline Fight"; Friedman, "Standing Rock Sioux Tribe Wins a Victory in Dakota
Access Pipeline Case"; "Standing Rock Asks Court to Shut Down Dakota Access Pipeline
as Company Plans to Double Capacity."

[105] Ridder, "The Appalachian Pipeline Resistance Movement: 'We're Not Going
Away'"; "Kenya Halts Lamu Coal Power Project at World Heritage Site," *BBC News*.

Tactic: Knowledge Is Power, the Flint Strategy

Generating and distributing knowledge in politically consequential ways is no special power of academic researchers. The response of residents to the water crisis in Flint, Michigan gives us an example of an organizing strategy that can even up the balance of power between those fighting for justice and those on the side of empire. The city of Flint is majority Black, and over 40 percent of its population are classified as "poor."[106] Financial problems led the state of Michigan to declare financial emergency and appoint unelected emergency managers to administer the city. One of these, Darnell Earley, oversaw the switching of the city's water source, against warnings that its treatment plant was not up to the job of rendering that much water safe for residents.[107] The state of Michigan's Department of Environmental Quality (MDEQ), a government body tasked with the support of "healthy communities," with a team of 50 trained scientists at its disposal, helped cover up the scale and gravity of the crisis by producing a doctored report claiming that the water was safe to drink.[108]

Residents got to work immediately, leading a "citizen science" campaign to counter the state department's attempt to paper over their problems, recruiting scientists to their cause and distributing sample kits to neighbors to test.[109] This step, along with the tireless work of residents to draw national condemnation of the issue, forced the state and local governments to replace the problematic service lines and force the state of Michigan to agree to a settlement of $600 million.[110]

The kind of alliance that residents, researchers, and lawyers participated in helped narrow the considerable gap in power between those fighting for environmental justice and the power structure aiming to deny it to them. But Michael Méndez points out a number of reasons why this approach doesn't happen more often: the "vast majority"

---

[106] CNN, "Flint, Michigan."
[107] "Flint's History of Emergency Management and How It Got to Financial Freedom," mlive.
[108] "Lead-Laced Water in Flint," NPR.
[109] Pieper et al., "Evaluating Water Lead Levels during the Flint Water Crisis."
[110] Fonger, "Neeley Gives Last Call—Sept. 18—to Sign up for Water Service Line Replacements in Flint"; Bosman, "Michigan to Pay $600 Million to Victims of Flint Water Crisis."

of environmental groups have fewer than five paid staff members and don't have the resources to commission technical research; their opponents, on the other hand, have industry experts and paid researchers; and states tend to address problems at a scale of people and geography that excludes neighborhood levels of analysis, even though this is the scale at which grassroots organizing often begins and at which environmental injustices are often realized.[111] In addition, a lot of public research capacity is available in university institutions, but these institutions and the incentives they create for career advancement and even continued funding powerfully tie researchers' projects to corporate agendas rather than popular ones.[112]

The Flint strategy of citizen-science linked to a political campaign helped mitigate some of these problems: it enlisted academic researchers who volunteered their time, and spun a campaign across multiple neighborhoods, enlarging the scope of the movement confronting state officials. Other knowledge producing strategies can also cause meaningful social change. In the case of sex abuse in the Church, legal campaigns and journalistic investigations led investigations of sex abuse in the Catholic Church that rocked one of the world's oldest and most powerful institutions on a global scale.[113] In Canadian "residential schools," this abuse was explicitly linked to a broader colonial project of eliminating First Nations' culture and languages. But by the time of the Boston Globe's famous 2002 investigation, prompted by decades of litigation, investigation, and other agitation by survivors of Church abuse, it was made clear to a wide audience that sex abuse was not confined to these institutions. Writing in 2019, legal scholar Mayo Moran reports that church leaders continue to "fall on an almost-daily basis" and that litigation around abuse

[111] Mendez, *Climate Change from the Streets: How Conflict and Collaboration Strengthen the Environmental Justice Movement*, 80–81.
[112] World Economic Forum, "Universities Need Philanthropy but Must Resist Hidden Agendas."
[113] February 14, 2019, and Comments139, "With So Much of Its Leadership Compromised, Is the Catholic Church Irredeemable?"; "Sex Abuse and the Catholic Church."

worldwide has cumulatively cost the Church billions of dollars and forced sweeping changes to its internal practices.[114]

In general, people who work in strategic parts of knowledge production and distribution (people in universities and news media outlets) have historically been important contributors to campaigns for justice. These kinds of connections are of immense strategic importance to fights for justice, and developing them is something we can start doing right now.

Tactic + Target: Deciding Together

A question that is equally apt for grassroots struggle and the formal halls of power: how do we decide on any of this?

Representative democracy has enjoyed pride of place as the dominant approach to political legitimacy in recent decades. But how representative is representative democracy? In much of the world, representative politics is plagued by elite capture: the manipulation of public institutions and resources by the most advantaged and well positioned, often to the detriment and irrelevance of everyone else.[115] As if that's not enough, many of the approaches to combating elite capture, including valorization of and organizing around marginalized identities ("identity politics") are likewise vulnerable to elite capture.[116]

A better alternative would emphasize the distribution of power itself, not mediated through representation. Johanna Bozuwa provides a helpful example in her summary of the work of many activists and community organizations, whose collective efforts she calls "energy democracy." Community control over the generation, transportation, and distribution of energy would shift the incentives governing how those important social advantages—and, importantly, the associated disadvantages of pollution—are controlled and managed. Publicly-owned utilities are no radical pipedream, even in the United

[114] Moran, "Cardinal Sins: How the Catholic Sexual Abuse Crisis Changed Private Law."
[115] Dutta, "Elite Capture and Corruption: Concepts and Definitions."
[116] Táíwò, "Identity Politics and Elite Capture."

States: they already serve small cities like Hammond, Wisconsin and big ones like Los Angeles, California, and Nashville, Tennessee.[117] But the community-level decision making and control over these still leaves much to be desired—beyond public ownership of energy, protection from elite capture is key to the pursuit of climate justice.

It is true but not enough to say that we should listen to the voices of marginalized peoples in making these decisions and controlling these sorts of initiatives. Each of us will have to decide, after all, which specific perspectives out of a variety to agree with. We shouldn't expect that process to be easy or without controversy. Groups including the Red Nation, an Indigenous-led organization; Cooperation Jackson in predominantly Black Mississippi; and the Pan African Climate Justice Alliance have each issued carefully developed statements offering broad direction as to what climate justice looks like in action.[118] But the devil is often in the details.

Identity issues further complicate an equally fundamental structural problem: the formal structures we have to work with are at the considerable disadvantage of responding to a global problem from a framework of responsibility that is bounded by borders. Environmental policy professor Michael Méndez details how a policy proposal for California to purchase "carbon offsets" split Indigenous groups in Brazil, with representatives from larger groups with legally recognized land like the Yawanawa speaking in favor of the proposal, and representatives from forest communities like the Apurina and Jaminawa speaking against.[119] Whatever decisions lawmakers make in such situations, none of these people, who live in Brazil, voted for the California legislators, and none of them are in a position to vote them out. As Méndez argues, we may need new "trans-local" ways of acting and thinking across largely different geographic and political contexts,

[117] Bozuwa, "Public Ownership for Energy Democracy."
[118] The Red Nation, "10 Point Program –"; Cooperation Jackson, "The Jackson Just Transition Plan"; Pan African Climate Justice Alliance, "African Climate Justice Manifesto."
[119] Mendez, *Climate Change from the Streets: How Conflict and Collaboration Strengthen the Environmental Justice Movement*, chap. 6.

ways that emphasize the importance of community level decision making and impacts.[120]

Outside of the formal levers of power, a promising process-based approach to the struggle of regular people against large corporations and governments was pioneered by workers' unions and community groups. This approach, called "bargaining for the common good," is "a conscious effort to tie union–community mobilization to the function that lies at the very heart of unionism: collective bargaining."[121] Typically workers negotiate with bosses over working conditions and compensation. But on this model, workers' organizations collaborate with community organizations to bargain with corporations over a wider set of demands that benefit the entire communities that workers come from and represent: that is, for the common good. Teachers' unions in Chicago and Los Angeles used this approach in 2019 to expand the local education budgets in favor of health care, language, and other social support services for their students.[122]

Its targets could be private commitments to local climate initiatives as well as things of global reach (especially when targeting multinational corporations). In March of 2020, workers of the Local 26 chapter of the Service Employees International Union, overwhelmingly immigrants of color, struck in Minneapolis. They demanded expanded training and use of "green cleaning," and issued a report with local progressive organizations like Minnesota Youth Climate Strike and the Minnesota Black, Indigenous, and People of Color Climate and Environmental Justice Table detailing the union's wider commitments to climate justice and goals for local policy.[123] This kind of approach, especially if done transnationally, can build the power necessary to build justice at a global scale as well.

Anyone in a union in a position to negotiate, or living in community with such a union, can join or help start an effort like this. In the United

[120] Mendez, *Climate Change from the Streets: How Conflict and Collaboration Strengthen the Environmental Justice Movement.*

[121] McCartin, "Bargaining for the Common Good."

[122] Century Foundation, "The Chicago Teachers Strike Is a Fight for the Common Good"; "Striking for the Common Good," *US News & World Report*; Campbell, "The 11-Day Teachers Strike in Chicago Paid Off."

[123] Brecher, "Did We Just Witness the First Union-Authorized Climate Strike in the United States?"

States, a group called Forge Organizing set up a database to help people identify opportunities to wage community and union joint campaigns for justice.[124] A like effort in other parts of the world would be a welcome contribution to climate politics.

Summing It All Up

In chapter 2, I mentioned that our discourse about how to change this social reality tends to offer "solutions" that are hopelessly out of scale to the size of the challenge. I gave the examples of personal philanthropy (even of Gates Foundation proportions) and NGOs. These can provide some starting contributions, but they aren't solutions. Slavery and colonialism built the world and its current basic scheme of social injustice, and philanthropy and NGOs were built within that scheme. The proper task of social justice is no smaller: it is to, quite literally, remake the world.

Adapting to climate change is likewise a project that can involve no less than the reordering of the globe. Beyond the fact that we can't protect our progress toward justice in the eco-apartheid world of unrestrained climate change, whether we accomplish a Green New Deal here will only save us if they manage something similar over there.

This scale can seem daunting and impossible. How are we supposed to win a political movement of that magnitude? But what I've attempted to argue throughout this book is that, for the past five hundred years, the task of justice has always been this large. The colonizers and conquerors of the world, from the US southern planter aristocracy to the Third Reich, have never been confused about the scale of their ambitions for injustice. It's time they met their match.

***

The 1835 the Malê continued a fight that we can help finish.

---

[124] The Forge, "Mapping Our Movement to Go on Offense."

6

The Arc of the Moral Universe

"Somewhere we must come to see that human progress never rolls in on the wheels of inevitability. It comes through the tireless efforts and the persistent work of dedicated individuals who are willing to be co-workers with God. And without this hard work, time itself becomes an ally of the primitive forces of social stagnation . . . We shall overcome because the arc of the moral universe is long, but it bends toward justice."
> —Dr. Martin Luther King, Jr., "Remaining Awake Through a Great Revolution"

"What we need to do . . . . is encourage groups of all kinds and all ages to participate in creating a vision of the future that will enlarge the humanity of all of us and then, in devising concrete programs on which they can work together, if only in a small way, to move toward their vision. In this unique interim time between historical epochs, this is how we can elicit the hope that is essential to the building of a movement and unleash the energies that in the absence of hope are turned against other people or even against oneself. . . . When people come together voluntarily to create their own vision, they begin wishing it to come into being with such passion that they begin creating an active path leading to it from the present. The spirit and the way to make the spirit live coalesce. Instead of seeing ourselves only as victims, we begin to see ourselves as part of a continuing struggle of human beings, not only to survive but to evolve into more human human beings."
> —Grace Lee Boggs, *Living for Change*

Reconsidering Reparations. Olúfẹ́mi O. Táíwò, Oxford University Press. © Oxford University Press 2022.
DOI: 10.1093/oso/9780197508893.003.0006

Takeshi Ueshiba is carefully surveying wood. He is careful because, although the material for his project literally does grow on trees, that's no small matter because he can't move forward with just any tree's wood. This 'Yoshino' cedar tree, and the wood it yields, could have been in the making for centuries.[1] He is careful because even a grand tree of this size—Yoshino cedar can easily grow to 50 feet or taller—will produce only four of the *kotsuki* planks necessary for his task, and the job requires forty.[2]

The task that Ueshiba and his team are responsible for is making *kioke*. These are wooden barrels, used in the production of sake (rice wine) and miso (a seasoning).[3] The pores of the Yoshino cedar, and the wood's steady resilience to a range of external temperatures, make the barrels fashioned out of it ideal environments for the ecosystem of microorganisms whose activity is crucial to the fermentation that give miso, sake, and soy sauce their flavor.

When the *kioke* are finished, it's Yasuo Yamamoto's turn. Yasuo Yamomoto is heir to five generations of this tradition.[4] While most manufacturers switched to using steel barrels after the Second World War, Yamamoto and others insist that fermentation in the kioke is the most essential ingredient in fermented Japanese foods—everything from miso to pickles. Yamamoto arranges the kioke he gets from Ueshiba's team, fills them with moromi mash, and waits for backup as the sauce ferments.

The fermentation stage of the process is ruled by enzymes, microorganisms, and the input of their environment. The wood in the kioke itself contributes many of the microorganisms that join those from the mash. Shodoshima's summers tend to get hot and muggy—when the weather cooperates in this way, the fermentation accelerates. Yamamoto listens closely to the audible gurgling sounds as he passes the kioke, gauging how the process is going.

Together, Yamamoto's grandfather and a neighbor planted the bamboo that produced the hoops for the kioke—an intervention that

---

[1] Tripp, "Yoshino': An Outstanding Cultivar of Japanese Cedar"; Pen Magazine International, "The Last Barrels of Tradition."
[2] Pen Magazine International, "The Last Barrels of Tradition."
[3] Pen Magazine International, "The Last Barrels of Tradition."
[4] SSENSE, "Yasuo Yamamoto's Trending Tradition."

proved necessary generations later, when Yasuo Yamamoto could not find suitable wood anywhere else.[5] The cedar trees Ueshiba used were planted as long ago, if not longer. The knowledge used by all these people has undergone literally millennia of development. There are references to the fermentation of soy going back at least as far as the second century in mainland China.[6] Yamamoto, Ueshiba, and all those who work with them are joining the cedar trees, the microorganisms, and countless people throughout Japan and the wider world in a 150 year arc of a millennia-long human practice: producing soy sauce.

Neither Yamamoto's neighbor nor his grandfather could have known what the future held. They couldn't have known, in Shodoshima in the 1920s, that there would be a Second World War—much less that the economic changes it brought would change Japanese food production so dramatically. Neither can Ueshiba know what will become of the physical kioke he produces or of his knowledge. During the same decades of the 1920s and 1930s, master kioke makers numbered in the tens of thousands.[7] At one point, Ueshiba was reported to be the last master craftsman of the barrels, but several Shodoshima carpenters—including Yamamoto himself—have studied under him to keep the craft alive. Above all: Ueshiba certainly cannot know what will happen to the weather, and thus to the trees on which the entire practice depends.

I like to think that Yamamoto and Ueshiba's ancestors acted in equal parts faith and responsibility. We don't have to think that they blindly assumed that kioke-based fermentation would never die. We can explain their responsibility in terms of what they did know for a fact: that the very possibility of enjoying a good, beautiful thing eighty years into the future depended on their actions today. And we can explain their trust in terms of that responsibility: they did their part in a larger, multigenerational project (planting cedar and bamboo) in faith and trust that the future would take up their contributions in a good and beautiful way. Ueshiba and Yamamoto inherited this faith and

[5] Hachisu, "Kioke."
[6] Shurtleff and Aoyagi, History of Soy Sauce (160 CE to 2012), 21.
[7] Hachisu, "Kioke."

responsibility from the generations that preceded them, and they are passing it on to the ones to come.

Reconstruction, Redemption

Ueshiba and Yamamoto might well succeed at a task their ancestors left for them. But there is also the possibility of defeats and setbacks. The twelve years following the US Civil War provide a powerful example of this: despite the centuries of racialized chattel slavery that preceded them, these were some of the most socially progressive years in American history.

The war brought massive upheaval in social relations. Thousands upon thousands of enslaved African Americans withdrew their labor from Confederate controlled territory in a "General Strike," which historians now acknowledge was in itself a major contribution to the Northern victory.[8] Moreover, some 180,000 of them also served in the Union Army as soldiers—a number nearly equivalent to the entire Union Army at the beginning of the war.[9] Despite racial discrimination in pay and promotion, these soldiers nevertheless enjoyed an elevated social status. It was in the military courts that Black people were first able to bear witness against whites in a court of law, and it was in the military schools where they first had access to a racially integrated education.[10]

For a time, it seemed as though there was no turning back the tide of these social changes. Historian Eric Foner quotes a northern official speaking toward the end of the Civil War: "No negro who has ever been a soldier . . . can again be imposed upon; they have learnt what it is to be free and they will infuse their feelings into others."[11]

The newly emancipated African-Americans worked alongside the Radical faction of the Republican party sto codify this massive social

---

[8] Foner, "Rights and the Constitution in Black Life during the Civil War and Reconstruction," 864.

[9] "Union Army," Encyclopedia.com.

[10] Foner, *A Short History of Reconstruction*, chap. 2.

[11] Foner, "Rights and the Constitution in Black Life during the Civil War and Reconstruction," 864.

change in feeling and recognition into law. The Radical Republicans rewrote the Constitutions of ten states, making massive structural changes in a progressive direction. In nine of these, married women were finally allowed to own property in their own name, and South Carolina had its first legal provision for divorce.[12] The radicals abolished the property qualification for voting and holding public office, and in some states eliminated imprisonment as a legal response to debt. The Fourteenth and Fifteenth Amendments established birthright citizenship and equal legal protection, and prohibited disenfranchisement on the basis of race—granting Black men the right to vote, at least as far as the letter of the law was concerned.[13] These legal changes also granted Black men the right to participate in government as elected officials: at the height of Reconstruction there were as many as eight Black Congressmen. In general, Black people wielded immense and unprecedented political power from 1865 to 1877, to an extent that would have been unthinkable as recently as a generation before, but that achievement would tragically return to "unthinkable" status in the years that followed.[14]

There were those who wanted to go even further. Some wanted to take the plantation lands upon which the enslaved had been forced to work, divide them up, and allocate plots to freedmen. Historian Ana Lucia Araujo points out that proponents of this radical land reform measure included formerly enslaved Black activists such as Sojourner Truth, who circulated a petition in 1870 demanding provision of land to freed people.[15] Likely owing to their activism and agitation, well-positioned elected officials among the Radical Republicans shared similar views, including Congressional Representative George W. Julian, the chairman of the House Committee on Public Lands.[16] Due to pressure from the Radical Republicans, Congress authorized

[12] Lebsock, "Radical Reconstruction and the Property Rights of Southern Women," 195–196.

[13] Araujo, *Reparations for Slavery and the Slave Trade: A Transnational and Comparative History*, 92.

[14] Foner, "Rights and the Constitution in Black Life during the Civil War and Reconstruction," chaps. 10–11.

[15] Araujo, *Reparations for Slavery and the Slave Trade: A Transnational and Comparative History*, 94.

[16] Foner, *A Short History of Reconstruction*, chap. 1.

the division of land abandoned or confiscated in the Civil War into forty-acre plots and established the Freedmen's Bureau to distribute food, fuel, clothing, and care for "all manner" of problems confronting newly freed Black Americans in the South.

But even during these years of progress, there were signs of trouble ahead. While these gains were being made, Southern states enacted state laws that would prove crucial to the later undoing of the progressive elements of Reconstruction: the Black Codes. Since the personal authority of the master-slave relationship had been abolished, planter elites and their allies turned to the government to provide the basis for coercive control over Black life, centering their efforts around coercive control of their labor. Mississippi required all Black people to have written evidence of employment for the next year and threatened any laborer leaving their job before the end of their contract with forfeiture of all the wages they had already earned. At one fell swoop, this measure prevented competition in the labor market from empowering Black workers—all but ensuring working conditions with unchecked exploitation and abuse—and barred Black entrepreneurship. Louisiana and Texas mandated that labor contracts "shall embrace the labor of all the members of the family able to work," eliminating gender protections for Black women. States crafted apprenticeship laws that functionally forced Black minors to work for white employers without pay at all.[17]

Free Black Americans, like their postrevolutionary counterparts in Haiti and the broader Caribbean, understood the political importance of land. The white planter elite of the South knew that they were right: that their ability to command coercive control of Black labor depended on their ability to control ownership of and access to the land of the plantation belt.[18] President Andrew Johnson's administration, which had been pardoning Confederates, blocked attempts to move forward with land redistribution.[19]

Since the promised provision of forty acres for freedmen never arrived, most of those who had been enslaved were condemned to

---

[17] Foner, *A Short History of Reconstruction*, chap. 5.
[18] Foner, *A Short History of Reconstruction*, chap. 4.
[19] Foner, *A Short History of Reconstruction*, chap. 4; Araujo, *Reparations for Slavery and the Slave Trade: A Transnational and Comparative History*, 92–93.

poverty. They, of course, had not had the ability to build capital while enslaved, and did not find white communities willing to extend them credit on other than grossly exploitative terms.[20] With the Black Codes, and without savings, property, or access to credit, Black Americans were forced into the market as wageworkers or sharecroppers.

As sharecroppers, they lived on and cultivated crops on land owned by a landowner, many of whom were previous slave owners. They paid rent to the landowner, often in the form of a share of the crop produced. As wage workers, they engaged in a more familiar transaction: the exchange of hours of work for dollars in compensation.

As formerly enslaved Black activist Frederick Douglass explained, both these dynamics between "capital and labor" and "landlords and tenants" were rife with exploitative possibilities. Landowners used the threat of eviction and control over the terms of rent to secure their profit and control tenant workers, just as factory and business owners used the threat of firing and control over wages to control wage workers. Douglass's explanation of the stakes of these relationships was unequivocal: "The man who has it in his power to say to a man you must work the land for me, for such wages as I choose to give, has a power of slavery as real, if not as complete, as he who compels toil over the lash. All that a man hath he will give for his life."[21] Confronted with these threats to their hard won freedom, Black Americans organized to bargain collectively: washerwomen in Jackson, factory workers in Richmond, mechanics in Columbus, and even sharecroppers on plantations all held strikes or petitioned collectively for better wages.[22]

Their efforts were stifled by a series of disasters beginning with an economic depression. In 1873, the postwar economic boom came to an abrupt end when an inability to market railroad bonds triggered a financial panic. By the following year, unemployment had reached 25 percent in New York City and half of the nation's iron furnaces had stopped production. The South was hardest hit: declining prices of cotton, tobacco, and sugar sent farmers hurtling into poverty.

---

[20] Foner, *A Short History of Reconstruction*, chap. 2.
[21] Douglass, "Address to the National Convention of Colored Men, Louisville, Ky.," 6.
[22] Foner, *A Short History of Reconstruction*, chap. 2; Foner, "Rights and the Constitution in Black Life during the Civil War and Reconstruction," 874.

The Democrats seized the political opportunity to defeat their Radical Republican rivals. This backlash to Reconstruction bears the chilling name "Redemption."

In white majority states, their machinations were primarily through the electoral process: associating higher taxes with programs that benefited Blacks, and waging a "race against race" campaign. In states with less favorable racial demographic numbers, defenders of white supremacy waged a calculated campaign of political terrorism, forming organizations explicitly dedicated to promoting white supremacy, like Louisiana's White League. These campaigns involved murdering Republican elected officials, disrupting court sessions, and driving Black workers from their homes.

The crisis escalated: by 1875, Democrats were murdering and robbing Black people indiscriminately in Mississippi and South Carolina. Though we may imagine the hooded figures of the Ku Klux Klan wielding torches in the dark when we imagine racial terrorism, these incidents occurred in broad daylight, with masses of unmasked, unhooded whites killing for supremacy. But in 1877, rather than supporting Black Southerners against this organized campaign of terrorism, President Rutherford B. Hayes ordered federal troops surrounding the statehouses of Louisiana and South Carolina to return to their barracks. The federal government lacked the will, not the opportunity, to intervene—a fact proven by the unprecedented federal intervention to put down labor uprisings by predominantly white workers in the Great Strike of 1877 that same year.[23]

The year 1877 marked the triumph of Redemption and southern "home rule" over the progressive legacy of Reconstruction. The surge of rapid social progress occasioned by the Civil War was interrupted by a political crisis, which provided the opportunity to erode Black people's hard-won rights and protections.

We often refer to gains in civil rights as historical progress, as if time and morality move together in lockstep. This is not so. The progress toward justice achieved in the social movements of the 1960s and 1970s—the liberatory anticolonial movements in Asia and Africa, the

[23] Foner, *A Short History of Reconstruction*, chap. 11.

Civil Rights Movement in the United States, transnational queer liberation and feminist movements—are not any more irrevocable than the
achievements of Reconstruction. They have been under attack since
the day they were won—1 million Black farm owners in the United
States have already been dispossessed of some 12 million acres worth
of land, and present-day voter suppression efforts continue to use tactics refined during the era of Jim Crow.[24] Forces opposed to justice
stand ready to reverse the gains of yesterday's struggles entirely, should
the opportunity present itself.

Acting Like an Ancestor

The ambitions of the worldmaking project recommended by the constructive view may make reparations appear beyond daunting. How
can we possibly succeed at a task as immense and contested as building
the just world? The unjust world order we have is the outcome of five
centuries of human action—it would be an incredible achievement
to undo this evil in half that time. And even that monumentally fast
achievement would still involve *centuries* of struggle, meaning generations and generations of people who have to act in their lifetimes in
pursuit of a good that may only materialize in someone else's.

Of course, it would be an immense and worthy achievement if those
of us alive today managed to do the whole thing: end oppression, build
a new social system, and set up safeguards that prevent the system
from backsliding into injustice. If we can do it, we should.

But we should resist all-or-nothing thinking about the struggle for
justice. No previous generation has won the struggle for justice outright, in one stroke—if they had, we wouldn't be in this position. The
fighters of the Haitian Revolution did not end the system of racialized
chattel slavery or the global racial empire it was predicated upon: they
eradicated its worst form from one island, the one they lived on. The

---

[24] "One Million Black Families in the South Have Lost Their Farms over the Past
Century"; Berman, "Voter Suppression"; Williams, "A Win against Voter Suppression
in the South"; NBC News, " 'Tidal Wave of Voter Suppression' Washes over States,
Lawyer Says"; "Georgia Election Fight Shows that Black Voter Suppression, a Southern
Tradition, Still Flourishes." PBS News Hour.

same is true of their abolitionist comrades-in-arms up north in the United States, who helped create the political conditions that eradicated racial slavery there. The work of replacing global racial empire with a just world order was not completed, but it was advanced.

Similarly, neither the French Revolution of 1789 nor the Russian Revolution of 1917 ushered in global political systems based on equality and fraternity: they *did* help uproot specific local systems of injustice and provided lessons and inspiration to future generations of freedom fighters. Those who participated in the twentieth century anti-colonial struggles did not bring to being the new world their struggle anticipated, or end global stratifications in wealth or political rights, but they did win national independence for much of Asia and Africa and thereby end formal colonial rule and domination in much of the world. The work of replacing global racial empire with a just world order was not completed, but it was advanced.

It often takes everything a generation has just to win the struggle immediately in front of them. But if they pass on the right things—and if we in the generations that follow pick up what they left for us—that can be enough.

Projects as lofty as bending the arc of the moral universe, becoming more "human" human beings, and ending deeply entrenched structures of racial injustice share something important in common with projects as mundane as making soy sauce. They both make use of this basic, often unnoticed yet miraculous capacity that we have: to join our actions up across time and space—even with those we have never met and may never know of.

Much of everyday life is the realization or continuation of multigenerational projects. The soy sauce Yamamoto makes owes its flavor to the kioke Ueshiba made to cook it in: the kioke owes the labor that constructed it to the skills imparted to Ueshiba and his team by their ancestors, and it owes the parts that make it up to the literal trees that they planted. Similarly, this very book I'm writing about reparations owes its existence to the courage of Black American students, teachers, and activists who fought to end racial apartheid in US education in the 1950s and 60s, and Africans who fought to end it on the African continent; both of whom owe their ability to win those struggles to the ancestors preceded them.

The struggle in front of our generation, I've argued in this book, is climate crisis. This crisis is existential—for humans and many non-human species, but especially for Black and Indigenous peoples, who may be set for wholesale destruction even in many of the scenarios where the human race as a whole makes it through the crisis. Any sober analysis of the implications of this fact cannot but recognize these further conclusions: if we fail in the struggle for climate justice, there's a serious risk that the gains our ancestors made will be lost. If we fail, our descendants may not have the resources or strategic position they need to right the ship. Depending on how we fail, our descendants may not have descendants of their own at all.

Then, there are questions we should ask of ourselves: how do we build the perspective, the culture, and the principles to use what our ancestors gave us? How do we will ourselves to do the hard work of actions that may only be completed by our descendants? One way to make progress on this is to recover an aspect of many cultures' moral life that modern cultural life, particularly given the kinds of cultural perspectives that circulate under capitalism, tends to deemphasize: the moral perspective of the ancestor.

I am a Yoruba person. I am not Yoruba by religion; my parents, like most Yoruba after British colonization, went to Christian churches and raised their children accordingly. I didn't even grow up speaking the language, given that doctors advised my parents to speak just one language at home in view of my older brother's speech delay and autism. Our home life followed an incomplete list of the full customs, as a degree of assimilation and acculturation into American society relaxed some traditions and bolstered others.

Like many middle class children of immigrants, I developed one sense of my culture at home with my parents and the wider Nigerian diaspora that raised me, and another sense of culture in university when I was privileged enough to access the time, space, and political sensibilities to study these things. Much of Yoruba culture, history, and religion is still foreign to me—if not quite as foreign as they would be to someone from another ethnic group or country, still foreign enough to temper most claims to knowledge or authority I could possibly pretend to make.

Yet, I am a Yoruba person. As with reparations, inheritance is enough.

After all: whatever I believe about them, I have ancestors. Religious studies scholar Dr. J. Omosade Awolalu explains that, according to the Yoruba, our ancestors are still here with us. The 'death' of their physical bodies only made them more powerful, releasing them from the constraints that confront us in the present day. From the other side of this life, they can control and direct the affairs of their descendants, looking out for the interests and steering them toward what they need. If illness befalls me, my ancestors must be asleep or inattentive; or, on the other hand, perhaps I haven't sacrificed as I should have.[25]

Unlike much of Yoruba thought and philosophy, *this* I find familiar. Yoruba culture is powerfully organized around age. For a powerful illustration: a speaker addressing an older person will use the same plural pronouns with which they address a group of people.[26] Indulge a philosopher's guess about the implied value underlying this linguistic fact: that to speak to someone older is to speak to history, and all its attendant accumulations. This guess may or may not be onto something. What is certain is that commitment to the continuity of the lives of past people with those of present people is a powerful framework for thinking about our place in the moral world.

The ancestor perspective can get us out of some ways of thinking about climate justice that are dead ends. Many people writing and thinking about social justice, especially from a systematic perspective, are insistent on and desperate for fast social change. This makes sense, since there's plenty of reason for haste and urgency: many of today's social ills are really intolerable, and some crises demand quick action to be resolved at all. Climate crisis is surely among these. But we do not need to win every fight to win some worth winning. We do not need a complete system transformation in our lifetime to nevertheless have achieved something important and notable in the longer historical fight for justice.

[25] Awolalu, "The Yoruba Philosophy of Life," 27.
[26] Adegbija, "A Comparative Study of Politeness Phenomena in Nigerian English, Yoruba and Ogori," 520.

There are many reasons people argue that effective solutions to climate crisis require a total system overhaul, but I suspect at least one comes down to our core motivations rather than technical arguments about policy and possibility. Revolution happens fast. Rapid social change allows us personally, in our lifetimes as individuals, to witness and receive some of the most prized fruits of our social justice labor and struggle. This would obviously be wonderful both for us and for the story of justice, but I suspect that embracing the ancestor perspective will make us less desperate in the face of more outcomes.

Many, correctly, blame capitalism—the distributive system built by global racial empire—for the climate crisis.[27] But others take it further, arguing that this means we have to completely end capitalism in our lifetimes in order to effectively respond to the climate crisis.[28] It wouldn't be the first time this has been tried: this gargantuan undertaking was, arguably, the subject of the Cold War, which defined politics for much of the twentieth century. Even in this contest, where the balance of power in capitalism's favor was much less decisive than in today's world, capitalism emerged undefeated and the results of the struggle left much to be desired.

The processes of accumulation that global racial empire built are vast and ever-moving. Even winning reparations in individual national or regional contexts, like the US Movement for Black Lives platform or the Caribbean nations' CARICOM reparations platform, would be a huge task. On a literal global scale the obstacles are even greater.

It's available to us to do the cultural work to think about this scale differently. The number of generations of our descendants who deal with this unjust world—in fact, who have a world to evaluate at all—depends on our successes or failures to provide intermediate wins or losses. Winning a global revolution against capitalism is of course one way that we could leave a better world on the long view of history. But this turns out to be just one way among many. If we should find that we can't do it in our generation it does not remotely follow that there is

---

[27] Left Voice, "Capitalism Is Responsible for Climate Change."
[28] For example, see Dawson, and a response by Chow: Dawson, "We Can't Beat Climate Change under Capitalism. Socialism Is the Only Way"; Chow, "We Don't Have Time to End Capitalism—but Growth Can Still Be Green."

204 RECONSIDERING REPARATIONS

nothing to do in this generation except burn the world down in frustration or resignation.

Our ancestors gave us the opportunities that we have, whether on purpose or by accident—but, we really ought to remember how much of it was on purpose. Many historical struggles were carried out by people operating in the full knowledge that they would never see the intended goal that they sweat and bled for. Dr. King, for his part, accepted this. The day before his murder, he addressed striking sanitation workers and the wider community of Memphis Tennessee at the Mason Temple. He told them: "I've seen the promised land. I may not get there with you. But I want you to know tonight, that we, as a people, will get to the promised land."[29] For Dr. King, his confidence in the eventual victory of the struggle was enough for him to continually contribute, up until and at the cost of his life. We can plant trees today with this same faith about tomorrow.

The ancestor perspective helps ground a kind of revolutionary patience while, at the same time, rejecting complacency. The arc of the moral universe will not bend itself (no matter how many times people take the Dr. King quote that serves as the epigraph for this chapter out of context). It will be bent by deliberate effort and political struggle if it will be bent at all—and there's no other hands to do it but ours. But, the point was (and is): we don't have to do it all at once.

This is a moral evaluative perspective that is just as available to us as it was for the generations of people who fought the fights to get us here. We can and ought to embrace the ancestor perspective, passing down tools to the next generation, putting in reach for our grandchildren things that are out of reach for us. We might not have to completely dismantle global racial empire to prevent climate change from rolling back the progress our ancestors fought for: we might just have to lower the concentration of greenhouse gases in our atmosphere.

Our ancestors were not gods. They had specific goals and perspectives, and were morally evaluable. While many of the Yoruba who came before me fought for freedom—particularly, but not

29 AFSCME, "'I've Been to the Mountaintop' by Dr. Martin Luther King, Jr.

exclusively, the thousands upon thousands of us who were sent on slave ships across the Atlantic—others were complicit in both indigenous and trans-Atlantic forms of slavery.[30] Some freed people even became slave owners themselves.[31]

In between the chapters of this book, I've told a history of the 1835 Malê revolt: a historically important revolt in Brazil led by people of my ethnic group. But the people in the Malê revolt, like all people, are not neatly divisible along identity lines. The wars and conflicts that led to a vast increase of people sold into racial slavery in South America were being fought on religious and national grounds in West Africa. The Malê revolt in Brazil was organized by Muslims and non-Muslims, by Yoruba and Hausa alike—that is, across the same very ethnic and religious identity lines that had waged the conflict that resulted in both of their enslavement. This was likely helped along by the fact that ethnic and religious categories did not split people up in mutually exclusive ways, and many of Yoruba in the city were Muslim. There were Yoruba amongst both those who contributed to the demise and amongst those who contributed to the defense of the racially unjust system that reigned in the empire of Brazil. Historically speaking, my inheritance includes both some of the people most morally responsible for events that helped construct the unjust world order we've inherited and some of that world order's fiercest opponents.[32]

But we don't have to take up everything our predecessors took up, we needn't accept their path as ours simply because it was theirs. As Cabral said, we should return only to the "upward" paths of our culture, the ones that lead toward something we have the responsibility to evaluate as justice.[33]

The trials and tribulations of my ancestors, colonized and enslaved, are of immense moral importance. So are the trials and tribulations of ancestors of the Tonton Macoute, the personal paramilitary force created by dictator François "Papa Doc" Duvalier in 1959. Duvalier ruled

[30] Robinson, *Black Marxism: The Making of the Black Radical Tradition*, 154–155.

[31] Reis, "Slave Resistance in Brazil: Bahia, 1807–1835," 129–130.

[32] Verdun, "If the Shoe Fits, Wear It: An Analysis of Reparations to African Americans."

[33] Cabral, "National Liberation and Culture."

over Haiti: where Christopher Columbus had landed and the same one where the fighters of the Haitian Revolution won a world-historical battle against global racial empire.

The Tonton Macoute under Duvalier inherited a noble lineage by ancestry, but an ignoble one by their actions: they enforced the rule of the Duvalier regime by way of terrorism, torture, and mass killings. Unsurprisingly, their murderous targeting of Haitian Communists earned the regime the material support of the US government—and that external meddling took this form because there were Haitians who stood ready to profit off of extreme violence to the people around them.[34]

The questions history asks of us are not the sort that we can answer with our ancestors' achievements, moral legacy, or suffering: as extraordinary and important as they might be. We can only answer them with our own actions, our own politics. I share the complex legacy of my ancestors with those in my immediate ethnic community who struggle for justice, with those who abuse their children and intimate partners, and with those who do both. What my ancestry adds to the moral character of our decisions is poorly treated as a moral inheritance and better described as a relationship of intergenerational mutual responsibility.

We should think about our ancestors. But we will win and lose our own ethical battles based on what we do for our descendants. We are defined by what kind of ancestors we choose to be.

This perspective is available to everyone. Most people's ancestors, in the genealogical sense, include a mix of people who were on right and wrong sides of history. But what makes someone a genuine ancestor, in the moral sense, is our relationship to them now: on the Yoruba view, whether we pay them respect of a certain kind. There are those who precede us in space and time whose imprint we reject. And then there are those who came before us whose projects we continue, whose steps order ours. Only these latter ones are ancestors, in the moral sense.

---

[34] Sprague, *Paramilitarism and the Assault on Democracy in Haiti*, 33–34.

This sense of moral and political inheritance relates me more directly and more powerfully to the white Quaker abolitionists and Haitian mixed-race creoles who struggled together with enslaved Africans of many nations against global racial empire than it does to the Yoruba rulers and traders who actively colluded with it. What defines our relationship to our ancestors is not what calls they made, but which of them we answer.

What is done is done. History has already built the pipes through which advantages and disadvantages flow. This sets which pipelines will have to be redirected, expanded, or destroyed if we want things to flow differently tomorrow and the next day. As Cabral explains: "I have the responsibility of deciding which of the paths I can inherit are the ones that lead upward."[35] That requires me to face the full truth about the legacies I inherit, but also the full truth about the legacy I am right now creating with my own actions and leaving for those who come after me. If I want to be an ancestor, I should take the kinds of steps worth following, and start or continue the kinds of projects worth finishing.

Many white people are descended from slaveholders, colonizers, or collaborators—but many are descendants of abolitionists, conscientious dissenters, and *their* collaborators. Their responsibility is no different from anyone else's: first, to decide which of those paths are available to follow. Second, to decide which of *those* lead upward, toward justice, and what actions they can take today to make the advancement of that path real—if not tomorrow, then perhaps the day after.

Regardless of what we've genealogically or even morally inherited, we can seek upward paths right now with our own actions. We can make our projects and decisions the source of moral inheritance for those who come after us. While many of us owe the responsibility to continue struggles for justice to our genealogical ancestors, all of us without exception owe it to our moral descendants—those who inherit the world that results from our successes and failures, regardless of parentage.

---

[35] Cabral, "National Liberation and Culture."

Some generations plant the trees, leaving it to others to build the barrels and taste what they brew. If we can do better than this, we should. But this is enough. If we want to achieve justice, in our lifetime or anyone's, we should act like ancestors.

For better or worse, our ancestors constructed this world in their image. We owe it to our descendants to rebuild it, in a new one.

APPENDIX A

The Malê Revolt

The 1835 Malê revolt in Brazil was centuries in the making.

It started in the Empire of Brazil, which had just won its independence from the Portuguese empire in 1822. The first peoples enslaved here were Indigenous, Tupi-speaking nations—soon after the arrival of the first Portuguese settlers in 1530. But disease quickly decimated the local population, and those who survived waged effective military resistance. Besides, the Jesuit missionaries among the early colonists preferred wage-working converts to slaves. Both to pacify the Company of Jesus and to fulfill labor demands, colonists conspired with the crown to traffic in Africans.[1] The first slave ships came from Africa in 1570. By the time the Malês revolted, the system they fought against had been in place for three centuries.

The world of the city of Salvador was like the wider Empire of Brazil: deeply stratified by race, slavery, and the plantation economy they built. There, the Yoruba and Hausa people, many of whom were abducted as a result of the wars in West Africa, became "Nagô" and "Haussá." A 1775 census found that whites made up 36% of the population, and enslaved Black and mixed-race people were 41% of the population.[2] The population boomed, especially among its African and "Afro-Bahian" (native Blacks descended from previous waves of trafficking) segments: by as early as 1807, free and enslaved Black peoples made up nearly three quarters of the city, a trend that likely continued by 1835. These numbers put the whole system at risk—they were good numbers for revolution.

The 1835 Malê revolt in Brazil was decades in the making.

It started in West Africa. Decades of immense social tensions in the north of the "Bight of Benin" region (of what is now Nigeria) came to a head in 1804. There, Fulani political leader and religious scholar Shehu Uthman dan Fodio led an uprising against the ruling Hausa elite: opposing their perceived heavy taxation, corruption, and intolerance of orthodox Islam.[3] The result of the revolution was a united Sokoto Caliphate, which became so large and powerful that by 1900 it had between 1 and 2.5 million slaves—a world historically large slave population, second only to the United States at its height (4 million by 1860).[4]

---

[1] Hébrard, *Slavery in Brazil: Brazilian Scholars in the Key Interpretive Debates.*

[2] Reis, *Rebelião Escrava No Brasil: A História Do Levante Dos Malês Em 1835*, 14–15.

[3] Ojo, "Beyond Diversity: Women, Scarification, and Yoruba Identity"; Nmah and Amanambu, "1804 Usman Dan Fodio's Jihad on Inter-Group Relations in the Contemporary Nigerian State"; Barcia, "'An Islamic Atlantic Revolution:' Dan Fodio's Jihād and Slave Rebellion in Bahia and Cuba, 1804–1844."

[4] McKay et al., *A History of World Societies, Combined Volume*, 755.

To the South of the newly born Sokoto Caliphate were kingdoms dominated by the kingdoms of Dahomey and Yorubaland. Since Dahomey had captured and tightly regulated trade (including human trafficking) to the west, Portuguese and other foreign traders moved eastward, cooperating with the Yoruba state of Oyo to establish a new port for trans-Atlantic slave traffic to the east, to this day referred to by the Portuguese word "Lagos." The captives of the war in the north who weren't sold into slavery in Yorubaland were transported to Lagos's Atlantic port for sale to North and South America.

These trends met over the decades from dan Fodio's 1804 jihad through the middle of the century. The Sokoto Caliphate's southward expansion produced conflict between the (now united) Hausa and Fulani militaries with Yoruba states. This expansion combined with civil and intra-ethnic wars throughout Yorubaland as the once powerful Yoruba Oyo Empire declined, generating a flood of fresh Muslim and non-Muslim captives to join the victims of slave raids and other conflicts.[5] The unlucky captured came from all of the region's ethnic groups, but the Yoruba were especially hard hit: as many as 1.62 million Yoruba were trafficked during the centuries of the trans-Atlantic slave trade, which had accelerated during this period.[6]

In West Africa, these peoples were called Hausas and Yoruba, and they were peoples divided by war. Salvador, a major city of Brazil's Bahia region and Brazil's colonial capital until 1763, was on the other side of the Atlantic—and of this political conflict.[7] There, people from these same ethnic groups met as "Nagô" and "Haussá," united by the combined condition of racialized chattel slavery. The politics on both sides of the Atlantic were linked by a system directly linking four continents in trade and politics: Africa, the site of the wars whose captives produced slaves for this growing economic and political system; Europe, via the imperial powers that secured and built the slave ports along Africa's western coast; and South America and North America.

These wars, and the human trafficking resulted from them, helped build the world. The 1835 Malê revolt in Brazil was decades in the making.

In Brazil, an important form of resistance to slavery emerged: the construction of alternative societies, where fugitives built a different social structure, aspiring toward forms of social organization based on solidarity, in response to the one premised on and sustained by slavery.[8] These were called quilombos or mocambos. The quilombos were made up of people born in Africa to different

[5] Barcia, "'An Islamic Atlantic Revolution:' Dan Fodio's Jihād and Slave Rebellion in Bahia and Cuba, 1804–1844," 7–8; Ojo, "The Organization of the Atlantic Slave Trade in Yorubaland, ca. 1777 to ca. 1856," 79–82.

[6] Eltis, "The Diaspora of Yoruba Speakers, 1650–1865: Dimensions and Implications," 25–28.

[7] Schwartz, "The 'Mocambo': Slave Resistance in Colonial Bahia."

[8] Barbosa, "O Poder de Zeferina No Quilombo Do Urubu Uma Reconstrução Histórica Político-Social," sec. 2.3.

*nations, but also Brazilian born people of African descent, Indigenous peoples—
even, in some cases, Portuguese-descended people.*[9] *The first of these in Bahia was a quilombo called Urubu. Urubu was built
in the woods on the outskirts of Salvador, on land granted to them by the
Indigenous Tupinambás.*[10] *There, the Bantu, Nagô, other ethnicities of Africans,
and Tupinambás joined forces. They sustained themselves with the help of
polycultural agricultural approach in a cooperative, fertile environment. From
this base, the quilombo mounted constant offensives to free enslaved people.*[11]

*Zeferina, a political and military leader armed with a bow and arrow, led the
fighting women and men of the Urubu quilombo against dismal odds. She and
her comrades were outnumbered more than four-to-one against a military force
equipped with firearms and horses.*[12] *Militarily, the confrontation ended in a devastating loss for Urubu—many of the surviving quilombolas were arrested and
died in prison, including Zeferina. But, viewed as part of resistance to Brazilian
slavery and colonialism, this battle was not the end of the story.*

The defeat of the 1835 Malê revolt in Brazil was mere days in the making.

*In 1791 on the French colony of Saint Domingue, revolution blossomed, and
the spiritual practice of Vodou paved the way. Boukman was a man of high
rank: he was both a Papaloi or High Priest of Vodou and a headman of a plantation. From this position he kept tabs on political developments among whites
and mixed-race Haitian creoles alike, and with this information the enslaved
Africans plotted to take the entire colony of Saint Domingue.*[13] *They set fire to
the plantations, destroying the symbolic and actual structures that had cemented
their slavery, and began fighting at once, liberating enslaved people as they went.
By 1804, they had the island—inspiring similar fights for independence from
slavery and colonialism throughout the Western Hemisphere that roared for the
remaining century.*[14]

*In 1835, in the Brazilian empire, it was Islam. Since the religion united
Africans from a variety of ethnic backgrounds, it was unsurprising that the Malê
revolt was organized in the madrassa, hidden in a rented house.*[15] *There, Manoel
Calafate and Aprígio, two free elderly Nagôs and religious leaders, engage intel-
lectually and spiritually with a predominantly enslaved set of Muslim students.*

[9] Barbosa, "O Poder de Zeferina No Quilombo Do Urubu Uma Reconstrução
Histórica Político-Social," sec. 2.1.
[10] Barbosa, "O Poder de Zeferina No Quilombo Do Urubu Uma Reconstrução
Histórica Político-Social," sec. 2.6.
[11] Barbosa, "O Poder de Zeferina No Quilombo Do Urubu Uma Reconstrução
Histórica Político-Social."
[12] Barbosa, "O Poder de Zeferina No Quilombo Do Urubu Uma Reconstrução
Histórica Político-Social," sec. 2.8.
[13] James, *The Black Jacobins: Toussaint L'Ouverture and the San Domingo
Revolution*, 86–87.
[14] James, *The Black Jacobins: Toussaint L'Ouverture and the San Domingo Revolution*.
[15] Rosa, "Du'as of the Enslaved."

But they were after more than religious development. They, along with Ahuna, an enslaved Nagô, spearheaded a plan to mount armed resistance, beginning on the last ten days of Ramadan. While the Malê revolt is often associated with Islam ("Malê" comes from the Yoruba imale, which would refer to a Muslim person), the revolt was remarkable in its breadth and organization. It included nearly equal numbers of freed and enslaved participants, and included substantial non-Muslim participation as well as participants "from virtually every ethnic group of African-born slaves and freedmen in Bahía."[16]

Their plan was foiled by the police. Sabina da Cruz, a freed Nagô, stumbled upon her husband at Manoel Calafate's iftar, discussing the plan for tomorrow's uprising. She alerted a friend, Guilhermina Rosa de Souza and fellow free Nagô. Rosa de Souza alerted the local government, including Francisco Gonçalves Martins—the chief of police, who put the police on high alert and ordered extra patrols in the parts of town identified by da Cruz. The next day, when the alliance of 600 Africans gathered for what they had hoped would be a surprise assault, they were confronted preemptively by a group of civilians, enslaved people loyal to the Crown, and soldiers who forced their way into their makeshift barracks.[17] They overcame this initial group and headed for the jail, hoping to free imprisoned comrades. They were repelled there. All told, the Africans were confronted by 1,500 police, cavalry, national guardsmen, and soldiers, most of whom were equipped with superior arms.[18] They were eventually routed and imprisoned.

The 1835 Malê revolt was defeated. It also succeeded.

From the beginning of dan Fodio's jihad until the middle of the 19th century, African-led insurrections (typically led by Hausa and/or Yoruba speaking people) were common throughout the parts of the world that those abducted in the conflict were sent—predominantly Brazil and Cuba. By 1835, the year of the Male revolt, the enslaved population of the city of Salvador was 42 percent of the population—nearly half. The situation was similar in Rio de Janeiro (then the capital of the Empire of Brazil), where the enslaved population was 38 percent. Nearly two-thirds of the enslaved population were African-born, and nearly all of these "New Negroes" ("negros novos") held freedom in their living memories, and a dangerous percentage of these had intricate knowledge of African warfare and tactics.[19]

This greatly concerned the empire of Brazil. They knew about the Haitian revolution, and knew that those they lorded over were aware as well. Some reports

---

[16]   Rosa; Graden, "An Act 'Even of Public Security': Slave Resistance, Social Tensions, and the End of the International Slave Trade to Brazil, 1835–1856," 256.

[17]   Reis, "Slave Resistance in Brazil: Bahia, 1807–1835," 125.

[18]   Reis, *Rebelião Escrava No Brasil: A História Do Levante Dos Malês Em 1835*, 89.

[19]   Graden, "An Act 'Even of Public Security': Slave Resistance, Social Tensions, and the End of the International Slave Trade to Brazil, 1835–1856," 254; Barcia and Paz, *West African Warfare in Bahia and Cuba: Soldier Slaves in the Atlantic World, 1807–1844*, 1–3; Reis, "Slave Resistance in Brazil: Bahia, 1807–1835," 124.

indicate that enslaved Brazilians spoke about Haiti boldly in Portuguese—indicating indifference to or courting of the possibility that passing whites would understand.[20] *They tried other measures: expanding the police to deport many freed Africans and bar those who remained from participating in specific religious activities; imposing a police curfew; and barring people of African descent from owning real estate.*[21] *But those efforts didn't work: year by year, the number of quilombos increased and "capoeira gangs" (practitioners of an Afro-Brazilian martial art) humiliated the police in the streets of Rio de Janeiro.*[22] *By 1850 they feared the writing was on the wall. They had been fortunate to survive the 1835 revolt. If slavery was maintained in the Empire of Brazil, they could expect to eventually meet the fate that the French met in the Haitian revolution.*

In 1850 they stopped the importation of Africans, hoping to cut off the flow of insurrectionary sentiment from abroad. But the rebellions kept coming, and the quilombos kept flourishing. In 1888, the Empire of Brazil—the last holdout in the Western hemisphere—finally abolished slavery.[23]

The 1835 Malê continued a fight that we can help finish.

---

[20]   Reis, "Slave Resistance in Brazil: Bahia, 1807–1835," 120–121.

[21]   Graden, "An Act 'Even of Public Security': Slave Resistance, Social Tensions, and the End of the International Slave Trade to Brazil, 1835–1856," 264.

[22]   Graden, "An Act 'Even of Public Security': Slave Resistance, Social Tensions, and the End of the International Slave Trade to Brazil, 1835–1856," 271–272.

[23]   Bucciferro, "A Lucrative End: Abolition, Immigration, and the New Occupational Hierarchy in Southeast Brazil."

Colonialism and Climate Vulnerability

Olúfẹ́mi O. Táíwò, Anna Saez de Tejada Cuenca, and Chun Hin Tsoi

Introduction and Data

The book contends that global racial empire helped establish patterns of accumulation that explain both racial and geopolitical stratifications (i.e., between the Global North and Global South) in key areas, including wealth and infrastructure. This broad perspective is outlined in chapter 2. In chapter 5, the book applies this general insight to environmental vulnerability, particularly as it relates to climate crisis. The figures used in that chapter come from preliminary results of the empirical analysis done by the co-authors of this Appendix and presented here.

To compute a climate change vulnerability index and study its relationship with colonial and economic indicators, we collect data from a number of different sources. As a starting point, we use the list of existing countries and territories, plus their ISO codes and geographical coordinates, compiled by Tadas Tamošauskas.[1] From this list, we only use entries corresponding to autonomous countries (as opposed to foreign territories of other countries).

Second, we include information on whether countries were colonized, colonized other countries, or both, from the ICOW Colonial History data set.[2] This list contains an entry for every country and territory, and detailed information on whether that country was ever ruled by a foreign colonial power, which one, the dates in which the colonial rule started and ended, the way in which independence was gained, etc. We discard observations corresponding to extinct countries or to foreign territories of current countries. In the case of countries that first were colonized, but after becoming independent went on to colonize others (Australia, Belgium, New Zealand, and the United States) we include them in the "Colonizer" category, given that colonizing others is the most recent event in their colonial history.

---

[1] Available at <https://gist.github.com/tadast/8827699>. Accessed on December 31, 2019.
[2] Paul R. Hensel. "ICOW Colonial History Data Set, version 1.1," 2018. <http://www.paulhensel.org/icowcol.html>. Accessed on December 31, 2019.

Two alternative classifications of countries, apart from whether they were colonized and whether they were colonizers, are the classification between Global North and Global South, which we take from the 2010–2015 Wikimedia strategic plan,[3] and the classification between developed and developing nations, for which we use the United Nations M49 list.[4]

The first economic indicator we use is each country's gross domestic product (GDP) per capita, taken from the World Bank (WB).[5] We take its most recent year of collection (2018). From the United Nations' Human Development Index (HDI) data,[6] we use several economic, social, health, and infrastructure indicators (listed in our description of the vulnerability index). For each indicator, we use the latest year for which there are data available; this is usually 2018, but some of the variables were collected in 2015 and the dataset lacks more recent values of them.

We use two sources of data to measure countries' freedom and governance. One is the Freedom House's (FH) data on political rights and civil liberties,[7] of which we use the 2018 rates. The other one is the governance data set collected by Kaufmann, Kraay, and Zoido-Lobaton (KKZ),[8] of which we also use the 2018 indicators (the most recent available).

Methods

Calculation of the Climate Change Vulnerability Index

We compute a climate change vulnerability index following Adger, Brooks, and Kelly (2015).[9] We use the following ten[10] variables (in parentheses, the

---

[3] Available at <https://strategy.wikimedia.org/wiki/Wikimedia_Movement_Strategic_Plan_Summary>. Accessed on April 12, 2020.

[4] Available at <https://unstats.un.org/unsd/methodology/m49>. Accessed on April 12, 2020.

[5] Available at <https://data.worldbank.org/indicator/NY.GDP.PCAP.CD>. Accessed on April 19, 2020.

[6] Available at <http://hdr.undp.org/en/data>. Accessed on December 31, 2019.

[7] Available at <https://freedomhouse.org/countries/freedom-world/scores>. Accessed on December 31, 2019.

[8] D. Kaufmann, A. Kraay, and P. Zoido. "Governance Matters." *World Bank Policy Research Working Paper* 2196 (1999). Data available at <http://info.worldbank.org/governance/wgi>. Accessed on December 31, 2019.

[9] N. Brooks, W. N. Adger, and P. M. Kelly. "The Determinants of Vulnerability and Adaptive Capacity at the National Level and the Implications for Adaptation." *Global Environmental Change* 15, no. 2 (2005), 151–163.

[10] The original index by Brooks et al. (2005) is based on 11 variables. However, we were unable to download data on the male/female literacy ratio, so we base our index

data set from which they are taken): life expectancy (HDI), maternal mortality ratio (HDI), dietary adequacy (HDI),[11] adult literacy rate (HDI), youth literacy rate (HDI), percentage of population with access to sanitation (HDI), government effectiveness (KKZ), voice and accountability (KKZ), civil liberties (FH), and political rights (FH).

Each one of these variables is measured on a different scale. To normalize them and build a composite index, we repeat the steps of Adger et al. (2005). First, for every one of these variables, we classify countries by its quintiles. Then, countries in the "best" quintile get a score of 1 in that variable; countries in the "second best" quintile receive a score of 2, etc. Countries in the "worst" quintile of that variable receive a score of 5. "Best" and "worst" are defined according to the variable's scale. For instance, in the case of life expectancy, the top quintile is the best; in the case of the FH's variables, where a score of 1 signifies the highest degree liberty and a score of 7 the lowest, the "best" quintile is that of the lowest numerical values of the variable. At this point, each country takes an integer value from 1 to 5 in each one of the variables, where 1 is the best possible score and 5 is the worst. Finally, for each country, we average its score over the different variables[12] to obtain an index between 1 and 5, where 1 is the lowest vulnerability (or the highest preparedness) to climate change, and 5 is the highest vulnerability (or lowest preparedness).

Results

Figure 5.1 shows the distribution of the climate change vulnerability index by country type (based on countries' colonial history). There is a stark difference between countries that colonized others, and those that were colonized. With the exception of three outliers (China, Russia, and Turkey, with vulnerability indices between 2.5 and 3), all countries that colonized others have vulnerability indices between 1 (the minimum value) and 1.625. In contrast, countries that were colonized have high values of the vulnerability index: among them, the index's percentile 25 equals to 2.70—in other words, 75 percent of the countries that were colonized now have a vulnerability index of 2.7 or higher. To see this more clearly, note that of the 155 countries that were colonized,

---

on 10 variables instead. Brooks et al., "The Determinants of Vulnerability and Adaptive Capacity at the National Level and the Implications for Adaptation."

[11] The original index by Brooks et al. (2005) uses caloric intake, which we were not able to find, so we substituted it for dietary adequacy data. Brooks et al., "The Determinants of Vulnerability and Adaptive Capacity at the National Level and the Implications for Adaptation."

[12] For some countries, data are available for fewer than 10 of the indicators. In those cases, we average over the variables for which data exist.

only seven have a vulnerability index of 1.6 or lower, that is, only seven of the colonized countries have a vulnerability index that overlaps with that of countries that were colonizers (with the exception of the three outliers mentioned above). Twenty-five percent of countries that were colonized have a climate change vulnerability index of 4.2 or higher. These are very high values of this index (recall that the maxim value it can take is 5). Countries that were neither colonized nor colonizers have a median vulnerability index that is fairly low (1.725), but they have the largest variability. Twenty-five percent of countries in the "neither" category have a climate change vulnerability index of 1.4 or lower, and 25 percent of them have an index of 3.275 or higher, with the rest falling between these two values.

Recall that, in our classification of countries by their colonial history, countries that first were colonized and then went on to colonize others had been counted as colonizers, given that colonizing others is the most recent of their colonial history events. To see how much our results change if we challenge this classification, we take those four countries (Australia, Belgium, New Zealand, and the United States) and create a separate colonial history category, which we call "Both." Figure 5. 2 shows the distribution of the vulnerability index using four categories, instead of three. As we can see, those four countries account for the lowest values of the vulnerability index, so when they are plotted separately, the percentiles of the index for the countries that colonized others ("Colonizer" box) increase, although the values of the index are still significantly lower than for colonized countries.

Two alternative classification systems between countries, with their respective vulnerability index distributions, are shown in Appendix B.1 and Appendix B.2. The former separates countries between the Global North and the Global South (Wikimedia), while the latter classifies them as developed or developing nations (UN M-49). The results of these two figures are extremely similar, as most countries classified as Global North are also classified as developed nations. All of the Global North's countries have a vulnerability index of 3 or lower, whereas 75 percent of the countries in the Global South have an index of 2.8 or higher.

In these three figures, we can see that countries that were colonized are much more vulnerable to climate change than those that colonized others, and that poorer countries are more vulnerable than wealthier ones. Is there a relationship between a country's colonial history and its current income? Appendix B.3 shows the distribution of GDP per capita by country colonial history. The difference in income between colonial powers and countries that were colonies is very clear. Among countries that were colonizers, the minimum GDP per capita is $8,759, and for 75 percent of them the GDP per capita is $21,437 or higher. Among countries that were colonized, the minimum GDP per capita is $293, and 75 percent of them have values of $9,689 or lower. So, although there exist a few wealthy countries that were colonized, the majority of former colonies have a lower GDP per capita than almost all of the colonizers. Again,

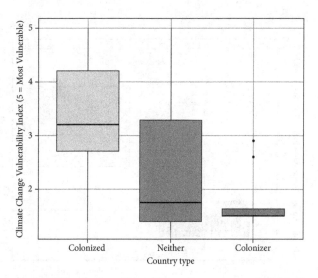

Appendix B.1 Distribution of the climate change vulnerability index, which ranges from 1 to 5 (with 5 being the most vulnerable), by country type based on colonial history. The left box contains the countries that were colonized by other countries; the right box, the countries that colonized others; the middle box contains the countries that neither colonized others nor were colonized.

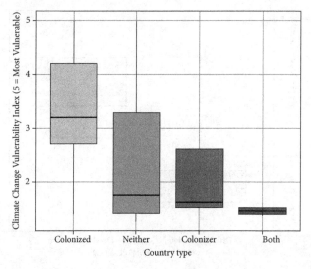

Appendix B.2 Distribution of the climate change vulnerability index by country type based on colonial history, where countries that both were colonized and colonized others are plotted separately from those that only colonized others.

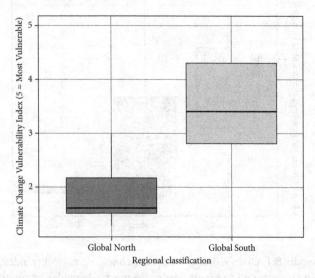

Appendix B.3 Distribution of the climate change vulnerability index by country type, using the Wikimedia 2010–2015 strategic plan's regional classification. The left box contains the Global North; the right box contains the Global South.

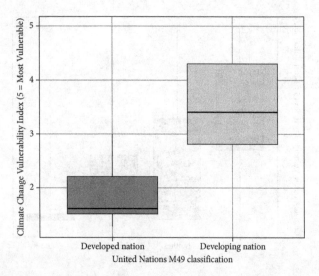

Appendix B.4 Distribution of the climate change vulnerability index by country type, using the United Nations' M-49 classification. The left box contains developed nations; the right box contains developing nations.

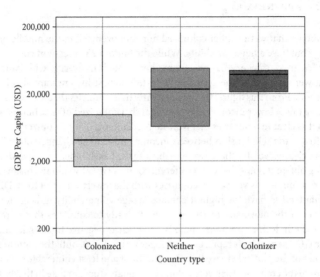

Appendix B.5 Distribution of GDP per capita in USD, represented in a logarithmic scale, by country type based on colonial history. The left box contains the countries that were colonized by other countries; the right box, the countries that colonized others; the middle box contains the countries that neither colonized others nor were colonized.

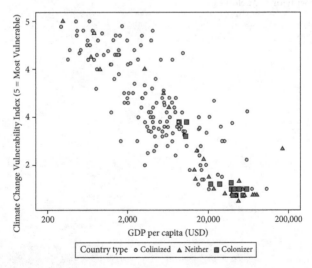

Appendix B.6 Relationship between income (GDP per capita in USD, in logarithmic scale; horizontal axis) and climate change vulnerability index (from 1 to 5, where 5 is the most vulnerable; vertical axis). Each circle represents a country that was colonized; each square represents a country that colonized other countries; each triangle represents a country that was neither a colonizer nor it was colonized.

countries that were neither colonized nor colonizers fall in the middle on average but have a huge variability. While the bottom 25 percent of countries in the "neither" category has an income low enough to overlap with countries that were colonized, the countries with the highest incomes are also in this category. From this figure, we can see clearly that countries that were colonized have a much lower income than countries that colonized others, but the story is not as clear for countries that were neither colonized nor colonizers.

To see the relationship between income and climate change vulnerability more clearly, we plot these two variables against each other in Appendix B.4, using different point shapes for different country types by colonial history. The correlation here is very clear: countries with the lowest values of the GDP per capita tend to have the highest climate change vulnerability indices (top left corner of the plot), and these correspond mostly to countries that were colonized (circles). From there, there is a very clear negative linear relationship (the GDP per capita is represented in logarithmic scale), until the bottom right corner of the plot, where we find the wealthiest and least vulnerable countries. Most of the countries that were colonizers (squares) accumulate in that bottom right corner, with the exception again of the three outliers (China, Russia, and Turkey), which lay around the middle of the scatter plot. Countries that were neither colonized nor colonizers (triangles) are dispersed across all the levels of income and vulnerability, but most of them lay on the wealthier, less vulnerable side, showing again that they have a higher overlap with colonial powers than with former colonies.

References

Aaronson, Daniel, Jacob Faber, Daniel Hartley, Bhashkar Mazumder, and Patrick Sharkey. "The Long-Run Effects of the 1930s HOLC 'Redlining' Maps on Place-Based Measures of Economic Opportunity and Socioeconomic Success." *Regional Science and Urban Economics* 86 (2020): 103622.

Abubakar, Y. Abdul-Rahman, Nasidi a Yahaya, and Turaki A. Hassan. "Nigeria: National Assembly Passes N4.6 Trillion Budget for 2010." allAfrica.com, March 26, 2010. https://allafrica.com/stories/201003260 735.html.

Acemoglu, Daron, Simon Johnson, and James Robinson. "The Rise of Europe: Atlantic Trade, Institutional Change, and Economic Growth." *American Economic Review* 95, no. 3 (2005): 546–579.

Adegbija, Efurosibina. "A Comparative Study of Politeness Phenomena in Nigerian English, Yoruba and Ogori." *Multilingua* 8, no. 1 (1989): 57–80.

Adigun, Olalekan Waheed. "A Critical Analysis of the Relationship between Climate Change, Land Disputes, and the Patterns of Farmers/Herdsmen's Conflicts in Nigeria." *Canadian Social Science* 15, no. 3 (2019): 76–89.

Adow, Mohamed. "The Climate Debt," April 14, 2020. https://www.foreignaffa irs.com/articles/world/2020-04-13/climate-debt.

AFSCME. "'I've Been to the Mountaintop' by Dr. Martin Luther King, Jr." Accessed April 23, 2020. https://www.afscme.org/about/history/mlk/moun taintop.

A Just Climate.org. October 2018. Accessed April 17, 2020. https://ajustclim ate.org.

Albritton Jonsson, Fredrik. "The Industrial Revolution in the Anthropocene." *Journal of Modern History* 84, no. 3 (2012): 679–696.

Alexander, Herbert B. "Brazilian and United States Slavery Compared." *Journal of Negro History* 7, no. 4 (1922): 349–364.

Algan, Yann, and Pierre Cahuc. "Inherited Trust and Growth." *American Economic Review* 100, no. 5 (2010): 2060–2092.

American Civil Liberties Union. "ACLU Report Details Horrors Suffered by Orleans Parish Prisoners in Wake of Hurricane Katrina." August 10, 2006. Accessed January 19, 2021. https://www.aclu.org/press-releases/aclu-rep ort-details-horrors-suffered-orleans-parish-prisoners-wake-hurricane-katrina.

Amin, Samir. "Underdevelopment and Dependence in Black Africa: Origins and Contemporary Forms." *The Journal of Modern African Studies* 10, no. 4 (1972): 503–524.

Anderson, M. Kat. *Tending the Wild: Native American Knowledge and the Management of California's Natural Resources*. Berkeley: University of California Press, 2013.

Anscombe, Frank J. "Rejection of Outliers." *Technometrics* 2, no. 2 (1960): 123–146.

Araujo, Ana Lucia. *Reparations for Slavery and the Slave Trade: A Transnational and Comparative History*. Bloomsbury Publishing, 2017.

Archibong, Belinda, and Nonso Obikili. "Convict Labor and the Costs of Colonial Infrastructure: Evidence from Prisons in British Nigeria, 1920–1938." Available at *Social Science Research Network, SSRN 3395458*, 2019.

Archibong, Belinda, and Nonso Obikili. "Prison Labor: The Price of Prisons and the Lasting Effects of Incarceration." *African Economic History Working Paper Series*, no. 52 (2020): 1–95.

Asch, Chris Myers, and George Derek Musgrove. *Chocolate City*. University of North Carolina Press, 2017. www.jstor.org/stable/10.5149/9781469635873_asch.

Autor, David H., David Dorn, and Gordon H. Hanson. "The China Shock: Learning from Labor-Market Adjustment to Large Changes in Trade." *Annual Review of Economics* 8, no. 1 (October 31, 2016): 205–240. https://doi.org/10.1146/annurev-economics-080315-015041.

Avalon Project. "Confederate States of America: Mississippi Secession." Accessed March 5, 2020. https://avalon.law.yale.edu/19th_century/csa_missec.asp.

Awolalu, J. Omosade. "The Yoruba Philosophy of Life." *Presence Africaine* 73, no. 1 (1970): 20–38.

Ayling, Julie, and Neil Gunningham. "Non-State Governance and Climate Policy: The Fossil Fuel Divestment Movement." *Climate Policy* 17, no. 2 (2017): 131–149.

Baer, Hans A. "Global Capitalism and Climate Change." In *Handbook on International Political Economy*, edited by Ralph Pettman, 395–414. World Scientific, 2012.

Baldwin, James. "The Black Scholar Interviews: James Baldwin." *The Black Scholar* 5, no. 4 (1973): 33–42.

Baldwin, James. *Notes of a Native Son*. Beacon Press, 1984.

Baldwin, James, and William F. Buckley, Cambridge Union Society (University of Cambridge), and National Educational Television and Radio Center. *Debate: Baldwin vs Buckley*. New York, NY: National Educational Television and Radio Center, 1965.

Balfour, Lawrie. "Reparations after Identity Politics." *Political Theory* 33, no. 6 (2005): 786–811.

Barbosa, Silvia. "O Poder de Zeferina No Quilombo Do Urubu." *Identidade!* 7, no. 7 (2005): 24–30.

Barbosa, Silvia Maria Silva. "O Poder de Zeferina No Quilombo do Urubu Uma Reconstrução Histórica Político-Social," 2003.

Barcia, Manuel. "'An Islamic Atlantic Revolution:' Dan Fodio's Jihād and Slave Rebellion in Bahia and Cuba, 1804–1844." *Journal of African Diaspora Archaeology and Heritage* 2, no. 1 (2013): 6–17.

Barcia, Manuel, and Manuel Barcia Paz. *West African Warfare in Bahia and Cuba: Soldier Slaves in the Atlantic World, 1807–1844.* Past & Present Book, 2014.

Barnes, Colin. "The Social Model of Disability: Valuable or Irrelevant." In *The Routledge Handbook of Disability Studies* edited by Nick Watson, Alan Roulstone, and Carol Thomas, 12–29. London: Routledge.

Barnes, Elizabeth. *The Minority Body: A Theory of Disability.* Oxford University Press, 2016.

Barragán, Rossana. "Working Silver for the World: Mining Labor and Popular Economy in Colonial Potosí." *Hispanic American Historical Review* 97, no. 2 (2017): 193–222.

Bauman, H.-Dirksen, and Joseph Murray. "Reframing: From Hearing Loss to Deaf Gain." *Deaf Studies Digital Journal* 1, no. 1 (2009): 1–10.

Bayly, Christopher Alan. *Indigenous and Colonial Origins of Comparative Economic Development: The Case of Colonial India and Africa.* The World Bank, 2008.

BBC East Midlands. "St Ann's Riot: The Changing Face of Race Relations, 60 Years On." *BBC News*, August 25, 2018, sec. Nottingham. https://www.bbc.com/news/uk-england-nottinghamshire-45207246.

Beckert, Sven. "Emancipation and Empire: Reconstructing the Worldwide Web of Cotton Production in the Age of the American Civil War." *The American Historical Review* 109, no. 5 (2004): 1405–1438.

Beeman, Richard R. "Labor Forces and Race Relations: A Comparative View of the Colonization of Brazil and Virginia." *Political Science Quarterly* 86, no. 4 (1971): 609–636.

Belafonte, Harry, and Michael Shnayerson. *My Song: A Memoir.* Vintage, 2011.

Bell, Derrick A. "Brown v. Board of Education and the Interest-Convergence Dilemma." *Harvard Law Review* 93, no. 3 (1980): 518–533. https://doi.org/10.2307/1340546.

Berger, Dan. "The Malcolm X Doctrine: The Republic of New Afrika and National Liberation on US Soil." *New World Coming: The Sixties and the Shaping of Global Consciousness* (2009): 46–55.

Berman, Ari. "Voter Suppression: The Confederacy Rises Again," September 4, 2012. https://www.thenation.com/article/archive/voter-suppression-confederacy-rises-again/.

Bevins, Vincent. *The Jakarta Method: Washington's Anticommunist Crusade and the Mass Murder Program that Shaped Our World.* Hachette UK, 2020.

Bidadanure, Juliana Uhuru. "The Political Theory of Universal Basic Income." *Annual Review of Political Science* 22, no. 1 (May 11, 2019): 481–501. https://doi.org/10.1146/annurev-polisci-050317-070954.

Billings, Stephen B., Emily Gallagher, and Lowell Ricketts. "Let the Rich Be Flooded: The Unequal Impact of Hurricane Harvey on Household Debt." *Available at SSRN 3396611*, 2019.

"Biloxi-Chitimacha-Choctaw Get $48 Million to Move off of Louisiana Island." Accessed April 14, 2020. https://indiancountrytoday.com/archive/biloxi-chitimacha-choctaw-get-48-million-to-move-off-of-louisiana-island-1T8 lBSRW6kSnY34zw0KElw.

Blackhawk, Ned. *Violence over the Land: Indians and Empires in the Early American West.* Harvard University Press, 2009.

BlackPast. "(1857) Frederick Douglass, 'If There Is No Struggle, There Is No Progress,'" January 25, 2007. https://www.blackpast.org/african-american-history/1857-frederick-douglass-if-there-no-struggle-there-no-progress/.

Blain, Keisha N. *Set the World on Fire: Black Nationalist Women and the Global Struggle for Freedom.* University of Pennsylvania Press, 2018.

Bosman, Julie. "Michigan to Pay $600 Million to Victims of Flint Water Crisis." *New York Times.* 2020. Accessed September 21, 2020. https://www.nytimes.com/2020/08/19/us/flint-water-crisis-settlement.html.

Boxill, Bernard. "Black Reparations." *Stanford Encyclopedia of Philosophy*, 2011. Accessed September 1, 2020. https://plato.stanford.edu/entries/black-reparations/.

Boxill, Bernard R. "A Lockean Argument for Black Reparations." *Journal of Ethics* 7, no. 1 (2003): 63–91.

Boxill, Bernard R. "The Morality of Reparation." *Social Theory and Practice* 2, no. 1 (1972): 113–123.

Bozuwa, Johanna. "Public Ownership for Energy Democracy." TheNextSystem.org, September 3, 2018. https://thenextsystem.org/learn/stories/public-ownership-energy-democracy.

Brading, David A., and Harry E. Cross. "Colonial Silver Mining: Mexico and Peru." *The Hispanic American Historical Review* 52, no. 4 (1972): 545–579.

Bradshaw, York W., and Jie Huang. "Intensifying Global Dependency: Foreign Debt, Structural Adjustment, and Third World Underdevelopment." *The Sociological Quarterly* 32, no. 3 (1991): 321–342.

Brecher, Jeremy. "Did We Just Witness the First Union-Authorized Climate Strike in the United States?" Common Dreams. 2020. Accessed April 18, 2020. https://www.commondreams.org/views/2020/03/01/did-we-just-witness-first-union-authorized-climate-strike-united-states.

Brida, Ange-Benjamin, Tom Owiyo, and Youba Sokona. "Loss and Damage from the Double Blow of Flood and Drought in Mozambique." *International Journal of Global Warming* 5, no. 4 (2013): 514–531.

Bridges, Linda, and John R. Coyne Jr. *Strictly Right: William F. Buckley Jr. and the American Conservative Movement.* John Wiley & Sons, 2007.

Brooks, Nick, W. Neil Adger, and P. Mick Kelly. "The Determinants of Vulnerability and Adaptive Capacity at the National Level and the Implications for Adaptation." *Adaptation to Climate Change: Perspectives across Scales* 15, no. 2 (July 1, 2005): 151–163. https://doi.org/10.1016/j.gloenvcha.2004.12.006.

Brophy, Alfred L. "Reparations Talk: Reparations for Slavery and the Tort Law Analogy." *BC Third World LJ* 24 (2004): 81.

Bucciferro, Justin R. "A Lucrative End: Abolition, Immigration, and the New Occupational Hierarchy in Southeast Brazil." *Cliometrica* (2020): 1–28.

Buccola, Nicholas. *The Fire Is upon Us: James Baldwin, William F. Buckley Jr., and the Debate over Race in America*. Princeton University Press, 2019.

Buckley Jr., William F. "Why the South Must Prevail." *National Review* 4, no. 7 (1957): 148–149.

Bullard, Robert D. *Dumping in Dixie: Race, Class, and Environmental Quality*. Routledge, 2018.

Bureau of Labor Statistics. "Optometrists." Accessed January 7, 2020. https://www.bls.gov/oes/current/oes291041.htm.

Burke, Teresa Blankmeyer. "Bioethics and the Deaf Community." *Signs and Voices: Deaf Culture, Identity, Language, and Arts* (2006): 63–74.

Butt, Daniel. "Repairing Historical Wrongs and the End of Empire." *Social & Legal Studies* 21, no. 2 (2012): 227–242.

Cabral, Amilcar. "National Liberation and Culture." *Transition*, no. 45 (1974): 12–17. https://doi.org/10.2307/2935020.

Cabral, Amílcar. "National Liberation and Culture." History Is a Weapon. Accessed November 10, 2019. https://www.historyisaweapon.com/defcon1/cabralnlac.html.

Calabresi, Guido. "Some Thoughts on Risk Distribution and the Law of Torts." *The Yale Law Journal* 70, no. 4 (1961): 499–553.

Campbell, Alexia Fernández. "The 11-Day Teachers Strike in Chicago Paid Off." Vox, November 1, 2019. https://www.vox.com/identities/2019/11/1/20943464/chicago-teachers-strike-deal.

Cappucci, Matthew, and Andrew Freedman. "Europe to See Third Major Heat Wave This Summer, as Temperatures Soar from France to Scandinavia." *Washington Post*, August 22, 2019, sec. Capital Weather Gang. https://www.washingtonpost.com/weather/2019/08/22/europe-see-third-major-heat-wave-this-year-temperatures-soar-france-scandinavia/.

Caribbean Community (CARICOM) Secretariat. "Reparations for Native Genocide and Slavery." Accessed July 11, 2017. http://www.caricom.org/reparations-for-native-genocide-and-slavery.

Caribbean Reparations Commission. "10-Point Reparation Plan." 10-Point Reparation Plan. Accessed November 26, 2020. https://caricomreparations.org/caricom/caricoms-10-point-reparation-plan/.

Center for Climate Change Communication. "America Misled: How the Fossil Fuel Industry Deliberately Misled Americans about Climate Change,"

October 14, 2019. https://www.climatechangecommunication.org/amer
ica-misled/.

Century Foundation. "The Chicago Teachers Strike Is a Fight for the Common
Good," October 28, 2019. https://tcf.org/content/commentary/chicago-
teachers-strike-fight-common-good/.

Chakravorti, Bhaskar, and Ravi Shankar Chaturvedi. "Ranking 42 Countries
by Ease of Doing Digital Business." *Harvard Business Review*, September 5,
2019. https://hbr.org/2019/09/ranking-42-countries-by-ease-of-doing-digi
tal-business.

Cheeseman, N., and J. Fisher. *Authoritarian Africa: Repression, Resistance, and
the Power of Ideas*. African World Histories. Oxford University Press, 2019.
https://books.google.com/books?id=zrFWxwEACAAJ.

Chertoff, Emily. "Occupy Wounded Knee: A 71-Day Siege and a Forgotten
Civil Rights Movement." The *Atlantic*, October 23, 2012. https://www.thea
tlantic.com/national/archive/2012/10/occupy-wounded-knee-a-71-day-
siege-and-a-forgotten-civil-rights-movement/263998/.

Chow, Tobita. "We Don't Have Time to End Capitalism—But Growth Can Still
Be Green." *In These Times*, April 15, 2019. http://inthesetimes.com/article/
21830/capitalism-economic-debates-alternatives-capitalism-green-gro
wth-investment.

Clark, Alexis. "Tulsa's 'Black Wall Street' Flourished as a Self-Contained Hub
in Early 1900s." *History*. Accessed September 24, 2020. https://www.history.
com/news/black-wall-street-tulsa-race-massacre.

"Climate Change Affected Australia's Wildfires, Scientists Confirm." *The
New York Times*. Accessed April 7, 2020. https://www.nytimes.com/2020/
03/04/climate/australia-wildfires-climate-change.html.

"Climate Change Is Contributing to California's Fires." *Science*, October 25,
2019. https://www.nationalgeographic.com/science/2019/10/climate-cha
nge-california-power-outage/.

Climate Home News. "Public Opinion on Climate Change Is Up but Let's Not
Forget Lessons from the Past," March 4, 2020. https://www.climatechangen
ews.com/2020/03/04/public-opinion-climate-change-lets-not-forget-less
ons-past/.

Climate Outreach. "Engaging the Public on Climate Risks and Adaptation."
Accessed April 7, 2020. https://climateoutreach.org/resources/engaging-
public-on-climate-risks-and-adaptation/.

Climate Reality. "The Climate Denial Machine: How the Fossil Fuel Industry
Blocks Climate Action.," September 5, 2019. https://www.climaterealityproj
ect.org/blog/climate-denial-machine-how-fossil-fuel-industry-blocks-
climate-action.

CNN, Michael Martinez. "Flint, Michigan: Neglected Because City Is Black,
Poor?" CNN. Accessed September 21, 2020. https://www.cnn.com/2016/
01/26/us/flint-michigan-water-crisis-race-poverty/index.html.

Coates, Ta-Nehisi. "The Case for Reparations." *The Atlantic*, June 2014. https://www.theatlantic.com/magazine/archive/2014/06/the-case-for-reparations/361631/.

Coates, Ta-Nehisi, and Coleman Hughes. "Should America Pay Reparations for Slavery? Ta-Nehisi Coates v. Coleman Hughes." *The Guardian*, June 19, 2019, sec. Opinion. https://www.theguardian.com/commentisfree/2019/jun/19/reparations-slavery-ta-nehisi-coates-v-coleman-hughes.

Coffey, Wallace, and Rebecca Tsosie. "Rethinking the Tribal Sovereignty Doctrine: Cultural Sovereignty and the Collective Future of Indian Nations." *Stanford Law & Policyy Review* 12 (2001): 191.

Cohen, Joshua, and Charles Sabel. "Extra Rempublicam Nulla Justitia?" *Philosophy & Public Affairs* 34, no. 2 (2006): 147–175.

Cook, John, Geoffrey Supran, Naomi Oreskes, Ed Maibach, and Stephan Lewandowsky. "Exxon Has Misled Americans on Climate Change for Decades. Here's How to Fight Back." *The Guardian*, October 23, 2019, sec. Opinion. https://www.theguardian.com/commentisfree/2019/oct/23/exxon-climate-change-fossil-fuels-disinformation.

Cooperation Jackson. "The Jackson Just Transition Plan." Accessed September 24, 2020. https://cooperationjackson.org/blog/2015/11/10/the-jackson-just-transition-plan.

Corlett, J Angelo. "Race, Racism, and Reparations." *Journal of Social Philosophy* 36, no. 4 (2005): 568–585.

Coulthard, Glen. "Place against Empire: Understanding Indigenous Anti-Colonialism." *Affinities: A Journal of Radical Theory, Culture, and Action*, 2010.

Crosby, Alfred W. "Columbian Exchange." *Food and History* 7, no. 1 (2009): 225.

Cuenca-Esteban, Javier. "India's Contribution to the British Balance of Payments, 1757–1812." *Explorations in Economic History* 44, no. 1 (2007): 154–176.

Curran, Robert Emmett. *The Bicentennial History of Georgetown University: From Academy to University, 1789–1889*. Vol. 1. Georgetown University Press, 1993.

Curtis, Mark. "The New Colonialism: Britain's Scramble for Africa's Energy and Mineral Resources War on Want," 2016. Accessed June 20, 2020. https://waronwant.org/resources/new-colonialism-britains-scramble-africas-energy-and-mineral-resources.

Danson, J. T. "On the Existing Connection between American Slavery and the British Cotton Manufacture." *Journal of the Statistical Society of London* 20, no. 1 (1857): 1–21.

Darity Jr., William A., and A. Kirsten Mullen. *From Here to Equality: Reparations for Black Americans in the Twenty-First Century*. UNC Press Books, 2020.

Darity, William. "Stratification Economics: The Role of Intergroup Inequality." *Journal of Economics and Finance* 29, no. 2 (2005): 144.

Darity, William, and Jessica Gordon Nembhard. "Racial and Ethnic Economic Inequality: The International Record." *American Economic Review* 90, no. 2 (2000): 308–311.

Dawson, Ashley. "We Can't Beat Climate Change under Capitalism. Socialism Is the Only Way." *In These Times*, April 15, 2019. http://inthesetimes.com/article/21837/socialism-anti-capitalism-economic-reform.

Deloria, Vine. *God Is Red: A Native View of Religion.* Fulcrum Publishing, 2003.

Deryugina, Tatyana, Laura Kawano, and Steven Levitt. "The Economic Impact of Hurricane Katrina on Its Victims: Evidence from Individual Tax Returns." *American Economic Journal: Applied Economics* 10, no. 2 (2018): 202–233.

Desmond, Matthew. "Eviction and the Reproduction of Urban Poverty." *American Journal of Sociology* 118, no. 1 (2012): 88–133.

Dickerman, Kenneth, and Simone Francescangeli. "Perspective: What Life Is Like for the Teenage Miners of Potosi, Bolivia." *Washington Post.* Accessed September 8, 2020. https://www.washingtonpost.com/news/in-sight/wp/2018/09/14/what-life-is-like-for-the-teenage-miners-of-potosi-bolivia/.

Dissent Magazine. "The Reparations Debate." Accessed April 26, 2020. https://www.dissentmagazine.org/online_articles/the-reparations-debate.

Dissent Magazine. "The Spanish-Speaking William F. Buckley." Accessed October 29, 2019. https://www.dissentmagazine.org/online_articles/span ish-speaking-william-f-buckley.

Docquier, Frédéric, Olivier Lohest, and Abdeslam Marfouk. "Brain Drain in Developing Countries." *The World Bank Economic Review* 21, no. 2 (2007): 193–218.

Dorninger, Christian, Alf Hornborg, David J. Abson, Henrik von Wehrden, Anke Schaffartzik, Stefan Giljum, John-Oliver Engler, Robert L. Feller, Klaus Hubacek, and Hanspeter Wieland. "Global Patterns of Ecologically Unequal Exchange: Implications for Sustainability in the 21st Century." *Ecological Economics* 179 (January 1, 2021): 106824. https://doi.org/10.1016/j.ecolecon.2020.106824.

Dörrie, Peter. "Europe Has Spent Years Trying to Prevent 'Chaos' in the Sahel. It Failed." *World Politics Review.* Accessed January 14, 2020. https://www.worldpoliticsreview.com/articles/27977/europe-has-spent-years-trying-to-prevent-chaos-in-the-sahel-it-failed.

Douglass, Frederick. "Address to the National Convention of Colored Men, Louisville, Ky." Louisville, 1883. Library of Congress. https://www.loc.gov/item/mfd.24003/.

Dubois, Laurent. "The Haitian Revolution and the Sale of Louisiana." *Southern Quarterly* 44, no. 3 (2007): 18.

Dutta, Diya. "Elite Capture and Corruption: Concepts and Definitions." *National Council of Applied Economic Research* (2009): 1–16.

Dworkin, Ronald. *Sovereign Virtue: The Theory and Practice of Equality.* Harvard University Press, 2002.

Dworkin, Ronald. "What Is Equality? Part 1: Equality of Welfare." *Philosophy & Public Affairs* (1981): 185–246.

Dworkin, Ronald. "What Is Equality? Part 2: Equality of Resources." *Philosophy & Public Affairs* (1981): 283–345.

Editors, History com. "Louisiana Purchase." History. Accessed January 18, 2021. https://www.history.com/topics/westward-expansion/louisiana-purchase.

Egbuta, Ugwumba. "Understanding the Herder-Farmer Conflict in Nigeria." *Conflict Trends* 2018, no. 3 (2018): 40–48.

Elbein, Saul. "These Are the Defiant 'Water Protectors' of Standing Rock." National Geographic, January 26, 2017. https://www.nationalgeographic.com/news/2017/01/tribes-standing-rock-dakota-access-pipeline-advancement/.

Eltis, David. "The Diaspora of Yoruba Speakers, 1650–1865: Dimensions and Implications." *The Yoruba Diaspora in the Atlantic World* (2004) 17–39.

Eltis, David. "The Volume and Structure of the Transatlantic Slave Trade: A Reassessment." *The William and Mary Quarterly* 58, no. 1 (2001): 17–46.

Engerman, Stanley L., Richard Sutch, and Gavin Wright. "Slavery." *Historical Statistics of the United States Millennial Edition*, 2003.

Epstein, Richard A. "A Theory of Strict Liability." *The Journal of Legal Studies* 2, no. 1 (1973): 151–204.

Equal Justice Initiative. "One Million Black Families in the South Have Lost Their Farms over the Past Century." Accessed October 17, 2019. https://eji.org/news/one-million-black-families-have-lost-their-farms.

Erevelles, Nirmala. *Disability and Difference in Global Contexts: Enabling a Transformative Body Politic.* Springer, 2011.

Estes, Nick. "Decolonization and Indigenous Liberation: The Remarkable Life and Work of John Redhouse." *La Jicarita* (blog), April 25, 2013. https://lajicarita.wordpress.com/2013/04/25/decolonization-and-indigenous-liberation-the-remarkable-life-and-work-of-john-redhouse/.

Estes, Nick, and Jaskiran Dhillon. *Standing with Standing Rock: Voices from the# NoDAPL Movement.* University of Minnesota Press, 2019.

"Faced with Existential Climate Threat, Small Island Nations Sound Climate Alarm at UN," UN News. September 27, 2014. https://news.un.org/en/story/2014/09/479412-faced-existential-climate-threat-small-island-nations-sound-climate-alarm-un.

Fausz, J. Frederick. "An 'Abundance of Blood Shed on Both Sides': England's First Indian War, 1609–1614." *The Virginia Magazine of History and Biography* 98, no. 1 (1990): 3–56.

Feinberg, Joel. "Collective Responsibility." *The Journal of Philosophy* 65, no. 21 (1968): 674–688.

Fenton, Adrian, Helena Wright, Stavros Afionis, Jouni Paavola, and Saleemul Huq. "Debt Relief and Financing Climate Change Action." *Nature Climate Change* 4, no. 8 (2014): 650.

Fields, Barbara Jeanne. "Slavery, Race and Ideology in the United States of America." *New Left Review* 181, no. 1 (1990): 95–118.

"Flint's History of Emergency Management and How It Got to Financial Freedom," mlive, January 16, 2018. https://www.mlive.com/news/flint/2018/01/city_of_the_state_flints_histo.html.

Florida, Richard. "The World's Knowledge Capitals? London and L.A." CityLab. Accessed April 14, 2020. http://www.citylab.com/work/2017/01/mapping-the-worlds-knowledge-hubs/505748/.

Flynn, Dennis O., and Arturo Giraldez. "Arbitrage, China, and World Trade in the Early Modern Period." *Journal of the Economic and Social History of the Orient* 38, no. 4 (1995): 429–448.

Flynn, Dennis O., and Arturo Giráldez. "Born with a Silver Spoon: The Origin of World Trade in 1571." *Journal of World History* 6, no. 2 (1995): 201–221.

Flynn, Dennis O., and Arturo Giráldez. "Cycles of Silver: Global Economic Unity through the Mid-Eighteenth Century." *Journal of World History* 13, no. 2 (2002): 391–427.

Foner, Eric. *A Short History of Reconstruction.* Harper Collins, 2015.

Foner, Eric. "Rights and the Constitution in Black Life during the Civil War and Reconstruction." *The Journal of American History* 74, no. 3 (1987): 863–883.

Fonger, Ron. "Neeley Gives Last Call—Sept. 18—to Sign up for Water Service Line Replacements in Flint." mlive, August 13, 2020. https://www.mlive.com/news/flint/2020/08/neeley-gives-last-call-sept-18-to-sign-up-for-water-service-line-replacements-in-flint.html.

Forman, James. "The Black Manifesto." *Africa Today* 16, no. 4 (1969): 21–24.

Fourie, Johan. "The Remarkable Wealth of the Dutch Cape Colony: Measurements from Eighteenth-Century Probate Inventories 1." *The Economic History Review* 66, no. 2 (2013): 419–448.

Francois, Patrick, and Jan Zabojnik. "Trust, Social Capital, and Economic Development." *Journal of the European Economic Association* 3, no. 1 (2005): 51–94.

Friedman, Lisa. "Standing Rock Sioux Tribe Wins a Victory in Dakota Access Pipeline Case." *The New York Times*, March 25, 2020, sec. Climate. https://www.nytimes.com/2020/03/25/climate/dakota-access-pipeline-sioux.html.

Frith, Nicola. "The Global Push for Reparations." *The Journal of Pan African Studies (Online)* 11, no. 5 (2018): 129.

Fullinwider, Robert K. "The Case for Reparations," Report From the Institute for Philosophy and Public Policy 20, no. 2 (2000): 1–8. http://www.lawrenceblum.net/uploads/2/7/5/8/27583233/fullinwider-on-reparations.pdf.

Galeano, Eduardo. *Las Venas Abiertas de América Latina.* Siglo xxi, 2004.

Gascoigne, Clark, and E. J. Fagan. "New AfDB-GFI Joint Report: Africa a Net Creditor to the Rest of the World." Global Financial Integrity. Accessed June 29, 2020. https://gfintegrity.org/press-release/new-afdb-gfi-joint-report-africa-net-creditor-rest-world/.

"Georgia Election Fight Shows that Black Voter Suppression, a Southern Tradition, Still Flourishes," PBS NewsHour, October 28, 2018. https://www. pbs.org/newshour/politics/georgia-election-fight-shows-that-black-voter-suppression-a-southern-tradition-still-flourishes.

Getachew, Adom. *Worldmaking after Empire: The Rise and Fall of Self-Determination*. Princeton University Press, 2019.

Ghosh, Jayati. "Stop Doing Business." Project Syndicate, September 10, 2020. https://www.project-syndicate.org/commentary/world-bank-should-scrap-doing-business-index-by-jayati-ghosh-2020-09.

Gilmore, Ruth Wilson. *Golden Gulag: Prisons, Surplus, Crisis, and Opposition in Globalizing California*. Vol. 21. University of California Press, 2007.

Glewwe, Paul, Albert Park, and Meng Zhao. "A Better Vision for Development: Eyeglasses and Academic Performance in Rural Primary Schools in China." *Poverty Action Lab*, May 2016. https://www.povertyac tionlab.org/sites/default/files/publications/424_542_A%20better%20vis ion%20for%20development_PaulGlewwe_May2016.pdf.

"Global Military Spending Remains High at $1.7 Trillion." SIPRI.org. Accessed September 20, 2020. https://www.sipri.org/media/press-release/2018/glo bal-military-spending-remains-high-17-trillion.

Government of Kenya (GOK). "National Climate Change Response Strategy." Nairobi, n.d. https://cdkn.org/wp-content/uploads/2012/04/National-Clim ate-Change-Response-Strategy_April-2010.pdf.

Graden, Dale T. "An Act 'Even of Public Security': Slave Resistance, Social Tensions, and the End of the International Slave Trade to Brazil, 1835–1856." *Hispanic American Historical Review* 76, no. 2 (1996): 249–282.

Grunwald, Michael. "Katrina: A Man-Made Disaster." Time, November 24, 2010. http://content.time.com/time/specials/packages/article/0,28804, 2032304_2032746_2035982,00.html.

Grunwald, Michael, and Susan B. Glasser. "The Slow Drowning of New Orleans." *Washington Post*, October 9, 2005. http://www.washingtonpost. com/wp-dyn/content/article/2005/10/08/AR2005100801458.html.

Hachisu, Nancy Singleton. "'Kioke': The Secret Ingredient of Soy Sauce." *The Japan Times Online*, July 29, 2016. https://www.japantimes.co.jp/life/2016/ 07/29/food/kioke-secret-ingredient-soy-sauce/.

Hadden, Sally E. *Slave Patrols: Law and Violence in Virginia and the Carolinas*. Harvard University Press, 2001.

Hamaji, Kate, Kumar Rao, Marbre Stahly-Butts, Janaé Bonsu, Charlene Carruthers, Roselyn Berry, and Denzel McCampbell. "Freedom to Thrive: Reimagining Safety & Security in Our Communities." *Center for Popular Democracy, Law for Black Lives, Black Youth Project* 100 (2017). https://populardemocracy.org/sites/default/files/Freedom%20To%20Thr ive%2C%20Higher%20Res%20Version.pdf.

Hanauer, Nick, David M. Rolf. "The Top 1% of Americans Have Taken $50 Trillion From the Bottom 90%—And That's Made the U.S. Less Secure."

Time, Sept. 14, 2020. Accessed September 20, 2020. https://time.com/5888 024/50-trillion-income-inequality-america/.

Handa, Sudhanshu, Luisa Natali, David Seidenfeld, Gelson Tembo, Benjamin Davis, and Zambia Cash Transfer Evaluation Study Team. "Can Unconditional Cash Transfers Raise Long-Term Living Standards? Evidence from Zambia." *Journal of Development Economics* 133 (2018): 42–65.

Hartung, William D., and Mandy Smithberger. "America's Defense Budget Is Bigger than You Think," May 7, 2019. https://www.thenation.com/article/ archive/tom-dispatch-america-defense-budget-bigger-than-you-think/.

Haushofer, Johannes, and Jeremy Shapiro. "The Short-Term Impact of Unconditional Cash Transfers to the Poor: Experimental Evidence from Kenya." *The Quarterly Journal of Economics* 131, no. 4 (2016): 1973–2042.

Hazareesingh, Sandip. "Cotton, Climate and Colonialism in Dharwar, Western India, 1840–1880." *Journal of Historical Geography* 38, no. 1 (2012): 1–17.

Hébrard, Jean M. *Slavery in Brazil: Brazilian Scholars in the Key Interpretive Debates*. Ann Arbor, MI: Michigan Publishing, University of Michigan Library, 2013.

Herman, Doug. "A Smithsonian Scholar Revisits the Neglected History of the Chesapeake Bay's Native Tribes." Smithsonian Magazine. Accessed January 21, 2020. https://www.smithsonianmag.com/smithsonian-institution/ following-footsteps-capt-john-smith-smithsonian-scholar-finds-neglec ted-history-180960984/.

Herrnstein, Richard J., and Charles Murray. *The Bell Curve: Intelligence and Class Structure in American Life*. Simon and Schuster, 2010.

Heyd, David. "Climate Ethics, Affirmative Action, and Unjust Enrichment." In *Climate Justice and Historical Emissions*, edited by Lukas H. Meyer and Pranay Sanklecha, 22–45. Cambridge: Cambridge University Press, 2017. https://doi.org/10.1017/9781107706835.002.

Heywood, Linda M. "Slavery and Its Transformation in the Kingdom of Kongo: 1491–1800." *Journal of African History* 50, no. 1 (2009): 1–22.

Heywood, Linda M., and John K. Thornton. *Central Africans, Atlantic Creoles, and the Foundation of the Americas, 1585–1660*. Cambridge University Press, 2007.

Higgins, Abigail. "Climate Change Could Devastate Africa. It's Already Hurting This Kenyan Town." *Washington Post*, January 30, 2016, sec. Africa. https://www.washingtonpost.com/world/africa/climate-change-could-devastate-africa-its-already-hurting-this-kenyan-town/2016/01/29/f77c8 e5a-9f58-11e5-9ad2-568d814bbf3b_story.html.

Higgins, Abigail. "How Corporate Landlords Helped Drive the Covid Evictions Crisis." Insider, March 26, 2021. https://www.businessinsider.com/how-corporate-landlords-helped-drive-the-covid-evictions-crisis-2021-3.

Higgins, Abigail, and Olúfẹ́mi O. Táíwò. "Enforcing Eviction," August 19, 2020. https://www.thenation.com/article/society/police-eviction-housing/.

Hinton, Elizabeth. *From the War on Poverty to the War on Crime.* Harvard University Press, 2016.

History Magazine. "400 Years Ago, Enslaved Africans First Arrived in Virginia," August 13, 2019. https://www.nationalgeographic.com/history/magazine/2019/07-08/virginia-first-africans-transatlantic-slave-trade/

Hobsbawm, Eric. *The Age of Revolution: 1789-1848.* New York, NY: Vintage Books, 1996.

Holz, Christian, Sivan Kartha, and Tom Athanasiou. "Fairly Sharing 1.5: National Fair Shares of a 1.5 °C-Compliant Global Mitigation Effort." *International Environmental Agreements: Politics, Law and Economics* 18, no. 1 (February 1, 2018): 117–134. https://doi.org/10.1007/s10784-017-9371-z.

Horn, James. "The Founding of English America: Jamestown." *OAH Magazine of History* 25, no. 1 (January 1, 2011): 25–29. https://doi.org/10.1093/oah mag/oaq003.

Hornborg, Alf. "Towards an Ecological Theory of Unequal Exchange: Articulating World System Theory and Ecological Economics." *Ecological Economics* 25, no. 1 (1998): 127–136.

Horowitz, Andy. *Katrina: A History, 1915–2015.* Harvard University Press, 2020.

Horton, Lois E. "From Class to Race in Early America: Northern Post-Emancipation Racial Reconstruction." *Journal of the Early Republic* 19, no. 4 (1999): 629–649.

"How Evo Morales Made Bolivia a Better Place . . . Before He Fled The Country." NPR.org. Accessed September 8, 2020. https://www.npr.org/secti ons/goatsandsoda/2019/11/26/781199250/how-evo-morales-made-boli via-a-better-place-before-he-was-forced-to-flee.

Hunter, Herbert M., and Sameer Y. Abraham. *Race, Class, and the World System: The Sociology of Oliver C. Cox.* Monthly Review Press, 1987.

Inikori, Joseph E. "Slavery and Atlantic Commerce, 1650–1800." *The American Economic Review* 82, no. 2 (1992): 151–157.

The Movement for Black Lives. "Invest-Divest," n.d. https://policy.m4bl.org/.

Irish, Jennifer L., Alison Sleath, Mary A. Cialone, Thomas R. Knutson, and Robert E. Jensen. "Simulations of Hurricane Katrina (2005) under Sea Level and Climate Conditions for 1900." *Climatic Change* 122, no. 4 (February 1, 2014): 635–649. https://doi.org/10.1007/s10584-013-1011-1.

Irwin, Douglas A. "Mercantilism as Strategic Trade Policy: The Anglo-Dutch Rivalry for the East India Trade." *Journal of Political Economy* 99, no. 6 (1991): 1296–1314.

Jacobs, Andrew. "A Simple Way to Improve a Billion Lives: Eyeglasses." *The New York Times,* May 5, 2018, sec. Health. https://www.nytimes.com/2018/05/05/health/glasses-developing-world-global-health.html.

James, Cyril Lionel Robert. *The Black Jacobins: Toussaint L'Ouverture and the San Domingo Revolution.* Penguin UK, 2001.

Jenkins, Destin. "Money and the Ghetto, Money in the Ghetto." *Journal of Urban History* 46, no. 3 (December 13, 2019): 494–499. https://doi.org/10.1177/0096144219891985.

Johansen, Bruce Elliott, and Roberto Maestas. *Wasi'chu: The Continuing Indian Wars*. Monthly Review Press, 1979.

Jones, Ben. "Credit Where Credit Is Due: Mary Eleanor Spear." Medium, August 9, 2019. https://medium.com/nightingale/credit-where-credit-is-due-mary-eleanor-spear-6a7a1951b8e6.

Jones, Matthew. "A 'Segregated' Asia?: Race, the Bandung Conference, and Pan-Asianist Fears in American Thought and Policy, 1954–1955." *Diplomatic History* 29, no. 5 (2005): 841–868.

Jubilee Debt Campaign UK. "Mozambique: Secret Loans and Unjust Debts." Accessed April 17, 2020. https://jubileedebt.org.uk/countries-in-crisis/mozambique-secret-loans-unjust-debts.

Jubilee Debt Campaign UK. "The Increasing Global South Debt Crisis and Cuts in Public Spending," January 9, 2020. https://jubileedebt.org.uk/report/the-increasing-global-south-debt-crisis-and-cuts-in-public-spending.

Julius, Alexander J. "Nagel's Atlas." *Philosophy & Public Affairs* 34, no. 2 (2006): 176–192.

Karp, Matthew. *This Vast Southern Empire*. Harvard University Press, 2016.

Kellenberg, Derek K. "An Empirical Investigation of the Pollution Haven Effect with Strategic Environment and Trade Policy." *Journal of International Economics* 78, no. 2 (2009): 242–255.

Kelley, Robin D. G. "What Did Cedric Robinson Mean by Racial Capitalism?" Text. Boston Review, January 12, 2017. https://bostonreview.net/race/robin-d-g-kelley-what-did-cedric-robinson-mean-racial-capitalism.

Kelley, Robin D. G. *Freedom Dreams: The Black Radical Imagination*. Beacon Press, 2002.

"Kenya Halts Lamu Coal Power Project at World Heritage Site." *BBC News*, June 26, 2019, sec. Africa. https://www.bbc.com/news/world-africa-48771519.

Khader, Serene J. *Decolonizing Universalism: A Transnational Feminist Ethic*. Studies in Feminist Philosophy, 2018.

Kelton, Paul. *Epidemics and Enslavement: Biological Catastrophe in the Native Southeast, 1492–1715*. Lincoln and London: University of Nebraska Press, 2007.

Khan, Farrukh I., and Dustin S. Schinn. "Triple Transformation." *Nature Climate Change* 3, no. 8 (August 1, 2013): 692–694. https://doi.org/10.1038/nclimate1965.

Killewald, Alexandra, and Brielle Bryan. "Falling behind: The Role of Inter- and Intragenerational Processes in Widening Racial and Ethnic Wealth Gaps through Early and Middle Adulthood." *Social Forces* 97, no. 2 (2018): 705–740.

King Jr., Martin Luther. *Where Do We Go from Here: Chaos or Community?* Vol. 2. Beacon Press, 2010.

King Jr, Martin Luther. "Remaining Awake through a Great Revolution." Oberlin College Archives for the Electronic Oberlin Group, February 11, 2009. https://www2.oberlin.edu/external/EOG/BlackHistoryMonth/MLK/CommAddress.html.

Klein Rosenthal, Joyce, Patrick L. Kinney, and Kristina B. Metzger. "Intra-Urban Vulnerability to Heat-Related Mortality in New York City, 1997–2006." *Health & Place* 30 (November 1, 2014): 45–60. https://doi.org/10.1016/j.healthplace.2014.07.014.

Koch, Alexander, Chris Brierley, Mark M. Maslin, and Simon L. Lewis. "Earth System Impacts of the European Arrival and Great Dying in the Americas after 1492." *Quaternary Science Reviews* 207 (March 1, 2019): 13–36. https://doi.org/10.1016/j.quascirev.2018.12.004.

Krzywinski, Martin, and Naomi Altman. "Points of Significance: Visualizing Samples with Box Plots," 2014.

Kumar, Rahul, and David Silver. "The Legacy of Injustice. Wronging the Future, Responsibility for the Past." *Justice in Time: Responding to Historical Injustice* (2004): 145–158.

Laakso, Liisa, and Adebayo Olukoshi. "The Crisis of the Post-Colonial Nation-State Project in Africa." *Challenges to the Nation-State in Africa, Uppsala: Nordic Africa Institute* (1996): 7–39.

Lawson, Bill E. "Moral Discourse and Slavery." *Between Slavery and Freedom: Philosophy and American Slavery* (1992): 71–89.

"Lead-Laced Water in Flint: A Step-by-Step Look at the Makings of a Crisis." NPR.org. Accessed June 21, 2016. http://www.npr.org/sections/thetwo-way/2016/04/20/465545378/lead-laced-water-in-flint-a-step-by-step-look-at-the-makings-of-a-crisis.Lebsock, Suzanne D. "Radical Reconstruction and the Property Rights of Southern Women." *Journal of Southern History* 43, no. 2 (1977): 195–216.

Lee, Robert, and Tristan Ahtone. "Land-Grab Universities." High Country News, March 30, 2020. https://www.hcn.org/issues/52.4/indigenous-affairs-education-land-grab-universities.

Leeming, David. *James Baldwin: A Biography.* Simon and Schuster, 2015.

Left Voice. "Capitalism Is Responsible for Climate Change." Accessed April 23, 2020. http://www.leftvoice.org/capitalism-is-responsible-for-climate-change.

Levitt, Jeremy. "Black African Reparations: Making a Claim for Enslavement and Systematic De Jure Segregation and Racial Discrimination under American and International Law." *Southern University Law Review* 25 (1997): 1.

Locke, John, and Crawford Brough Macpherson. *Second Treatise of Government.* Hackett Publishing, 1980.

Lowcountry Digital History Initiative (LDHI). "African Laborers for a New Empire: Iberia, Slavery, and the Atlantic World. The Early Trans-Atlantic Slave Trade: Nicolas Ovando." Accessed January 18, 2021. http://ldhi.libr ary.cofc.edu/exhibits/show/african_laborers_for_a_new_emp/early_trans _atlantic_slave_tra.

Lu, Catherine. "Reconciliation and Reparations." *The Oxford Handbook of Ethics of War*, October 2015. https://doi.org/10.1093/oxfordhb/9780199943 418.013.17.

Lumumba, Chokwe, Imari Abubakari Obadele, and Nkechi Taifa. 1989. *Reparations, Yes!: The Legal and Political Reasons Why New Afrikans, Black People in North America, Should Be Paid Now for the Enslavement of Our Ancestors: Articles*. Washington, DC: House of Songhay, Commission for Positive Education, 1989.

Lustgarten, Abrahm. "Where Will Everyone Go?" ProPublica, July 23, 2020. https://features.propublica.org/climate-migration/model-how-climate-refugees-move-across-continents/.

Lyerly, Anne Drapkin, Margaret Olivia Little, and Ruth Faden. "The Second Wave: Toward Responsible Inclusion of Pregnant Women in Research." *IJFAB: International Journal of Feminist Approaches to Bioethics* 1, no. 2 (2008): 5–22.

Magill, Bobby. "Katrina: Lasting Climate Lessons for a Sinking City." Accessed January 18, 2021. https://www.climatecentral.org/news/katrina-climate-change-sinking-ground-19370.

Mann, Charles C. *1493: Uncovering the New World Columbus Created*. Vintage, 2011.

Manning, Patrick. "Contours of Slavery and Social Change in Africa." *The American Historical Review* 88, no. 4 (1983): 835–857.

The Forge. "Mapping Our Movement to Go on Offense: An Interactive Tool for Common Good Organizing," April 29, 2020. https://forgeorganizing.org/ article/mapping-our-movement-go-offense-interactive-tool-common-good-organizing.

Martinez, Doreen E. "The Right to Be Free of Fear: Indigeneity and the United Nations." *Wicazo Sa Review* 29, no. 2 (2014): 63–87.

Marx, Karl. 1847. "The Poverty of Philosophy." Accessed August 2, 2020. https://www.marxists.org/archive/marx/works/1847/poverty-philosophy/ ch02.htm.

Marx, Karl. 1852. "18th Brumaire of Louis Bonaparte. Accessed November 4, 2019. https://www.marxists.org/archive/marx/works/1852/18th-brumaire/ ch01.htm.

Marx, Karl. 1867. "Capital, Volume I." 1867. https://www.marxists.org/arch ive/marx/works/1867-c1/.

Mazrui, Ali A. "Global Africa: From Abolitionists to Reparationists." *African Studies Review* 37, no. 3 (1994): 1–18.

McCartin, Joseph A. "Bargaining for the Common Good." *Dissent* 63, no. 2 (2016): 128–135.

McCracken, John. "Underdevelopment in Malawi: The Missionary Contribution." *African Affairs* 76, no. 303 (1977): 195–209.

McKay, John P., Bennett D. Hill, John Buckler, Roger B. Beck, Patricia Buckley Ebrey, Clare Haru Crowston, and Merry E. Wiesner-Hanks. *A History of World Societies, Combined Volume.* Macmillan, 2011.

McKinney, Rachel Ann. "Extracted Speech." *Social Theory and Practice* 42, no. 2 (2016): 258–284.

Means, Russell, and Marvin Wolf. *Where White Men Fear to Tread: The Autobiography of Russell Means.* Macmillan, 1995.

Meissner, Shelbi Nahwilet. "Reclaiming Rainmaking from Damming Epistemologies: Indigenous Resistance to Settler Colonial Contributory Injustice." *Environmental Ethics* 42, no. 4 (2020): 353–372.

Mendez, Michael Anthony. *Climate Change from the Streets: How Conflict and Collaboration Strengthen the Environmental Justice Movement.* Yale University Press, 2020.

Mendy, Peter Karibe. *Amílcar Cabral: A Nationalist and Pan-Africanist Revolutionary.* Ohio University Press, 2019.

Merton, Robert K. "The Matthew Effect in Science: The Reward and Communication Systems of Science Are Considered." *Science* 159, no. 3810 (1968): 56–63.

Meyer, Robinson. "A Major but Little-Known Supporter of Climate Denial: Freight Railroads." The Atlantic, December 13, 2019. https://www. theatlantic.com/science/archive/2019/12/freight-railroads-funded-clim ate-denial-decades/603559/.

"Milestones: 1945–1952."—Office of the Historian, US Department of State. Accessed December 10, 2019. https://history.state.gov/milestones/1945-1952/asia-and-africa.

Milkoreit, Manjana, Jennifer Hodbod, Jacopo Baggio, Karina Benessaiah, Rafael Calderón-Contreras, Jonathan F. Donges, Jean-Denis Mathias, Juan Carlos Rocha, Michael Schoon, and Saskia E. Werners. "Defining Tipping Points for Social-Ecological Systems Scholarship—an Interdisciplinary Literature Review." *Environmental Research Letters* 13, no. 3 (2018): 033005.

Millimet, Daniel L., and Jayjit Roy. "Empirical Tests of the Pollution Haven Hypothesis When Environmental Regulation Is Endogenous." *Journal of Applied Econometrics* 31, no. 4 (2016): 652–677.

Mills, Charles W. "Kant and Race, Redux." *Graduate Faculty Philosophy Journal* 35, no. 1/2 (2014): 125–157.

Mills, Charles W. *The Racial Contract.* Ithaca: Cornell University Press, 1997.

"Misleading Reports of Lawlessness after Katrina Worsened Crisis, Officials Say." *The Guardian.* Accessed January 19, 2021. https://www.theguardian. com/us-news/2015/aug/16/hurricane-katrina-new-orleans-looting-viole nce-misleading-reports.

Moellendorf, Darrel. "Cosmopolitanism and Compatriot Duties." *The Monist* 94, no. 4 (2011): 535–554.

Moore, W. Gyude. "A New Cold War Is Coming. Africa Should Not Pick Sides." *The Mail & Guardian* (blog), August 21, 2020. https://mg.co.za/africa/2020-08-21-a-new-cold-war-is-coming-africa-should-not-pick-sides/.

Moran, Mayo. "Cardinal Sins: How the Catholic Sexual Abuse Crisis Changed Private Law." *Georgetown Journal of Gender and Law* 21 (2019): 95.

Morrison, Toni. "A Humanist View." Portland State University, 1975. https://www.mackenzian.com/wp-content/uploads/2014/07/Transcript_Portland State_TMorrison.pdf.

Morrow, David. *Values in Climate Policy*. Rowman & Littlefield International, 2019.

Morse, Joel N., and Jetaime Ross. "A Forensic Economics Approach to Reparations." baltimoresun.com. Accessed January 30, 2020. https://www.baltimoresun.com/opinion/op-ed/bs-ed-op-0107-slavery-reparations-20180103-story.html.

Movement for Black Lives. "Economic Justice," n.d. https://m4bl.org/policy-platforms/economic-justice/.

Movement for Black Lives. "Reparations." Accessed July 21, 2017. https://policy.m4bl.org/reparations/.

Mueller, Jennifer C. "The Social Reproduction of Systemic Racial Inequality," 2013. Doctoral dissertation, Texas A & M University. Available electronically from https://hdl.handle.net/1969.1/172973.

Murphy, Colleen. *The Conceptual Foundations of Transitional Justice*. Cambridge University Press, 2017.

Murphy, Michael Warren, Jackie Smith, Patrick Manning, and Ruth Mostern. "Introduction: World History and the Work of Reparations." *Journal of World-Systems Research* 26, no. 2 (2020): 143–150.

Nash, George H. *The Conservative Intellectual Movement in America since 1945*. Open Road Media, 2014.

Natanson, Hannah. "Two Centuries Ago, University of Virginia Students Beat and Raped Enslaved Servants, Historians Say." *Washington Post*. Accessed October 6, 2019. https%3A%2F%2 Fwww.washingtonpost.com%2Fhistory%2F2019%2 F10%2F06%2 Ftwo-centuries- ago-university-virginia- students-beat-raped-enslaved- servants-historians-say%2F.

National Coalition of Blacks for Reparations in America (NCOBRA). "The Abuja Proclamation (Pan-African Conference on Reparations,- 1993, Abuja, Nigeria)." Accessed July 11, 2017. http://www.ncobraonline.org/the-abuja-proclamation/.

National Coalition of Blacks for Reparations in America (NCOBRA). "Reparations Means Full Repair: For 400 Years of Terror, and Other Egregious Crimes," March 17, 2019. https://www.ncobraonline.org/reparations-means-full-repair-for-400-years-of-terror-and-other-egregious-crimes/.

National Geographic News. "The First Official Climate Refugees in the U.S. Race Against Time," May 25, 2016. https://www.nationalgeographic.com/news/2016/05/160525-isle-de-jean-charles-louisiana-sinking-climate-cha nge-refugees/.

National Indian Brotherhood. *Indian Control of Indian Education: Policy Paper Presented to the Minister of Indian Affairs and Northern Development.* The Brotherhood, 1972.

NBC News. "'Tidal Wave of Voter Suppression' Washes over States, Lawyer Says." Accessed April 14, 2020. https://www.nbcnews.com/news/nbcblk/presidential-voting-season-tidal-wave-voter-suppression-washing-over-multiple-n1128041.

New Internationalist. "Cotton: A History," April 1, 2007. https://newint.org/features/2007/04/01/history.

Newkirk II, Vann R. "The Great Land Robbery." *The Atlantic*, September 2019. https://www.theatlantic.com/magazine/archive/2019/09/this-land-was-our-land/594742/.

Ngugi, Mukoma wa. "The Pitfalls of Symbolic Decolonization." Accessed February 3, 2020. https://africasacountry.com/2020/01/the-pitfalls-of-symbolic-decolonization.

Nkrumah, Kwame. "Neo-Colonialism: The Last Stage of Imperialism," 1967.

Nmah, Patrick Enoch, and Uchenna Ebony Amanambu. "1804 Usman Dan Fodio's Jihad on Inter-Group Relations in the Contemporary Nigerian State." *Journal of Religion and Human Relations* 9, no. 1 (2017): 47–71.

Nunn, Nathan. "The Long-Term Effects of Africa's Slave Trades." *The Quarterly Journal of Economics* 123, no. 1 (February 1, 2008): 139–176. https://doi.org/10.1162/qjec.2008.123.1.139.

Nunn, Nathan, and Leonard Wantchekon. "The Slave Trade and the Origins of Mistrust in Africa." *American Economic Review* 101, no. 7 (2011): 3221–3252.

Nuti, Alasia. *Injustice and the Reproduction of History: Structural Inequalities, Gender and Redress.* Cambridge University Press, 2019.

Nyerere, Julius K. "The Plea of The Poor: New Economic Order Needed For the World Community." *New Directions* 5, no. 1 (1977): 8.

Obikili, Nonso. "The Trans-Atlantic Slave Trade and Local Political Fragmentation in Africa." *The Economic History Review* 69, no. 4 (2016): 1157–1177.

Ochieng'Opalo, Ken. *Legislative Development in Africa: Politics and Postcolonial Legacies.* Cambridge University Press, 2019.

Ogle, Vanessa. "'Funk Money': The End of Empires, the Expansion of Tax Havens, and Decolonization as an Economic and Financial Event." *Past & Present* 248, no.1 (2020): 213–249. Accessed February 1, 2021. https://doi.org/10.1093/pastj/gtaa001.

Ogle, Vanessa. "Tax Havens: Legal Recoding of Colonial Plunder." LPE Project, November 10, 2020. Accessed February 1, 2021. https://lpeproject.org/blog/tax-havens-legal-recoding-of-colonial-plunder/.

Ojo, Olatunji. "Beyond Diversity: Women, Scarification, and Yoruba Identity." *History in Africa* 35 (2008): 347–374.

Ojo, Olatunji. "The Organization of the Atlantic Slave Trade in Yorubaland, ca. 1777 to ca. 1856." *The International Journal of African Historical Studies* 41, no. 1 (2008): 77–100.

Ojwang, Jackton B. "The Residue of Legislative Power in English and French-Speaking Africa: A Comparative Study of Kenya and the Ivory Coast." *International & Comparative Law Quarterly* 29, no. 2–3 (1980): 296–326.

Olberding, Amy. *The Wrong of Rudeness: Learning Modern Civility from Ancient Chinese Philosophy*. New York: Oxford University Press, 2019.

Onazi, Oche. "Disability Justice in an African Context: The Human Rights Approach." In *An African Path to Disability Justice*, 39–72. Springer, 2020.

Osabu-Kle, Daniel Tetteh. "The African Reparation Cry: Rationale, Estimate, Prospects, and Strategies." *Journal of Black Studies* 30, no. 3 (2000): 331–350.

Otto, Ilona M., Jonathan F. Donges, Roger Cremades, Avit Bhowmik, Richard J. Hewitt, Wolfgang Lucht, Johan Rockström, et al. "Social Tipping Dynamics for Stabilizing Earth's Climate by 2050." *Proceedings of the National Academy of Sciences* 117, no. 5 (February 4, 2020): 2354. https://doi.org/10.1073/pnas.1900577117.

Pacto Ecosocial del Sur. "For a Social, Ecological, Economic and Intercultural Pact for Latin America." OpenDemocracy. Accessed May 13, 2021. https://www.opendemocracy.net/en/democraciaabierta/social-ecological-econo mic-intercultural-pact-latin-america/.

Pan African Climate Justice Alliance. "African Climate Justice Manifesto." PACJA, 2011. http://climate-justice.info/wp-content/uploads/2011/07/Afri can-Climate-Justice-Manifesto-PACJA-version2.pdf.

Parron, Tâmis. "Capital e raça: Os segredos por trás dos nomes." Revista Rosa. Accessed November 13, 2020. http://revistarosa.com/2/capital-e-raca.

Parthasarathi, Prasannan. *Why Europe Grew Rich and Asia Did Not: Global Economic Divergence, 1600–1850*. Cambridge: Cambridge University Press, 2011.

Pearce, Fred. "The African Queen." New Scientist. Accessed July 13, 2020. https://www.newscientist.com/article/mg16322035-100-the-african-queen/.

Peischel, Will. "A Judge Handed the Standing Rock Tribes a Big Win in Their Dakota Access Pipeline Fight." *Mother Jones* (blog). Accessed November 29, 2020. https://www.motherjones.com/environment/2020/07/a-judge-just-handed-the-standing-rock-tribe-a-big-win-in-their-dakota-access-pipel ine-fight/.

Pember, Mary Annette. "The Catholic Church Siphoned Away $30 Million Paid to Native People for Stolen Land." *In These Times*. Accessed August 14,

2020.   https://inthesetimes.com/article/catholic-church-mission-schools-investigation-treaty-ojibwe-native-people.

Pen Magazine International. "The Last Barrels of Tradition." Accessed October 10, 2019. https://pen-online.com/food/nihonshu-02/.

Pew Research Center. "U.S. Concern about Climate Change Is Rising, but Mainly among Democrats." *Pew Research Center* (blog). Accessed April 7, 2020.   https://www.pewresearch.org/fact-tank/2019/08/28/u-s-concern-about-climate-change-is-rising-but-mainly-among-democrats/.

Pfeffer, Fabian T., and Alexandra Killewald. "Generations of Advantage. Multigenerational Correlations in Family Wealth." *Social Forces* 96, no. 4 (2018): 1411–1442.

Pfeffer, Fabian T., and Alexandra Killewald. "Intergenerational Wealth Mobility and Racial Inequality." *Socius* 5 (2019): 2378023119831799.

Pieper, Kelsey J., Rebekah Martin, Min Tang, LeeAnne Walters, Jeffrey Parks, Siddhartha Roy, Christina Devine, and Marc A. Edwards. "Evaluating Water Lead Levels during the Flint Water Crisis." *Environmental Science & Technology* 52, no. 15 (2018): 8124–8132.

Piketty, Thomas, and Gabriel Zucman. "Capital Is Back: Wealth-Income Ratios in Rich Countries 1700–2010." *The Quarterly Journal of Economics* 129, no. 3 (2014): 1255–1310.

Plato. *Republic*. Translated by C. D. C. Reeve. Indianapolis/Cambridge: Hackett Publishing Co., Inc., 2004.

Pogge, Thomas. *Realizing Rawls*. Cornell University Press, 1989.

Pogge, Thomas. "The Role of International Law in Reproducing Massive Poverty." In *The Philosophy of International Law*. Oxford University Press, 2010.

Pogge, Thomas. "World Poverty and Human Rights." *Ethics & International Affairs* 19, no. 1 (2005): 1–7.

Pogge, Thomas. *World Poverty and Human Rights: Cosmopolitan Responsibilities and Reforms*. Cambridge:Polity Press, 2002. [Published online by Cambridge University Press, 2012.]

Popova, Maria. "The Doom and Glory of Knowing Who You Are: James Baldwin on the Empathic Rewards of Reading and What It Means to Be an Artist." *Brain Pickings* (blog), May 24, 2017. https://www.brainpickings.org/2017/05/24/james-baldwin-life-magazine-1963/.

"Porto-Novo." INOSAAR. Accessed January 20, 2021. https://www.inosaar.llc.ed.ac.uk/en/activity/porto-novo.

Potter, Gary. "The History of Policing in the United States." Eastern Kentucky University. Accessed July 14, 2020. https://plsonline.eku.edu/insidelook/history-policing-united-states-part-1.

"Pregnant Women in DRC Finally Receive Ebola Vaccine." Devex. Accessed February 17, 2020. https://www.devex.com/news/pregnant-women-in-drc-finally-receive-ebola-vaccine-95204.

Preston, William. "Serpent in Eden: Dispersal of Foreign Diseases into Pre-Mission California." *Journal of California and Great Basin Anthropology* (1996) 2–37.

Preston, William. "Serpent in the Garden: Environmental Change in Colonial California." *California History* 76, no. 2–3 (1997): 260–298.

Price, Carter C., and Kathryn A. Edwards. "Trends in Income from 1975 to 2018," September 14, 2020. https://www.rand.org/pubs/working_papers/WRA516-1.html.

Pro Market. "Prison Labor Can Create Perverse Incentives for Incarceration and Reduce Trust in Legal Institutions," July 14, 2020. https://promarket.org/2020/07/14/prison-labor-can-create-perverse-incentives-for-incarceration-and-reduce-trust-in-legal-institutions/.

Rawls, John. *A Theory of Justice*. Revised Edition. Cambridge: Harvard University Press, 1999.

Rawls, John. *A Theory of Justice*. Harvard university Press, 2009.

Rawls, John. "The Basic Structure as Subject." *American Philosophical Quarterly* 14, no. 2 (1977): 159–165.

Rawls, John. *The Law of Peoples: With, the Idea of Public Reason Revisited*. Harvard University Press, 2001.

Red Black and Green New Deal. "A National Black Climate Agenda." May 11, 2021. Accessed May 13, 2021. https://redblackgreennewdeal.org/#about.

Reed, Adolph L. "The Case Against Reparations." *Nonsite.Org* (blog), February 11, 2016. https://nonsite.org/editorial/the-case-against-reparations.

Reed, Adolph L., and Merlin Chowkwanyun. "Race, Class, Crisis: The Discourse of Racial Disparity and Its Analytical Discontents." *Socialist Register* 48 (2012): 149–175.

Rego, Antonio da Silva. "Portuguese Colonization in the Sixteenth Century: A Study of the Royal Ordinances (Regimentos)," 1965.

The Red Nation. "10 Point Program." Accessed September 24, 2020. https://therednation.org/10-point-program/.

Reis, João José. *Rebelião Escrava No Brasil: A História Do Levante Dos Malês Em 1835*. Companhia das Letras, 2003.

Reis, João José. "Slave Resistance in Brazil: Bahia, 1807–1835." *Luso-Brazilian Review* 25, no. 1 (1988): 111–144.

The Movement for Black Lives. "Reparations." Accessed July 21, 2017. https://policy.m4bl.org/reparations/.

National Coalition of Blacks for Reparations in America (NCOBRA). "Reparations." Accessed November 26, 2020. https://www.ncobraonline.org/reparations/.

Restall, Matthew. *When Montezuma Met Cortés: The True Story of the Meeting that Changed History*. HarperCollins, 2018.

Rezendes, Michael. 2019, updated Feb. 14. "With So Much of Its Leadership Compromised, Is the Catholic Church Irredeemable? *The Boston Globe*." BostonGlobe.com. Accessed September 24, 2020. https://www.bostongl

obe.com/ideas/2019/02/14/with-much-its-leadership-compromised-catho
lic-church-irredeemable/O5oTVEuu57QUoFe8GGEuHM/story.html.

Rice, James D. "War and Politics: Powhatan Expansionism and the Problem of Native American Warfare." *The William and Mary Quarterly* 77, no. 1 (2020): 3–32.

Richter, Daniel K. *Trade, Land, Power: The Struggle for Eastern North America.* University of Pennsylvania Press, 2013.

Ridder, Kevin. "'The Appalachian Pipeline Resistance Movement: 'We're Not Going Away.'" Appalachian Voices, October 28, 2020. https://appvoices.org/2020/10/28/the-appalachian-pipeline-resistance-movement/.

Rigaud, Kanta Kumari, Alex de Sherbinin, Bryan Jones, Jonas Bergmann, Viviane Clement, Kayly Ober, Jacob Schewe, Susana Adamo, Brent McCusker, and Silke Heuser. "Groundswell: Preparing for Internal Climate Migration," Washington, DC: World Bank, 2018.

Rios, Victor M. *Punished: Policing the Lives of Black and Latino Boys.* New York University Press, 2011.

Rivlin, Gary. "White New Orleans Has Recovered from Hurricane Katrina. Black New Orleans Has Not." Talk Poverty, August 29, 2016. https://talkpoverty.org/2016/08/29/white-new-orleans-recovered-hurricane-katrina-black-new-orleans-not/.

Roberts, J. Timmons, Sujay Natson, Victoria Hoffmeister, Alexis Durand, Romain Weikmans, Jonathan Gewirtzman, and Saleemul Huq. "How Will We Pay for Loss and Damage?" *Ethics, Policy & Environment* 20, no. 2 (2017): 208–226.

Roberts, J. Timmons, and Bradley C. Parks. "Ecologically Unequal Exchange, Ecological Debt, and Climate Justice: The History and Implications of Three Related Ideas for a New Social Movement." *International Journal of Comparative Sociology* 50, no. 3–4 (2009): 385–409.

Robeyns, Ingrid. "The Capability Approach." In *The Stanford Encyclopedia of Philosophy,* edited by Edward N. Zalta, Winter 2016. Metaphysics Research Lab, Stanford University, 2016. https://plato.stanford.edu/archives/win2016/entries/capability-approach/.

Robinson, Cedric J. *Black Marxism: The Making of the Black Radical Tradition.* University of North Carolina Press, 1983.

Rodney, Walter. "How Europe Underdeveloped Africa." *Bogle-L'Ouverture Publications, London and Dar Es Salaam,* 1972.

Rogers, Melvin L. "Introduction: Disposable Lives." *Theory & Event* 17, no. 3 (2014).

Rogers, Melvin L. "The People, Rhetoric, and Affect: On the Political Force of Du Bois's *The Souls of Black Folk.*" *American Political Science Review* 106, no. 1 (2012): 188–203. https://doi.org/10.1017/S0003055411000578.

Rollins, Judith. "Part of a Whole: The Interdependence of the Civil Rights Movement and Other Social Movements." *Phylon (1960–)* 47, no. 1 (1986): 61–70.

Rosa, Margarita. "Du'as of the Enslaved: The Malê Slave Rebellion in Bahía, Brazil." Yaqeen Institute for Islamic Research, April 5, 2018. https://yaqe eninstitute.org/margarita-rosa/duas-of-the-enslaved-the-male-slave-rebell ion-in-bahia-brazil/.

Rossi, Enzo, and Olúfẹmi O. Táíwò. "What's New about Woke Racial Capitalism (and What Isn't)." Spectre Journal. Accessed January 16, 2021. https://spectrejournal.com/whats-new-about-woke-racial-capitalism-and-what-isnt/.

Rountree, Helen C. *Pocahontas's People: The Powhatan Indians of Virginia through Four Centuries*. Vol. 196. University of Oklahoma Press, 1990.

Rugh, Jacob S., Len Albright, and Douglas S. Massey. "Race, Space, and Cumulative Disadvantage: A Case Study of the Subprime Lending Collapse." *Social Problems* 62, no. 2 (2015): 186–218.

"Russia's VTB Sues Mozambique over Loan in $2 Billion Debt Scandal." *Reuters*, January 7, 2020. https://www.reuters.com/article/us-mozambique-credit-suisse-vtb-idUSKBN1Z527M.

Salau, Mohammed Bashir. *Plantation Slavery in the Sokoto Caliphate: A Historical and Comparative Study*. Vol. 80. Rochester Studies in African H, 2018.

Sampson, Robert J., and John H. Laub. "A Life-Course Theory of Cumulative Disadvantage and the Stability of Delinquency." *Developmental Theories of Crime and Delinquency* 7 (1997): 133–161.

Sangiovanni, Andrea. "Global Justice, Reciprocity, and the State." *Philosophy & Public Affairs* 35, no. 1 (2007): 3–39.

Schleifstein, Mark. "15 Years after Katrina, New Orleans Levees Are in the Best Shape Ever. Experts Say It's Not Enough." NOLA.com. Accessed January 25, 2021. https://www.nola.com/news/environment/article_80c27be8-e3e7-11ea-bbf9-1731ebdd9171.html.

Schmidt, Elizabeth. *Foreign Intervention in Africa after the Cold War: Sovereignty, Responsibility, and the War on Terror*. Ohio University Press, 2018.

Schwartz, David A. "Clinical Trials and Administration of Zika Virus Vaccine in Pregnant Women: Lessons (That Should Have Been) Learned from Excluding Immunization with the Ebola Vaccine during Pregnancy and Lactation." *Vaccines* 6, no. 4 (December 4, 2018): 81. https://doi.org/10.3390/vaccines6040081.

Schwartz, Stuart B. "'The Mocambo': Slave Resistance in Colonial Bahia." *Journal of Social History* (1970): 313–333.

Scott, Joyce Hope. "Reparations, Restitution, Transitional Justice." *Journal of World-Systems Research* 26, no. 2 (2020): 168–174.

Sen, Amartya. "Famines." *World Development* 8, no. 9 (1980): 613–621.

Sen, Amartya. "Ingredients of Famine Analysis: Availability and Entitlements." *The Quarterly Journal of Economics* 96, no. 3 (1981): 433–464.

Sen, Amartya Kumar. *Inequality Reexamined*. Oxford University Press, 1992.

Sewell, Summer. "There Were Nearly a Million Black Farmers in 1920. Why Have They Disappeared?" *The Guardian*, April 29, 2019, sec. Environment. https://www.theguardian.com/environment/2019/apr/29/why-have-ameri cas-black-farmers-disappeared.

"Sex Abuse and the Catholic Church." *BBC News*, February 26, 2019, sec. World. https://www.bbc.com/news/world-44209971.

Shakespeare, Tom. *Disability Rights and Wrongs Revisited.* Routledge, 2013.

Shapiro, Ben. *The Right Side of History: How Reason and Moral Purpose Made the West Great.* Broadside Books, 2019.

Shavell, Steven. "The Mistaken Restriction of Strict Liability to Uncommon Activities." *Journal of Legal Analysis* 10 (2018).

Shelby, Tommie. *Dark Ghettos: Injustice, Dissent, and Reform.* Harvard University Press, 2016.

Sherwin, Emily. "Reparations and Unjust Enrichment." *Boston University Law Review* 84 (2004): 1443.

Shiffrin, Seana Valentine. "Reparations for US Slavery and Justice over Time." In *Harming Future Persons*, 333–339. Springer, 2009.

Shiffrin, Seana Valentine. "Wrongful Life, Procreative Responsibility, and the Significance of Harm." *Legal Theory* 5, no. 02 (1999): 117–148.

Shilliam, Robbie. "The Atlantic as a Vector of Uneven and Combined Development." *Cambridge Review of International Affairs* 22, no. 1 (2009): 69–88.

Shivji, Issa G. *The Rise, the Fall, and the Insurrection of Nationalism in Africa.* Durban: Center for Civil Society, 2004. http://www.nu.ac.za/ccs/default. asp?3,45,10,1059.

Shuey, Kim M., and Andrea E. Willson. "Cumulative Disadvantage and Black-White Disparities in Life-Course Health Trajectories." *Research on Aging* 30, no. 2 (2008): 200–225.

Shurtleff, William, and Akiko Aoyagi. *History of Soy Sauce (160 CE to 2012).* Soyinfo Center, 2012.

Silva, Luciana Lucia da. "Paulo Dias de Novais e o Desenvolvimento Das Relações Entre Os Portugueses e o Ndongo, Século XVI Paulo Dias de Novais and the Development of Relations between the Portuguese and Ndongo, 16th Century," n.d.

Singer, Peter. "Famine, Affluence, and Morality." *Philosophy & Public Affairs* (1972): 229–243.

Smith, Anna V. "Tribal Nations Demand Response to Climate Relocation." *High Country News*, April 1, 2020. https://www.hcn.org/issues/52.4/ind igenous-affairs-justice-tribal-nations-demand-response-to-climate-rel ocation.

Solow, Barbara L. "Capitalism and Slavery in the Exceedingly Long Run." *Journal of Interdisciplinary History* 17, no. 4 (1987): 711–737. https://doi. org/10.2307/204651.

Solow, Barbara L. "Caribbean Slavery and British Growth: The Eric Williams Hypothesis." *Journal of Development Economics* 17, no. 1–2 (1985): 99–115.

Sprague, Jeb. *Paramilitarism and the Assault on Democracy in Haiti.* New York University Press, 2012.

SSENSE. "Yasuo Yamamoto's Trending Tradition," March 16, 2020. https://www.ssense.com/en-us/editorial/culture/yasuo-yamamotos-trending-tradition.

"Standing Rock Asks Court to Shut Down Dakota Access Pipeline as Company Plans to Double Capacity," Inside Climate News. August 20, 2019. https://insideclimatenews.org/news/20082019/standing-rock-dakota-access-pipel ine-impact-assessment-court-double-capacity.

Staub, Michael E. "The Mismeasure of Minds." *Boston Review,* May 8, 2019. https://bostonreview.net/race/michael-e-staub-mismeasure-minds.

Stolberg, Sheryl Gay. "At Historic Hearing, House Panel Explores Reparations." *The New York Times,* June 19, 2019, sec. U.S. https://www.nytimes.com/2019/06/19/us/politics/slavery-reparations-hearing.html.

Story, Molly Follette, James L. Mueller, and Ronald L. Mace. *The Universal Design File: Designing for People of All Ages and Abilities.* Raleigh, NC: School of Design, the Center for Universal Design, NC State University, 1998.

"Striking for the Common Good." *US News & World Report.* Accessed April 18, 2020. https://www.usnews.com/news/the-report/articles/2019-11-01/chicago-teachers-strike-adds-safety-net-to-demands.

Tabellini, Guido. "Institutions and Culture." *Journal of the European Economic Association* 6, no. 2–3 (2008): 255–294.

Táíwò, Olúfẹ́mi. *How Colonialism Preempted Modernity in Africa.* Indiana University Press, 2010.

Táíwò, Olúfẹ́mi. "States Are Not Basic Structures: Against State-Centric Political Theory." *Philosophical Papers* 48, no. 1 (2019): 59–82.

Táíwò, Olúfẹ́mi O. "Climate Apartheid Is the Coming Police Violence Crisis." Dissent Magazine, August 12, 2020. https://www.dissentmagazine.org/onli ne_articles/climate-apartheid-is-the-coming-police-violence-crisis.

Táíwò, Olúfẹ́mi O. "Cops, Climate, COVID: Why There Is Only One Crisis." The Appeal. Accessed September 24, 2020. https://theappeal.org/cops-clim ate-covid-why-there-is-only-one-crisis/.

Táíwò, Olúfẹ́mi O. "Crisis, COVID-19, and Democracy." *Blog of the APA* (blog), June 2, 2020. https://blog.apaonline.org/2020/06/02/crisis-covid-19-and-democracy/.

Táíwò, Olúfẹ́mi O. "Green New Deal Policies Could Exacerbate a Burgeoning Climate Colonialism." *Slate Magazine,* March 1, 2019. https://slate.com/tec hnology/2019/03/green-new-deal-climate-colonialism-energy-land.html.

Táíwò, Olúfẹ́mi O. "Identity Politics and Elite Capture." *Boston Review,* May 7, 2020. https://bostonreview.net/race/olufemi-o-taiwo-identity-politics-and-elite-capture.

Taylor, M. Scott. "Unbundling the Pollution Haven Hypothesis." *Advances in Economic Analysis & Policy* 3, no. 2 (2004).

Theobald, Brianna. "A 1970 Law Led to the Mass Sterilization of Native American Women. That History Still Matters." Time. Accessed February 18, 2020. https://time.com/5737080/native-american-sterilization-history/.

Thompson, A. C. "Post-Katrina, White Vigilantes Shot African-Americans with Impunity." ProPublica. Accessed September 24, 2020. https://www.pro publica.org/article/post-katrina-white-vigilantes-shot-african-americans-with-impunity.

Thomson, Ryan, Johanna Espin, and Tameka Samuels-Jones. "Green Crime Havens: A Spatial Cluster Analysis of Environmental Crime." *Social Science Quarterly*, 2020.

Thornton, John. "The African Experience of the '20. and Odd Negroes' Arriving in Virginia in 1619." *The William and Mary Quarterly* 55, no. 3 (1998): 421–434.

Toney, Heather McTeer. "Opinion | Black Women Are Leaders in the Climate Movement."| Black Women Are Leaders in the Climate Movement." *The New York Times*, July 25, 2019, sec. Opinion. https://www.nytimes.com/2019/07/25/opinion/black-women-leaders-climate-movement.html.

Tripp, Kim E. "'Yoshino': An Outstanding Cultivar of Japanese Cedar." *Arnoldia* 63, no. 4 (2005): 13–14.

"Trump Derides Protections for Immigrants from 'Shithole' Countries." *The Washington Post*. Accessed October 6, 2019. https://www.washingtonpost.com/politics/trump-attacks-protections-for-immigrants-from-shithole-countries-in-oval-office-meeting/2018/01/11/bfc0725c-f711-11e7-91af-31ac729add94_story.html?utm_term=.02ee26f49a8e.

"Union Army." Encyclopedia.com." Accessed January 19, 2021. https://www.encyclopedia.com/social-sciences-and-law/political-science-and-governm ent/military-affairs-nonnaval/union-army.

World Economic Forum. "Universities Need Philanthropy but Must Resist Hidden Agendas." Accessed September 21, 2020. https://www.weforum.org/agenda/2018/02/universities-need-philanthropy-but-must-resist-hid den-agendas/.

UN News. "World Faces 'Climate Apartheid' Risk, 120 More Million in Poverty: UN Expert," June 25, 2019. https://news.un.org/en/story/2019/06/1041261.

University of Virginia. President's Commission on Slavery and the University, Marcus L. Martin, Meghan S. Faulkner, and Kirt Von Daacke. *President's Commission on Slavery and the University: Report to President Teresa A. Sullivan, 2018.* University of Virginia, 2018.

"UPDATE 1-IMF: Mozambique Debt Talks with VTB Almost Finalized, Cyclone Hits Growth." *Reuters*, May 17, 2019. https://www.reuters.com/arti cle/mozambique-debt-vtb-idUSL5N22T34O.

US Census Bureau. "World Population Day: July 11, 2018." The United States Census Bureau. Accessed January 7, 2020. https://www.census.gov/newsroom/stories/2018/world-population.html.

"US Dollar to Nigerian Naira Spot Exchange Rates for 2010." Accessed June 29, 2020. https://www.exchangerates.org.uk/USD-NGN-spot-exchange-rates-history-2010.html.

Van Wingen, John, and Herbert K. Tillema. "British Military Intervention after World War II: Militance in a Second-Rank Power." *Journal of Peace Research* 17, no. 4 (1980): 291–303.

Verdun, Vincene. "If the Shoe Fits, Wear It: An Analysis of Reparations to African Americans." *Tulane Law Review* 67 (1992): 597.

Vision Impact Institute. "The Social and Economic Impact of Poor Vision." Vision Impact Institute, May 2012. https://vii-production.s3.amazonaws.com/uploads/research_article/pdf/51356f5ddd57fa3f6b000001/VisionImpactInstitute-WhitePaper-Nov12.pdf.

Vogel, W. H., and A. Berke. *Brief History of Vision and Ocular Medicine.* Amsterdam,Netherlands: Kugler Publications, 2009. http://ebookcentral.proquest.com/lib/georgetown/detail.action?docID=449441.

Wade, Lisa. "Who Didn't Evacuate for Hurricane Katrina?" Pacific Standard. Accessed January 19, 2021. https://psmag.com/environment/who-didnt-evacuate-for-hurricane-katrina.

Walker, Margaret Urban. *Moral Repair: Reconstructing Moral Relations after Wrongdoing.* Cambridge University Press, 2006.

Wamba-dia-Wamba, Ernest. "The National Question in Zaire: Challenges to the Nation-State Project." *Challenges to the Nation-State in Africa*, 1996.

Warren, Dorian. "Reparations and Basic Income." *Work, Inequality, Basic Income* (2017): 56–60.

Warrior, Robert Allen. "Intellectual Sovereignty and The Struggle for An American Indian Future. Chapter 3 of Tribal Secrets: Vine Deloria, John Joseph Mathews, and the Recovery of American Indian Intellectual Traditions." *Wicazo Sa Review* 8, no. 1 (1992): 1–20. https://doi.org/10.2307/1409359.

Weber, Max. *The Protestant Ethic and the Spirit of Capitalism.* Routledge, 2013.

Welch, Michael Patrick. "Hurricane Katrina Was a Nightmare for Inmates in New Orleans." Vice. Accessed January 19, 2021. https://www.vice.com/en/article/5gjdxn/hurricane-katrina-was-a-nightmare-for-inmates-in-new-orleans-829.

Wells-Barnett, Ida B. *Southern Horrors: Lynch Law in All Its Phases.* Good Press, 2019.

Wells-Barnett, Ida B. *The Red Record Tabulated Statistics and Alleged Causes of Lynching in the United States.* 2012.

Whatley, Warren. "Up the River: The International Slave Trades and the Transformations of Slavery in Africa." *Ann Arbor* 1001 (2020): 48109.

Whatley, Warren C. "The Gun-Slave Hypothesis and the 18th Century British Slave Trade." *Explorations in Economic History* 67 (2018): 80–104.

Wickham, Hadley, and Lisa Stryjewski. "40 Years of Boxplots." *American Statistician*, 2011.

Williams, Casey. "A Win Against Voter Suppression in the South." *In These Times*, January 31, 2020. http://inthesetimes.com/article/22256/voter-suppression-black-northcarolina-africanamericans-smithrec-hbcu.

Williams, Eric. *Capitalism and Slavery*. University of North Carolina Press Books, 2014.

Williams, Nikesha Elise. "Katrina Battered Black New Orleans. Then the Recovery Did It Again." *Washington Post*. Accessed January 18, 2021. https://www.washingtonpost.com/outlook/katrina-battered-black-new-orleans-then-the-recovery-did-it-again/2020/08/27/193d2420-e7eb-11ea-bc79-834454439a44_story.html.

Williams, Robert Franklin. *Negroes with Guns*. Wayne State University Press, 1998.

Wolfe, Patrick. "Settler Colonialism and the Elimination of the Native." *Journal of Genocide Research* 8, no. 4 (2006): 387–409.

Wolff, Robert S. "Da Gama's Blundering: Trade Encounters in Africa and Asia during the European 'Age of Discovery,' 1450–1520." *The History Teacher* 31, no. 3 (1998): 297–318.

Woods, Clyde Adrian. *Development Arrested: The Blues and Plantation Power in the Mississippi Delta*. Verso, 1998.

Wright, Erik Olin. "Can the Universal Basic Income Solve Global Inequalities?" UNESCO Inclusive Policy Lab, February 14, 2020. https://en.unesco.org/inclusivepolicylab/news/can-universal-basic-income-solve-global-inequalities.

Wynter, Sylvia. "No Humans Involved: An Open Letter to My Colleagues." *Institute NHI*, Forum NHI: Knowledge for the 21st Century, 1, no. 1 (1992): 42–74.

Xu, Chi, Timothy A. Kohler, Timothy M. Lenton, Jens-Christian Svenning, and Marten Scheffer. "Future of the Human Climate Niche." *Proceedings of the National Academy of Sciences* 117, no. 21 (May 26, 2020): 11350. https://doi.org/10.1073/pnas.1910114117.

Xue, Yi, and Richard Larson. "STEM Crisis or STEM Surplus? Yes and Yes: Monthly Labor Review: U.S. Bureau of Labor Statistics." Bureau of Labor Statistics. Accessed February 17, 2020. https://www.bls.gov/opub/mlr/2015/article/stem-crisis-or-stem-surplus-yes-and-yes.htm.

Young, Iris Marion. "Responsibility and Global Justice: A Social Connection Model." *Social Philosophy and Policy* 23, no. 1 (2006): 102–130.

Zuckerman, Harriet. "Accumulation of Advantage and Disadvantage: The Theory and Its Intellectual Biography." *Robert K. Merton and Contemporary Sociology* (1998): 139–161.

Zucman, Gabriel. *The Hidden Wealth of Nations: The Scourge of Tax Havens*. University of Chicago Press, 2015.

Index

fossil fuels, 160
  oil and Hurricane Katrina, 152–53
free trade, 50
freedom. *See* political rights
Freedman's Bureau (U.S.), 195–96
French empire. *See* Haiti
Fulani. *See* Malê revolt

GDP, and climate change
    vulnerability, 218–22
gender
  and discrimination in medical
    research, 98
  under colonialism, 31–32
Georgetown University, 113–17
Getachew, Adom, 4, 72, 73, 99
Gilmore, Ruth Wilson, 165–66
Global Racial Empire
  definition, 30–31
  relation to history, 74–75
  See also colonialism
global warming. *See* climate change
globalization. *See* world order
grassroots organizing. *See* Flint, Michigan
Great Dying, 46–47, 159
Great Society, 64–65
Green Climate Fund, 177–94
green crime havens, 166, 215

habits. *See* moral norms
Haiti
  colonial history & Revolution, 151–52
  Duvalier regime, 205–6
Halliburton, 60
Hausa. *See* Malê revolt
Hazareesingh, Sandip, 42–43
headright system, 110
heatwave mortality, 161–62
Heyd, David, 85–86
Heywood, Linda, 109, 119
Higgins, Abigail, 58
Hinton, Elizabeth, 64–65
Hispaniola. *See* Haiti; history
history as process, 20–25, 85, 150
Home Owners Loan Corporation
    (U.S.), 154
Home Relief Bureau (U.S.), 15
Horn, James, 108

Housing and Home Finance Agency
    (U.S.), 58–59
housing injustice
  in America, 58
  in New Orleans, 154, 156–57
HSBC, 60
Hughes, Coleman, 2
Hurricane Betsy (1965), 153
Hurricane Harvey (2017), 161–62
Hurricane Katrina (2003), 150–57
  deep historical context, 151–52
  and housing injustice, 154, 156–57
  and incarceration, 156
  and oil extraction, 152–53
  responsibility for, 153, 154–57
hygiene and mortality, 40

ICOW Colonial History data set, 215
identity, author's, 201–2
Igbo, 32
incarceration
  and disadvantage, 28
  and Hurricane Katrina, 156
  in colonial Nigeria, 55
  in U.S., 64–65
India, colonial
  and cotton production, 35
  collectorate system, 42
India, precolonial
  Vasco da Gama, 38
Indian Removal Act of 1830 (U.S.), 152
Indigenous Americans
  American Indian Movement, 62
  broken treaties, 107
  child mortality, 50
  Creek War of 1813, 33–34
  forced sterilization, 50
  land theft, 41–42
  mission schools, 116
  Native trust funds, 116
  removal from Louisiana, 152
  reservations, 50
  Standing Rock, 183–84
  See also Jamestown
Indigenous peoples
  of Brazil, xiii, 188–89
  as climate refugees, 161–62
  connection to Black peoples, 17–18